IMAGES
of America

LORTON PRISONS

ON THE COVER: Leaving behind the dirty, rat-infested cells of the DC Jail, the minimum-security prisoners sentenced to the Workhouse lived dormitory style, much like military barracks, as the Progressive movement sought to implement more humane ways of dealing with prisoners. (Courtesy of DC Archives.)

IMAGES
of America

LORTON PRISONS

Alice Reagan and Kenena Hansen Spalding

ARCADIA
PUBLISHING

ISBN 978-1-4671-0934-5

Published by Arcadia Publishing
Charleston, South Carolina

Printed in the United States of America

Library of Congress Control Number: 2022942575

For all general information, please contact Arcadia Publishing:
Telephone 843-853-2070
Fax 843-853-0044
E-mail sales@arcadiapublishing.com
For customer service and orders:
Toll-Free 1-888-313-2665

Visit us on the Internet at www.arcadiapublishing.com

Dedicated to the Workhouse Prison Museum Committee and docents who created, funded, and staffed a temporary museum while preparing for its future home across the quad

Contents

ACKNOWLEDGMENTS

We are grateful for the many people who stepped forward to help make the book Irma Clifton planned to publish become a reality after her death. Their encouragement, suggestions, and leads were invaluable.

We relied heavily upon Mary Oakey's book *Journey from the Gallows* and articles Irma wrote for local news outlets, as well as newspapers and periodicals from the era. The Prints and Photograph Division of the Library of Congress, the District of Columbia Archives (DC Archives), the Virginia Room of the Fairfax County Public Library, the People's Archive at the DC Public Library, the Fairfax County Park Authority, the Fairfax County Department of Planning and Development, the Fairfax County Department of Fire and Rescue, and Sally Lyons, Mary Lipsey, and Lynne Garvey Hodge from the Fairfax County History Commission were all supportive in locating or scanning material.

We are grateful to Eleanor Lally and Jennifer McConnell, who edited the captions, and to Larry Rood for his photographic expertise in getting the proper resolution for the pictures. John Ferrari, Chris Bright, Stefan Hembre, William Koch, Alan McKie, Laura McKie, Larry Clark, Doug Spalding, Joe Rodriguez, Neal McBride, Charles Albert Huckins, and Don Sweeney all shared pictures from their files.

We want to give special recognition to Patrick O'Neill who, in partnering with us, went above and beyond with his guidance, time, patience, advice, and photographic contributions. His technical skills greatly eased putting together the final product.

Appreciation also goes to Arcadia Publishing, which recognized this as the story of a unique place that reflects the history of its time and is worth telling.

Introduction

I met Irma Clifton, the leader of efforts to preserve the history of the Lorton Prison complex and create a museum to accomplish that goal when she and some of her colleagues from the recently established Lorton Arts Foundation visited our Northern Virginia Community College (NVCC) Woodbridge campus in the fall of 2005. A lifelong resident of Lorton, Irma was the chair of the Lorton Arts Foundation, which sought to reimagine the site of the former Lorton Correctional Complex in Fairfax County, Virginia. Not only had Irma grown up just up the road from the prison complex, but she also worked there, managing supplies for many years. Most of the group wanted to meet with our art faculty, but Irma was looking for a women's historian. When she asked if there was anyone who taught women's history, everyone pointed to me. She explained that the planned Lorton Arts Center would include a museum, and one of its focuses would be the suffragists who were imprisoned in 1917 by the Woodrow Wilson administration for picketing the White House in their efforts to pass the 19th Amendment. She recruited me on the spot to help create the museum.

I quickly learned that Irma was one of the driving forces behind the preservation of the Lorton Prison site. After the Occoquan Workhouse opened in 1910, a number of institutions that became the Lorton Prison Complex followed. At its height in the 1960s, the Lorton Complex also included a reformatory, penitentiary, women's workhouse, and youth facility. At various times, it also included a NIKE missile site (the largest in the United States) and an alcohol rehabilitation center. Celebrated for its unusual treatment of inmates, with no bars or cells in its early years, it attracted corrections officials from all over the country. By the 1960s, forces of social change in the United States—including the rise of Islam among the inmates, the protests against the Vietnam War, and the Poor People's Campaign—left their marks on the Lorton Complex. A major court decision in 1966 that declared alcoholism a disease, not a crime, nearly emptied the Workhouse and led to the closing of many farming operations and brick-making efforts that allowed the prison to be self-supporting. With the crack cocaine epidemic of the 1980s, Lorton found itself overwhelmed. In spite of the addition of towers, razor wire, and fences, there were too many inmates (44 percent overcrowding) and not enough financial resources to keep the complex afloat. For many neighbors who had arrived as suburbia spread to Lorton, the fire set by the prisoners in 1985 was the last straw, and they began a 10-year effort to close Lorton. In 1997, a law passed by Congress did just that, and Fairfax County acquired the site.

Irma was part of the community group that recommended the establishment of the Lorton Arts Foundation and the repurposing of the Workhouse campus as an arts center after the Lorton Prison complex closed in 2001. Irma began her efforts to preserve the prison complex's history while she was still employed there. She had a small museum in her office at the prison. She also was instrumental in the Workhouse being added to the National Register of Historic Places. She served as the longtime president of the Lorton Heritage Society, a group that was instrumental in the creation of the Lorton Arts Foundation (LAF), and she served as its first chairman.

Irma was driven, passionate, and focused in her efforts to create what became the Lucy Burns Museum—call it her passion project. She quickly organized a group of six who began plans to organize the museum and run its day-to-day operations. What began as a cubicle on the second floor of the Administration Building during Women's History month in 2009 eventually opened in January 2020 as the Lucy Burns Museum. Along the way, Irma tirelessly advocated for the museum, be it with local history organizations, business or political groups, or the Workhouse Arts Center board. She also helped create the Museum and History Committee that became the driving force for the museum's establishment. She was responsible for much of the fundraising for Building No. 2's renovation and repurposing as the Lucy Burns Museum. Along the way, Irma received countless honors from the community and local history groups for her efforts to preserve and promote the history of the Lorton Prison complex.

One of Irma's unfinished projects was the creation of a book about the prison's history. She planned to publish a pictorial history of Lorton, but she died of cancer in the fall of 2019 before the museum opened. Before her passing, she asked Kenena Spalding and me to help her edit the captions. After her death, we decided to complete the book in her memory.

—Alice Reagan
Woodbridge, Virginia
July 2022

One

The Beginning Years

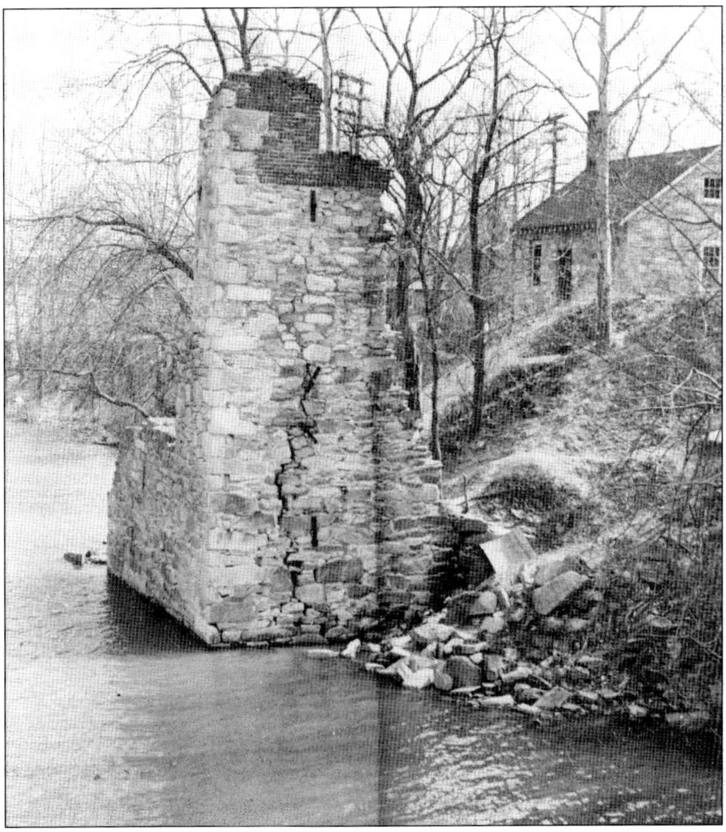

At the dawn of the 20th century, the United States was still mostly rural with a few big cities. The country was bursting with optimism and reveling in new inventions that were quickly following one another. Its energy was embodied by its youthful president, Theodore Roosevelt. He was bursting with Progressive ideas for how to make things better. When he focused on crime, it changed the landscape and lives of the villages of Lorton and Occoquan and the surrounding area. (Courtesy of the Library of Congress.)

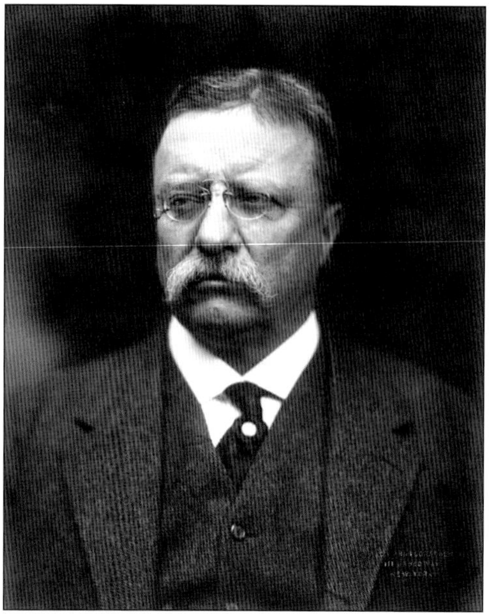

After learning of poor conditions at the DC Jail, Pres. Theodore Roosevelt appointed a three-person commission to consider reform of the penal system in the District of Columbia as part of his Progressive agenda. Their report, issued in 1909, recommended a workhouse for offenders who had committed minor crimes. This type of institution was predicated on "hard work for every able-bodied prisoner, together with humane treatment, fresh air, wholesome food, and sanitary living conditions." (Courtesy of the Library of Congress.)

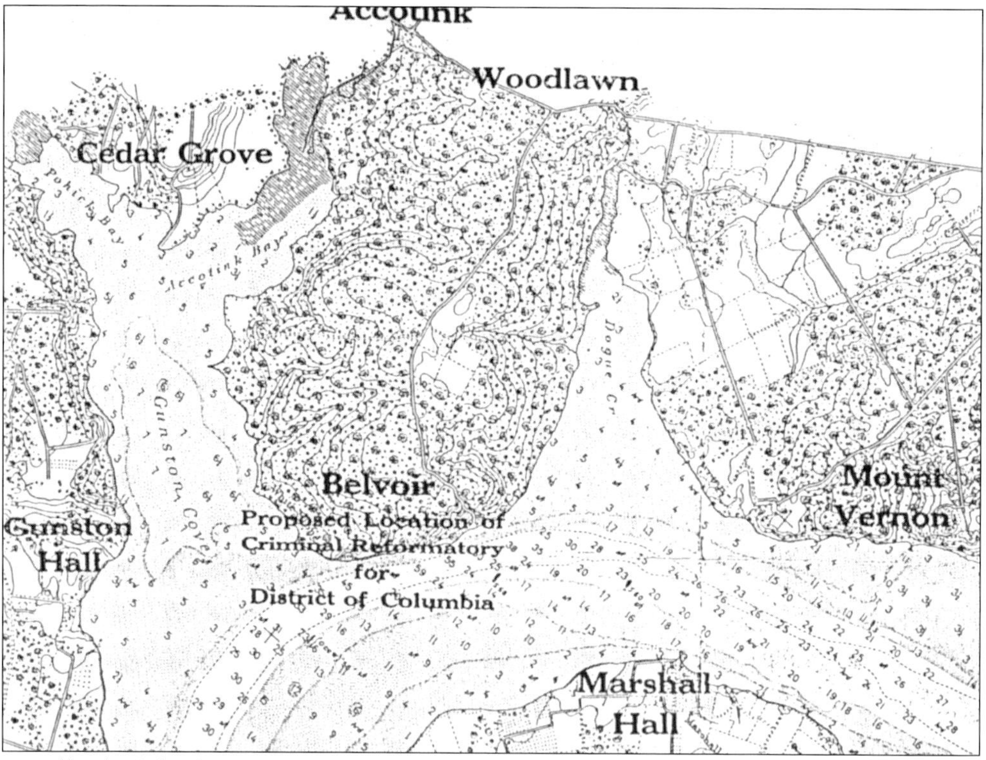

Initially, the federal government purchased 1,500 acres, including the foundations of the Fairfax home, as a location for the new District of Columbia Workhouse. When the Mount Vernon Ladies Association became aware of this, they made a spirited and public protest against it. An arrangement was made with the Army to swap for land along the Occoquan River. This land became Fort Belvoir; the former Army land was used to build the DC Workhouse. (Courtesy of Patrick O'Neill.)

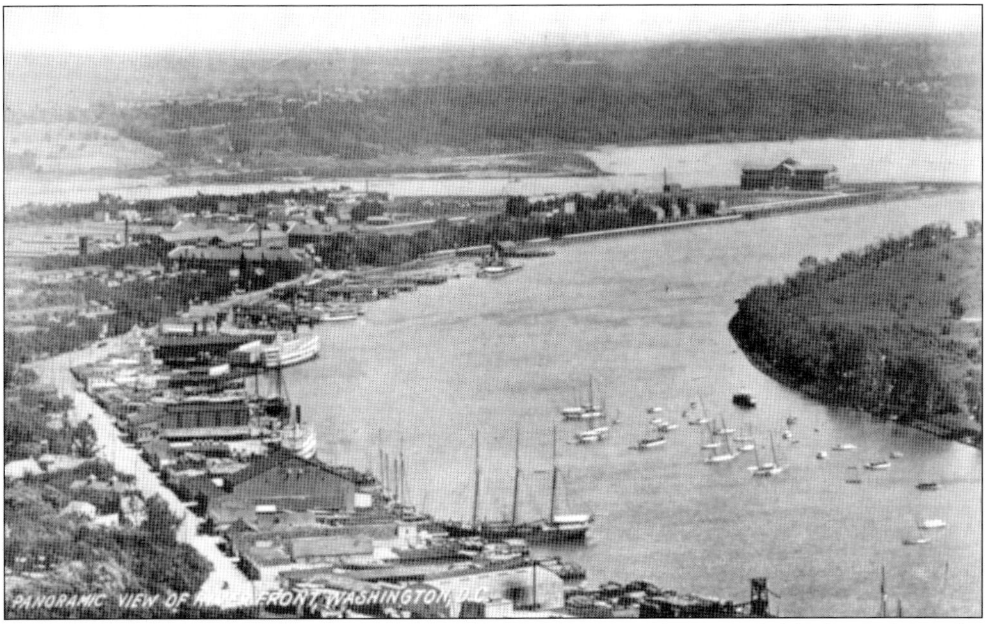

Twenty-nine prisoners left the DC Jail in the summer of 1910. They traveled by barge down the Potomac River and about a half mile up the Occoquan River to a landing site selected for the new workhouse. By the end of August, they erected and equipped tents to live in, cut down trees from the site, set up a portable sawmill, and used the lumber to build a stockade. They then prepared to build the temporary wooden structures that would become the Workhouse at Occoquan. They continued to cut trees on site and stockpiled the lumber; horses and oxen would later be used to ferry the building materials from the sawmill at the wharf to the top of the hill. Meanwhile, they lived in their tents and caught fish in the river to supplement their diets. (Above, courtesy of John Ferrari; below, courtesy of William Koch.)

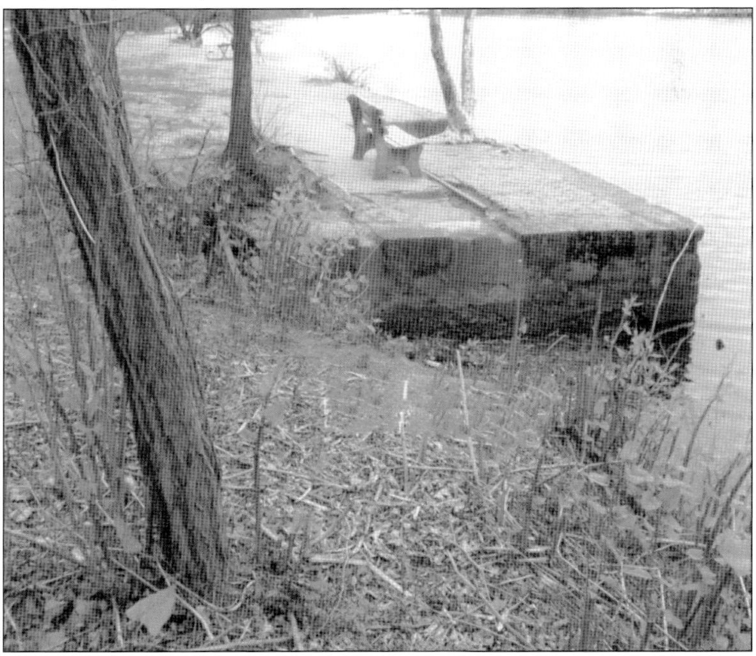

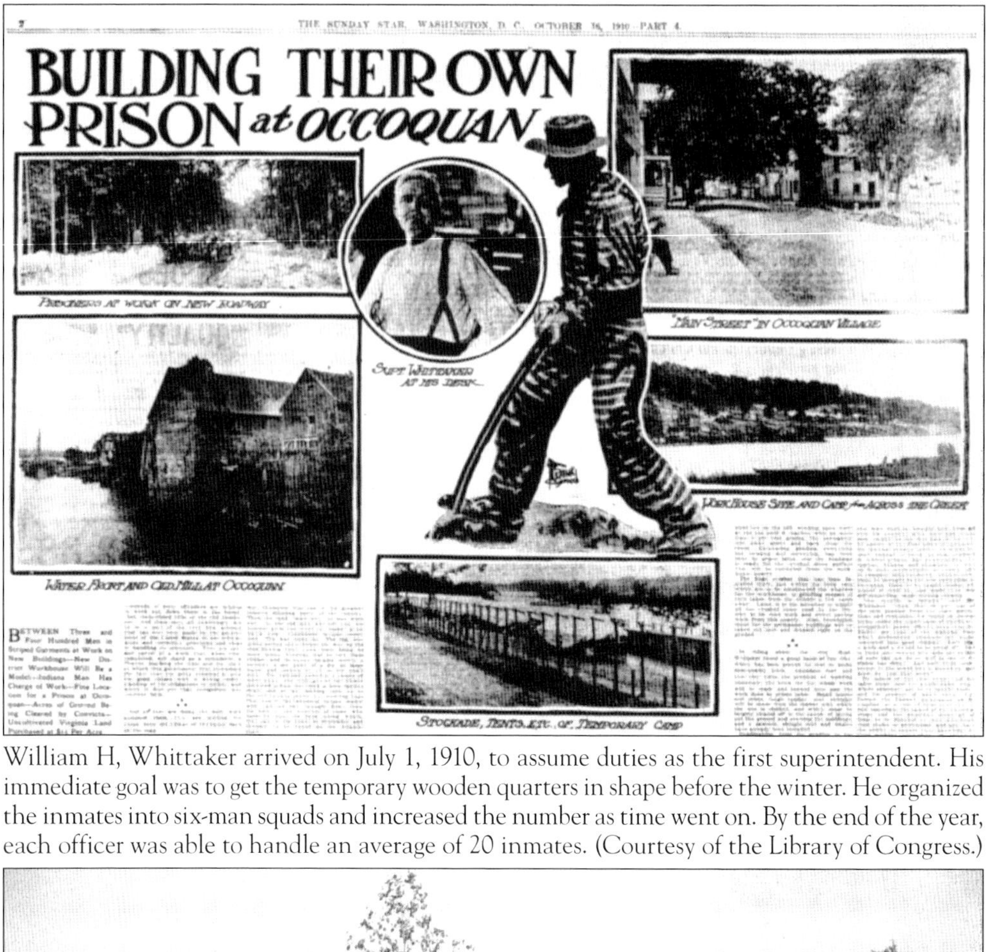

THE SUNDAY STAR, WASHINGTON, D. C., OCTOBER 16, 1910—PART 4.

BUILDING THEIR OWN PRISON at OCCOQUAN

PRISONERS AT WORK ON NEW ROADWAY

SUPT WHITTAKER AT HIS DESK

MAIN STREET IN OCCOQUAN VILLAGE

WATER FRONT AND OLD MILL AT OCCOQUAN

WORKHOUSE SITE AND CAMP ACROSS THE CREEK

STOCKADE, TENTS, ETC. OF TEMPORARY CAMP

BETWEEN Three and Four Hundred Men in Striped Garments at Work on New Buildings—New District Workhouse Will Be a Model—Indiana Man Has Charge of Work—Fine Location for a Prison at Occoquan—Acres of Ground Being Cleared by Convicts—Uncultivated Virginia Land Purchased at $13 Per Acre.

William H, Whittaker arrived on July 1, 1910, to assume duties as the first superintendent. His immediate goal was to get the temporary wooden quarters in shape before the winter. He organized the inmates into six-man squads and increased the number as time went on. By the end of the year, each officer was able to handle an average of 20 inmates. (Courtesy of the Library of Congress.)

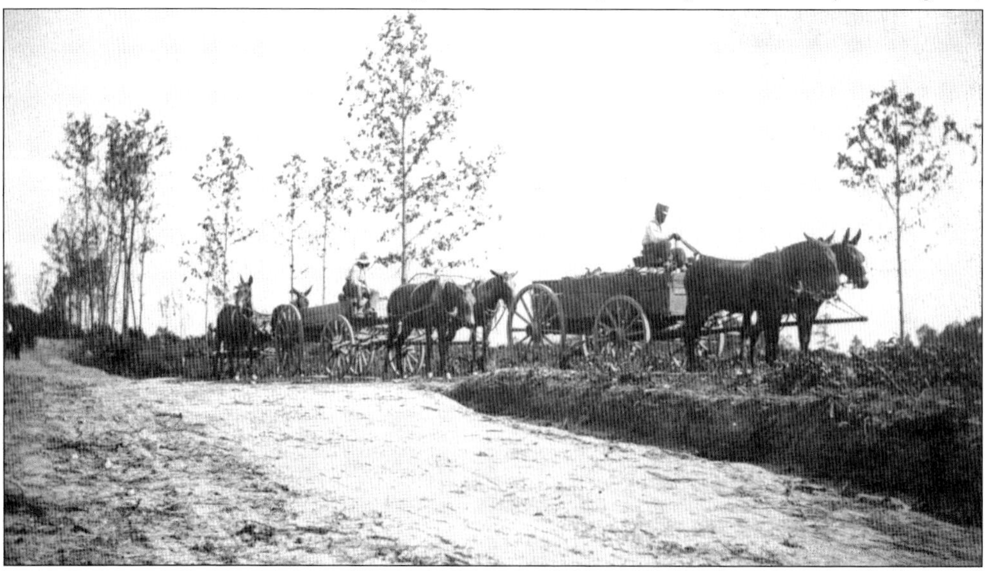

First, they needed to build a road from the encampment on the bank of the Occoquan River to the permanent location near the center of the tract. The selected building site was about a mile and a half north and up the steep hill. Mules were brought in to help. (Courtesy of Virginia Room, Fairfax County Library.)

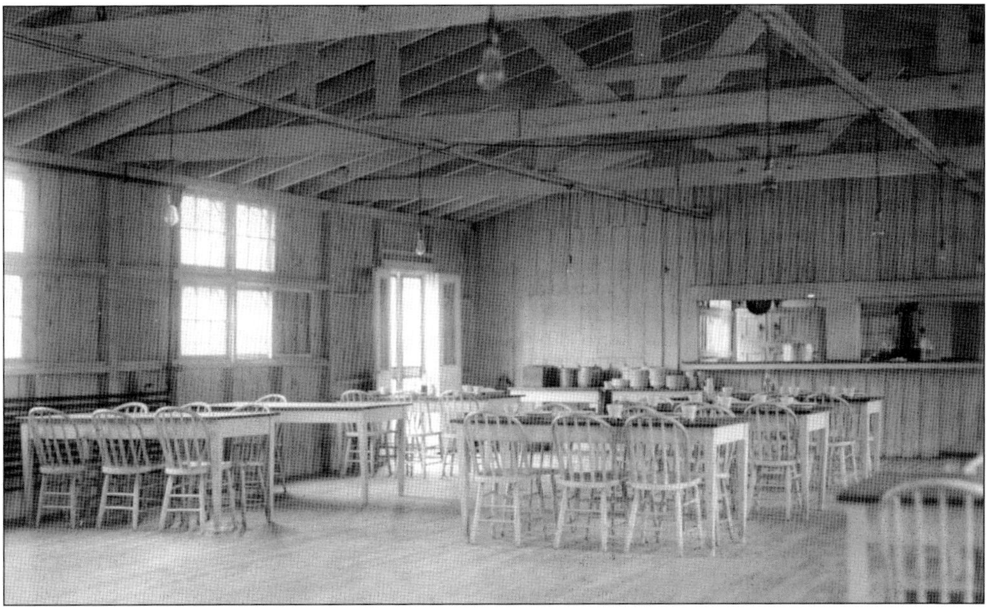

By 1914, thirty temporary one-story wooden buildings had been constructed, including three dormitories, a dining room, a lounging hall, a hospital, and horse and dairy barns. There were no walls, cells, locks, or bars in the institution. All the buildings were equipped with steam heat, electric lights, and both hot and cold water and sewage systems. (Courtesy of DC Archives.)

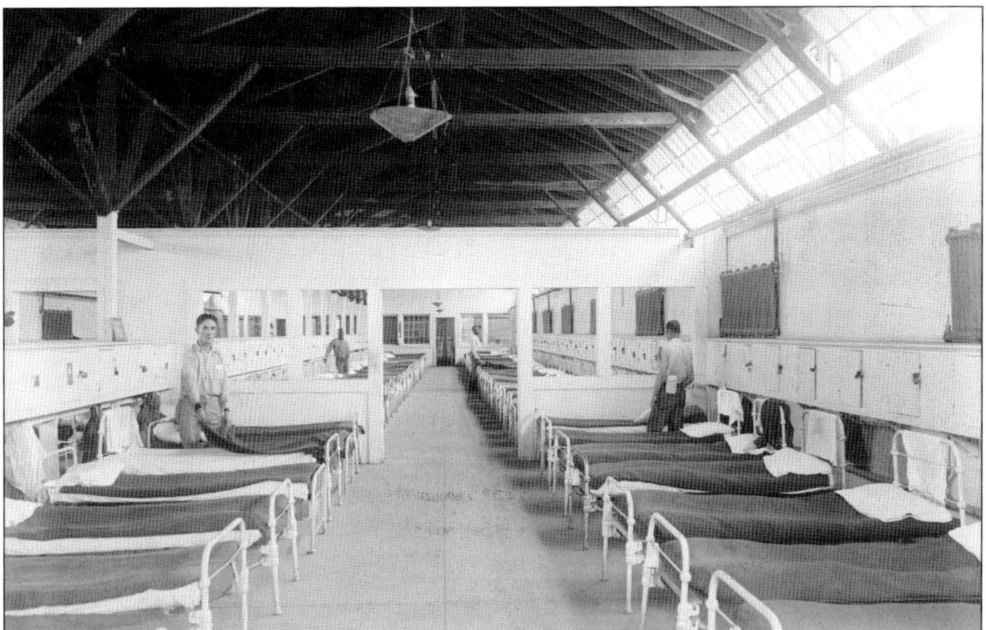

The interior of a men's dormitory in about 1911 shows cots arranged side-by-side on raised platforms. Each prisoner was given a straw mattress made at the prison, a pillow, sheets, a blanket, and "comfort." The site soon housed 500 inmates. They built offices for the workhouse, dining hall, laundry, bathroom, bake shop, storeroom, ice plant, and a hospital. The buildings were all of the simple one-story frame construction using lumber cut on site. (Courtesy of DC Archives.)

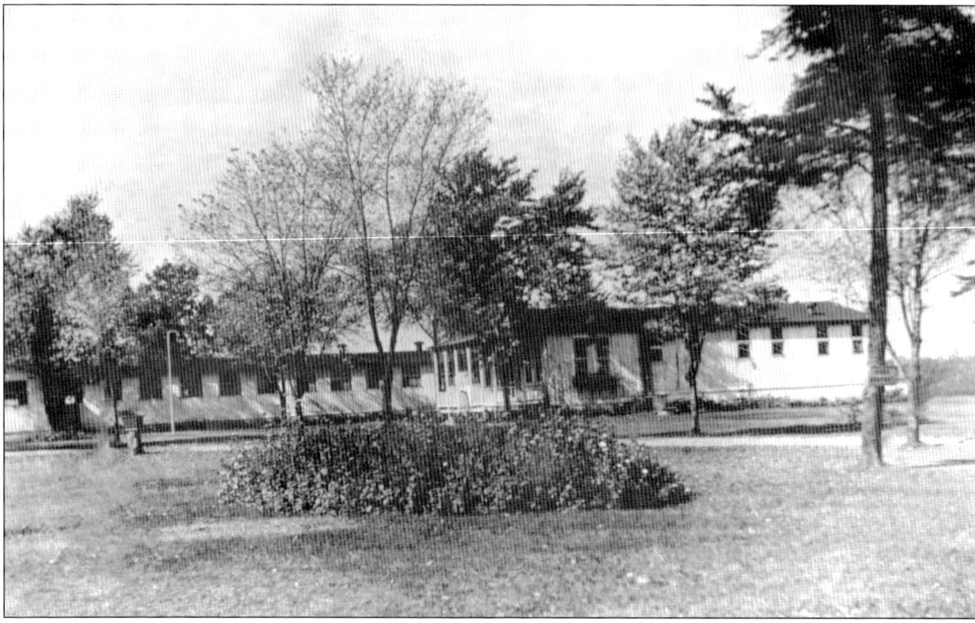

The Women's Workhouse opened in June 1912, across the road from where the men were housed. By the end of the year, it could accommodate 100 women arrested and sentenced in the District of Columbia. Minnie Herndon was named assistant superintendent and, along with the matrons, supervised the day-to-day activities of inmates. (Courtesy of DC Archives.)

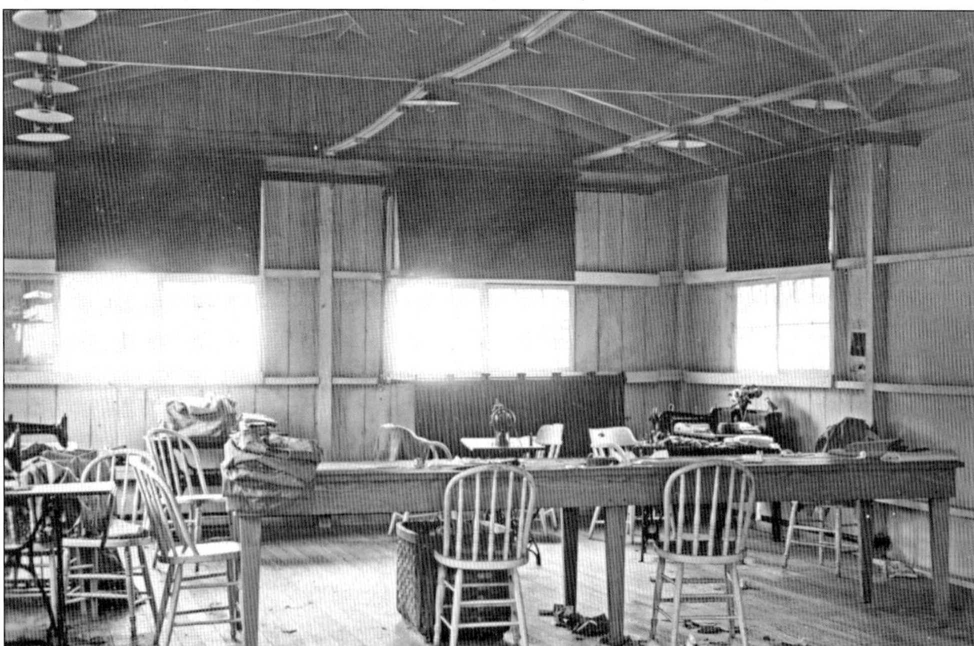

The women were expected to do a full day's work. They painted, cooked, cleaned, and worked on the lawns and gardens. Two operations were also set up that serviced both institutions. In the sewing room, they made all the clothes worn at the prison as well as truck covers, tablecloths, towels, and pillowcases. (Courtesy of DC Archives.)

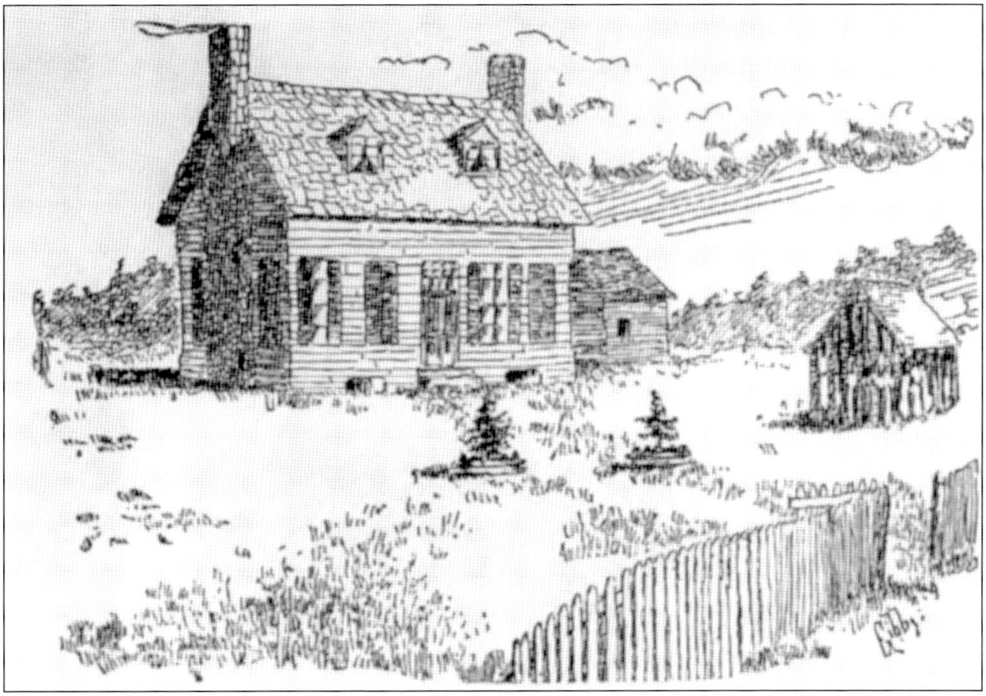

In 1914, a total of 150 acres of the old Laurel Hill Plantation were acquired for a reformatory. Major William Lindsay was *aide de camp* to George Washington during the Revolutionary War. The Lindsay home, called Laurel Hill House, became the home of the superintendent of the Lorton facility in 1916. Prison labor made the needed repairs. The house continued as a residence for prison superintendents until the mid-1930s. (Courtesy of Virginia Room, Fairfax County Library.)

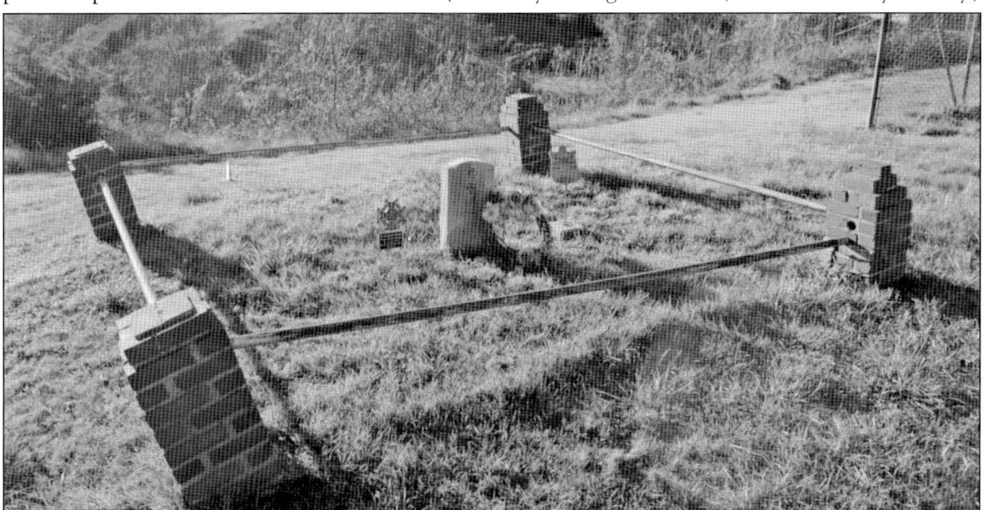

The graves of Major Lindsay and his wife remain on the property and are carefully maintained. In the 1930s, prison labor was used to construct classically designed gardens adjacent to the house using bricks made by the prisoners as the primary material for creating the tiers. A cultural landscape report on the property and gardens was done between 2007 and 2009. No action was taken on the recommendations. (Courtesy of Stefan Hembre.)

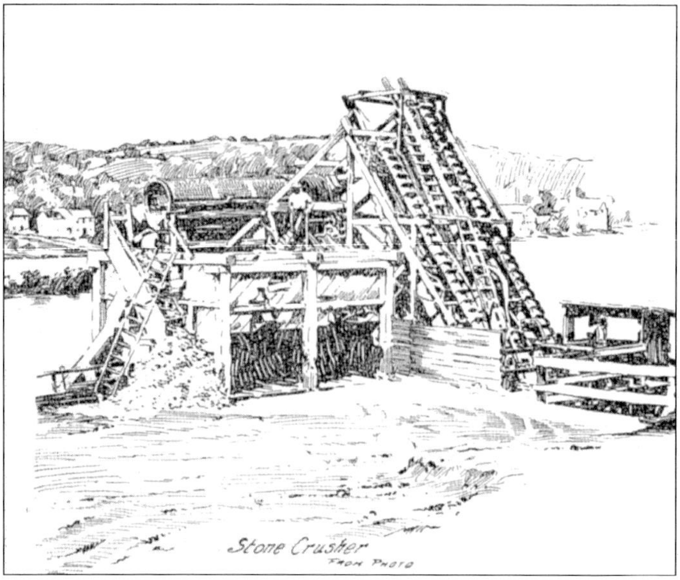

Valuable clay deposits at the Occoquan site were recognized by DC prior to purchasing the land. Other ingredients needed to make bricks; sand, clay, shale, and water were nearby. A small stone-crushing operation was already running on the land when it was purchased. Adjacent to it, the prison opened a brickyard and planned the construction of two kilns with plans to add 10 more. (Courtesy of Patrick O'Neill.)

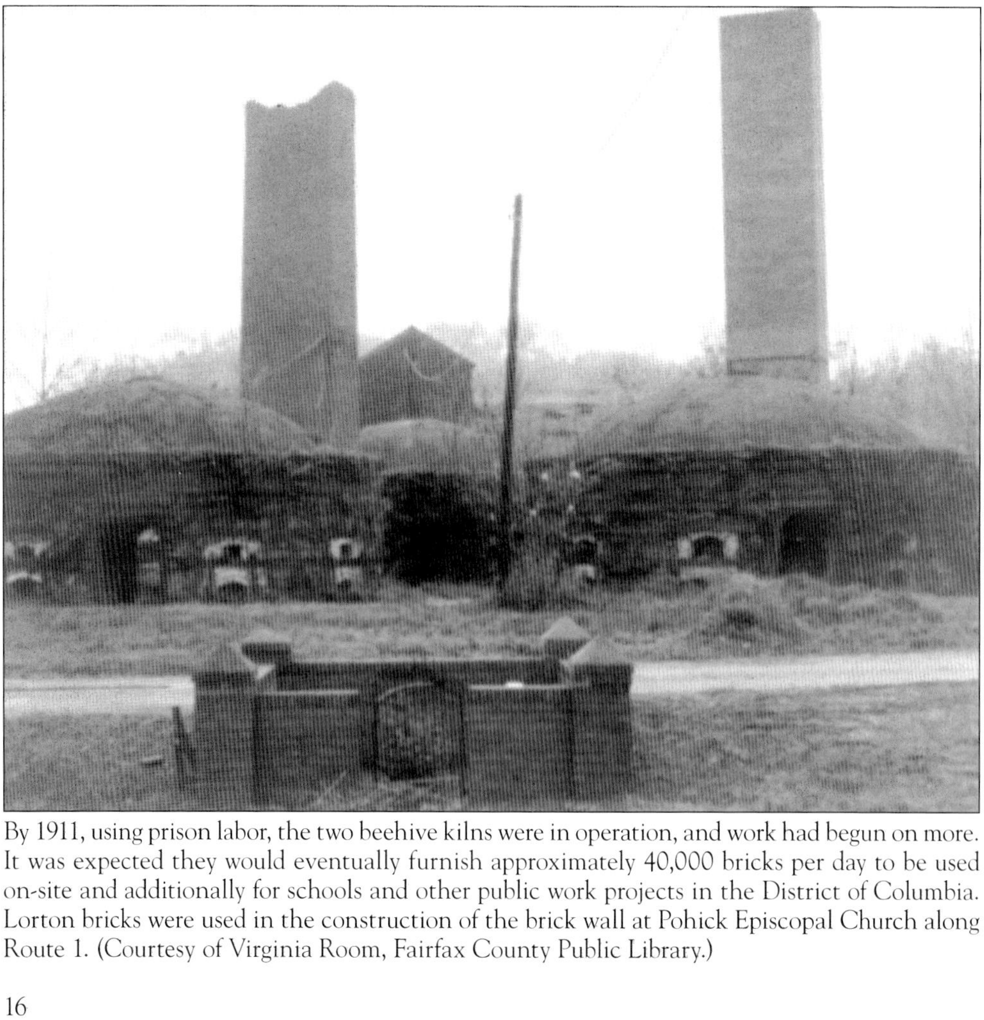

By 1911, using prison labor, the two beehive kilns were in operation, and work had begun on more. It was expected they would eventually furnish approximately 40,000 bricks per day to be used on-site and additionally for schools and other public work projects in the District of Columbia. Lorton bricks were used in the construction of the brick wall at Pohick Episcopal Church along Route 1. (Courtesy of Virginia Room, Fairfax County Public Library.)

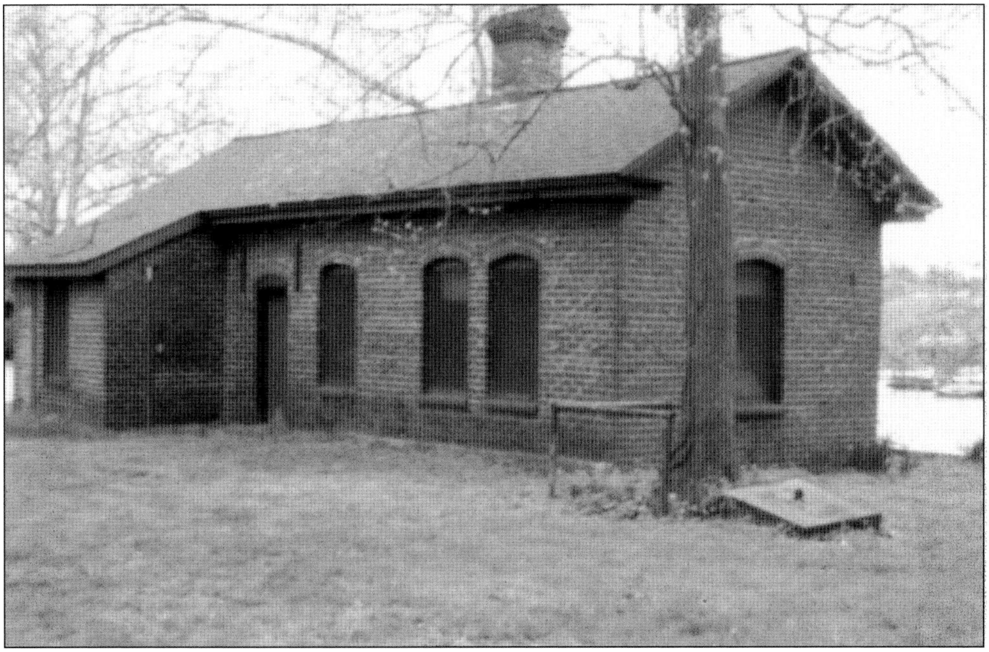

Bricks needed to be carefully stacked in a particular way inside the kiln to dry properly. To be the prisoner in charge of the process was considered an important job. The controls for temperatures were in the nearby kiln-house. Bricks were not standardized until the mid-20th century, and Lorton bricks were a little thicker and heavier. (Courtesy of Fairfax County Department of Planning and Development.)

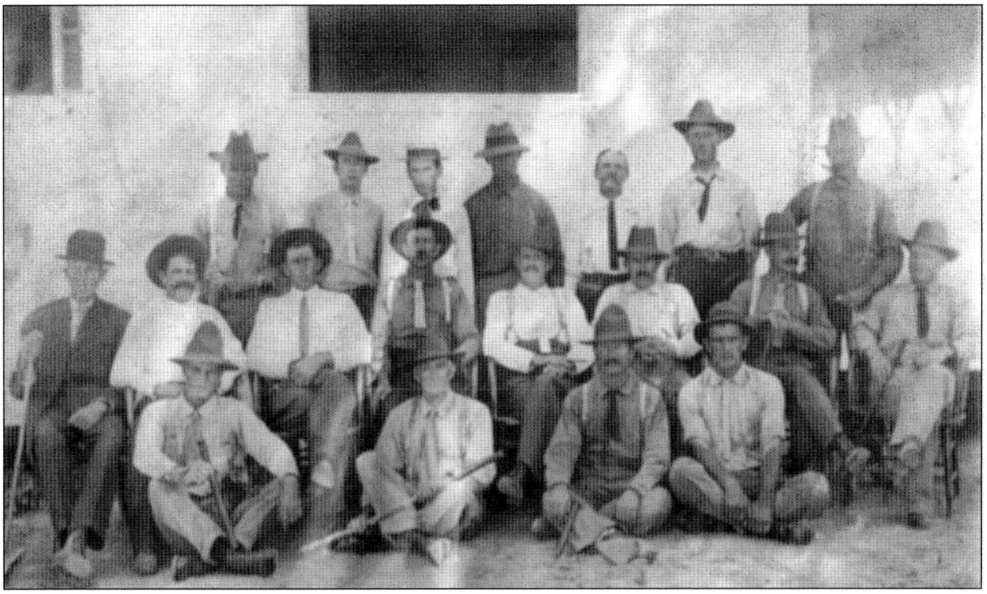

The Workhouse employed men from nearby families. Some sold their land for the prison. They were paid better wages than could be earned elsewhere and it became a major source of employment for the area. The prison provided a nearby market for the farmers' goods and the community also benefited from the prisoner-built road from the Lorton to Occoquan providing access to the Richmond, Fredericksburg & Potomac Railroad train stop. (Courtesy of the Pegelow family.)

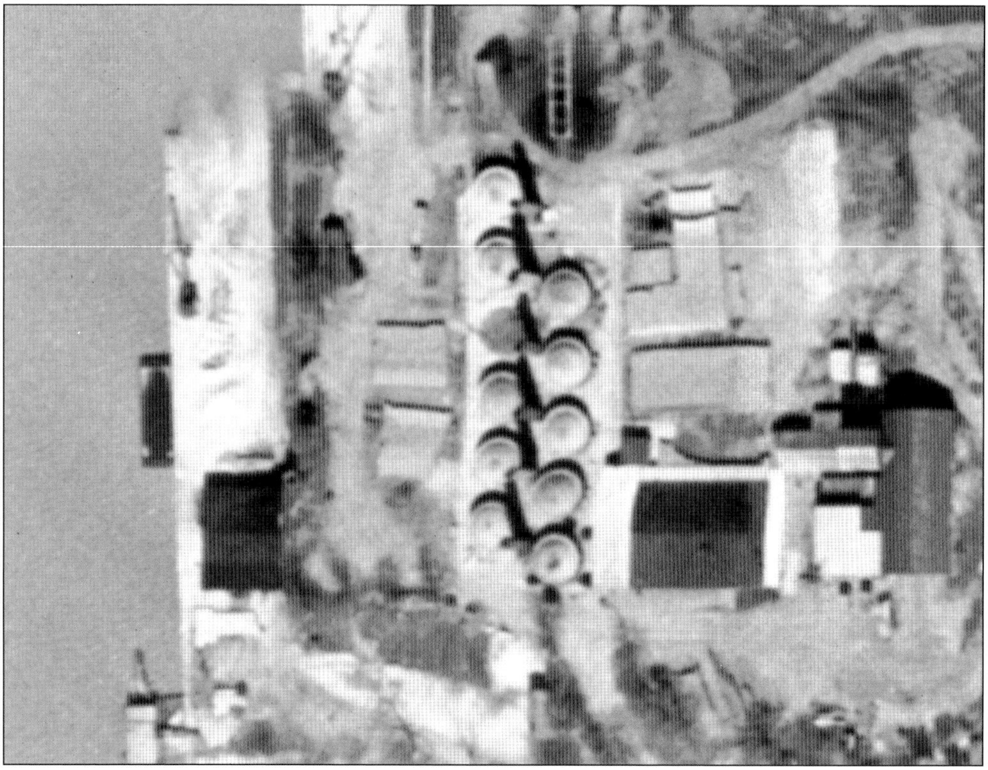

During the construction of a brick kiln at Occoquan, a work crew discovered crumbling, unreadable tombstones. Work was temporarily halted. Local patriot societies believed the mound near the water contained bodies of the soldiers who died fighting Lord Dunmore to protect Martha Washington and Mount Vernon. They sought to permanently halt the construction. The kilns were built. (Courtesy of Virginia Room, Fairfax County City Library.)

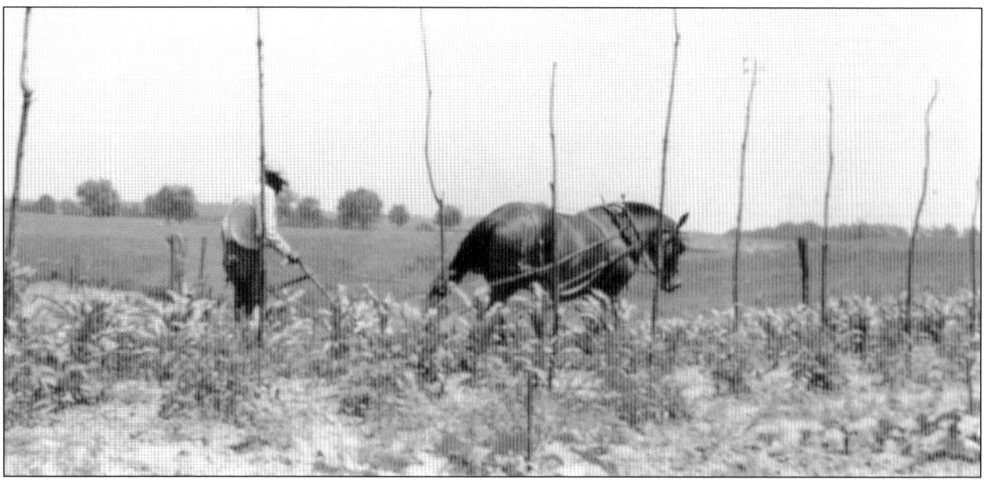

Before crops could be grown, it was necessary to clear and cultivate the soil to prepare it for planting. To fertilize the farmland, animal manure collected on the streets of Washington was sent down the Potomac River by barge and off-loaded at the newly built prison wharf on the Occoquan River. At first, it was a subsistence farm and most of the produce was eaten on site or preserved for future use. (Courtesy of DC Archives.)

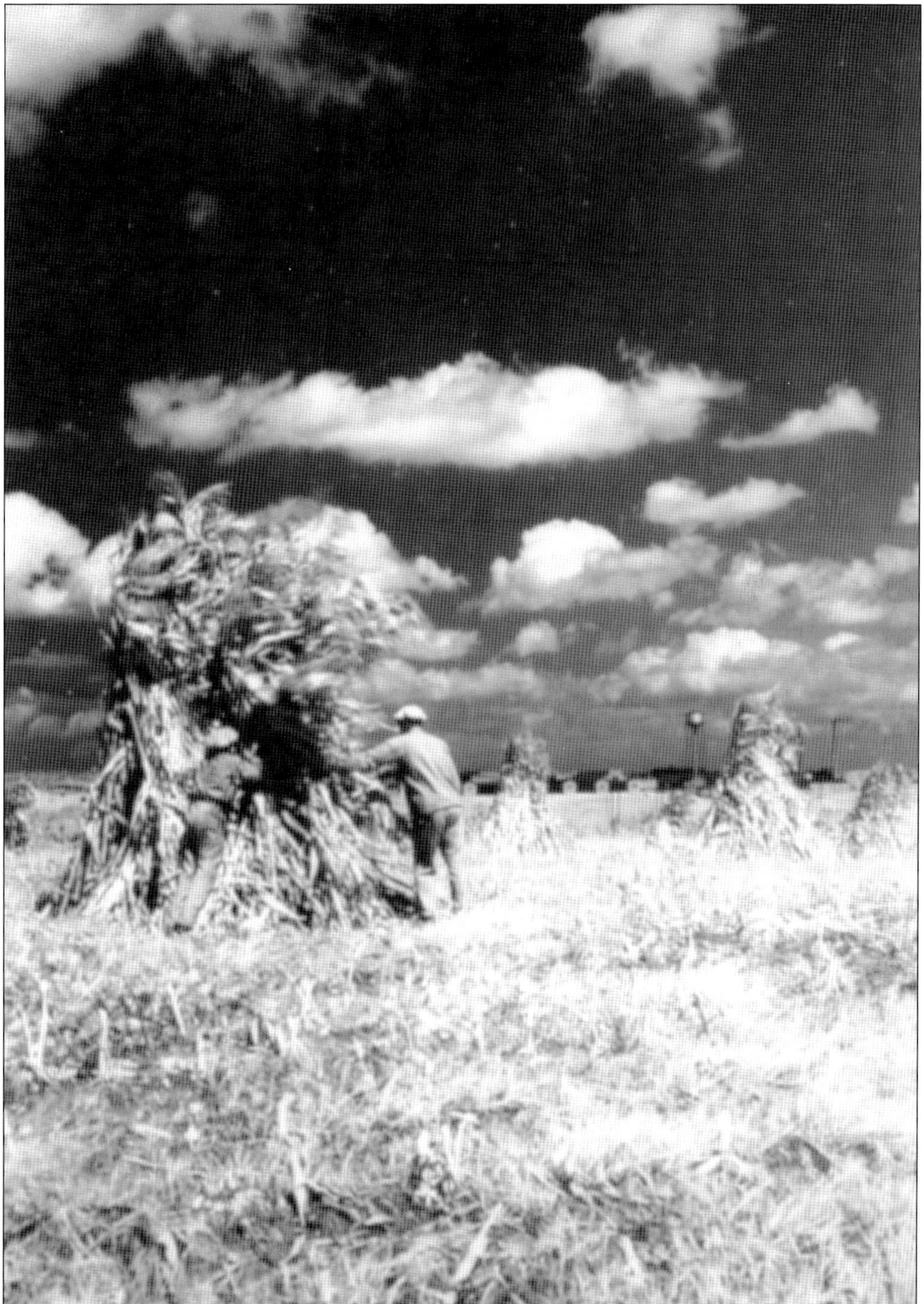

The Workhouse farm continued to be a subsistence farm. Most of the produce was eaten on-site or preserved for winter use. All kinds of vegetables were grown and the orchards started to provide a variety of fruits. Beef and dairy cattle, pigs, chickens, and geese were raised. Corn, wheat, and hay were grown to feed the animals. (Courtesy of DC Archives.)

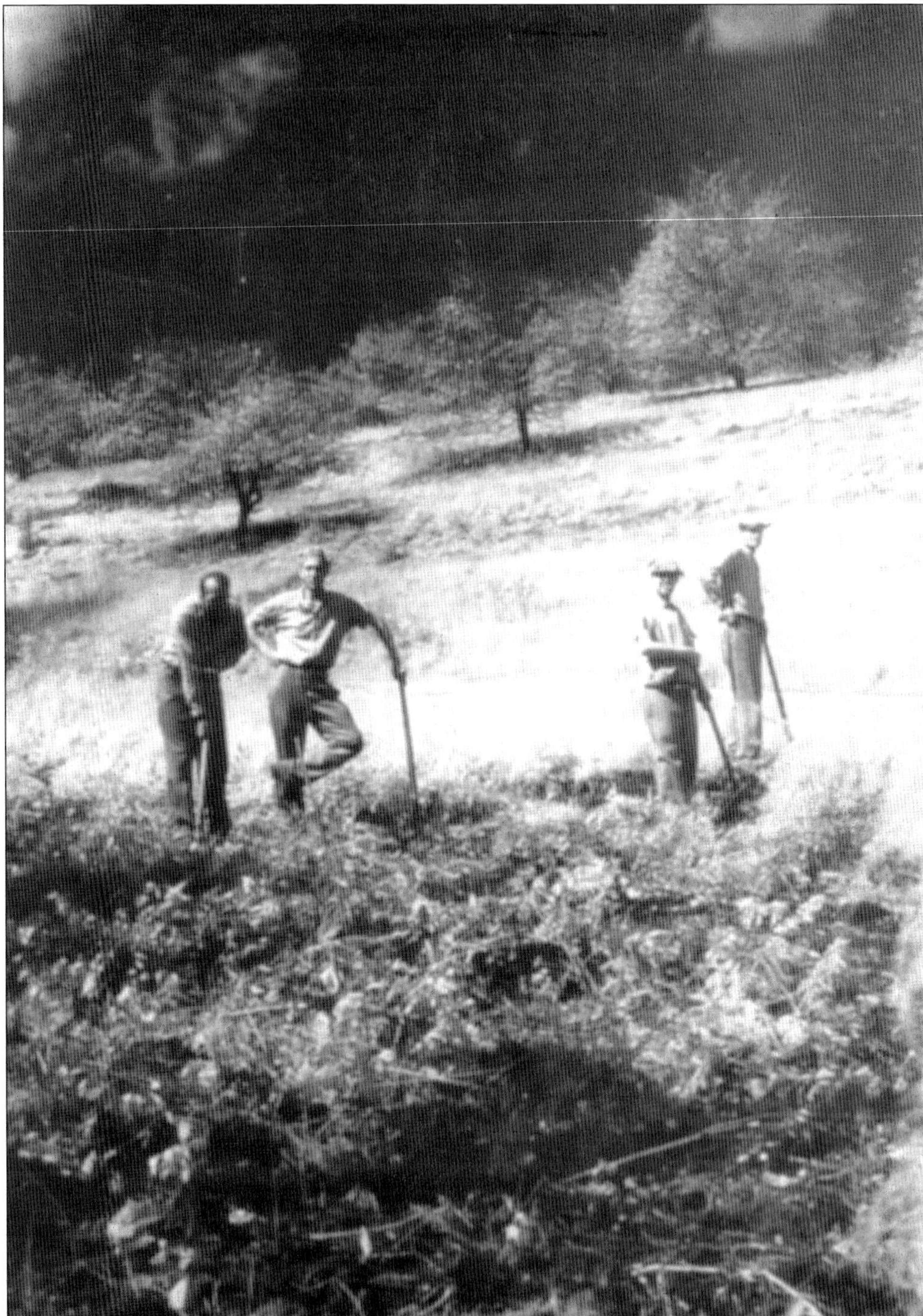

The orchard they created along both sides of Lorton Road provided apples and a variety of other fruits for the prison diet. A large apple storage barn was built along Furnace Road until it was unfortunately lost to arson in the 1970s. Many longtime residents of Lorton still refer to that area as Apple Orchard Hill. (Courtesy of DC Archives.)

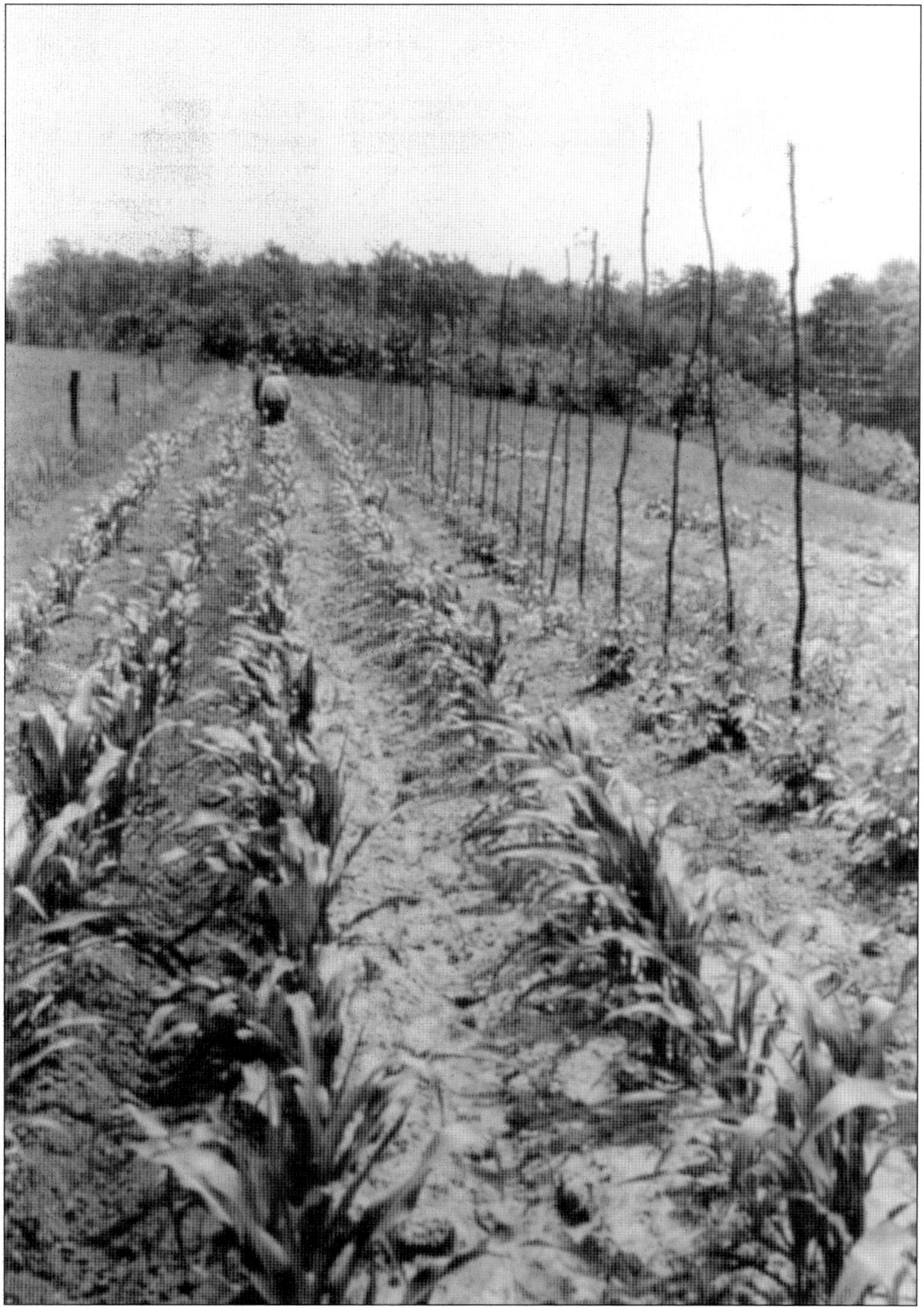

Years later, a guard recalled early days at the industrial farm: "Prisoners had to carry everything themselves. We planted from 8 a.m. 'til 12 noon. We planted cabbages—oh Lord—we planted everything. We killed hogs on Monday, killed beef cattle—oh, let me see—on Thursday. Inmates planted impatiens, of course the shrubbery, roses, pansies, that kind of thing. They planted the grass and mowed the grass. They took care of it all." (Courtesy of DC Archives.)

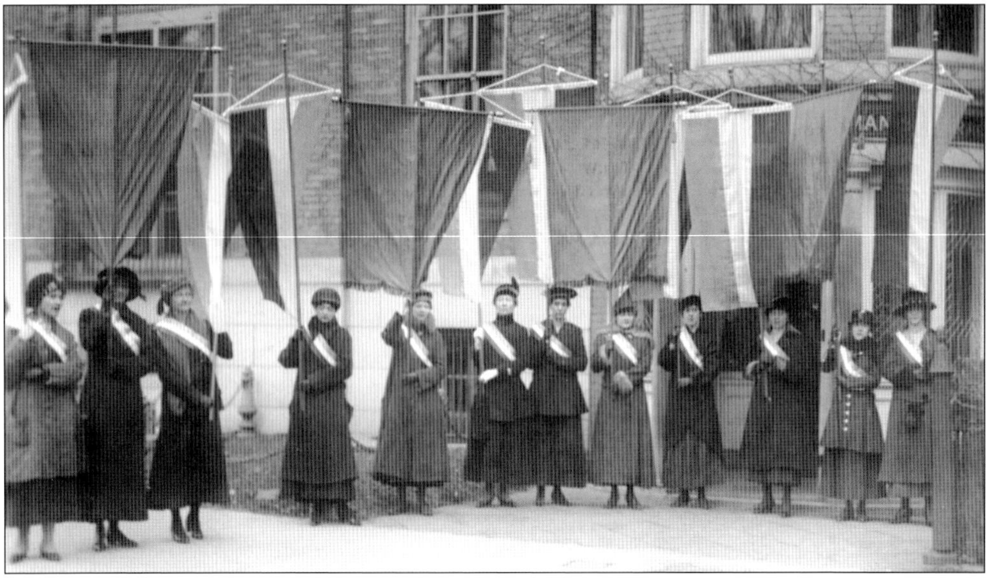

Women suffragists demanding the right to vote began picketing the White House in January 1917 in an effort to pressure the president to persuade Congress to bring the 19th Amendment up for a vote. They showed up with their banners every day but Sunday and became a crowd favorite with the tourists. They were unmolested for five months. (Courtesy of the Library of Congress.)

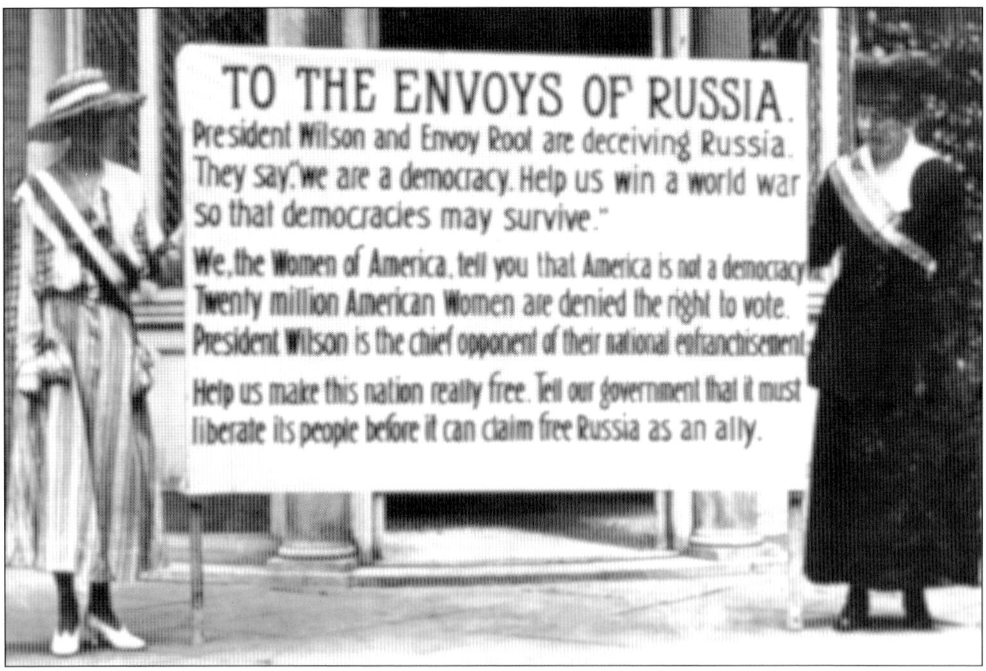

Things changed in June when Katherine Morey (left) and Lucy Burns (right) unfurled the Russian banner as the Russian envoy was entering the White House to confer with Pres. Woodrow Wilson. The women were taken into custody; their banner was confiscated. They were released and warned to cease picketing. More women continued to return with new banners with the same message. Finally, they were arrested and twice sentenced to five days in the DC Jail. (Courtesy of the Library of Congress.)

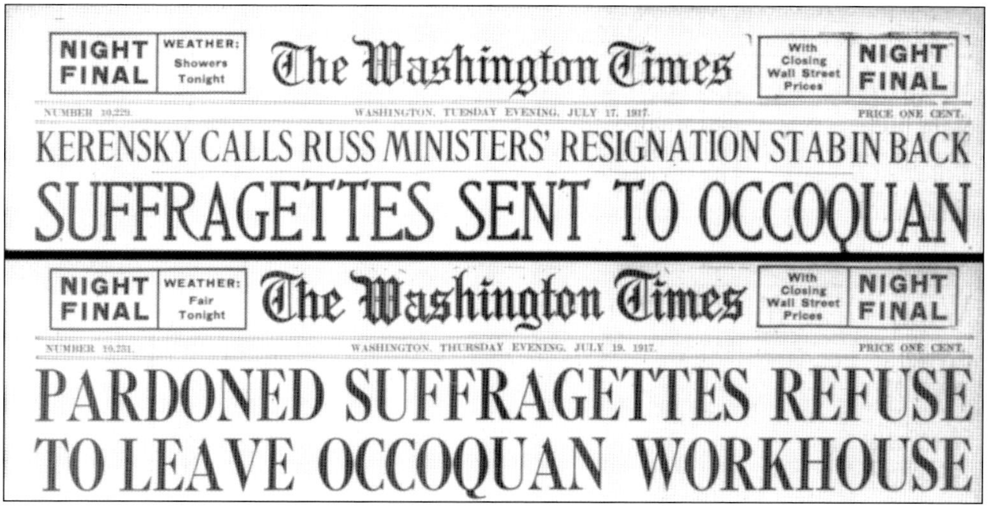

NIGHT FINAL | WEATHER: Showers Tonight | The Washington Times | With Closing Wall Street Prices | NIGHT FINAL

WASHINGTON, TUESDAY EVENING, JULY 17, 1917. PRICE ONE CENT.

KERENSKY CALLS RUSS MINISTERS' RESIGNATION STAB IN BACK

SUFFRAGETTES SENT TO OCCOQUAN

NIGHT FINAL | WEATHER: Fair Tonight | The Washington Times | With Closing Wall Street Prices | NIGHT FINAL

WASHINGTON, THURSDAY EVENING, JULY 19, 1917. PRICE ONE CENT.

PARDONED SUFFRAGETTES REFUSE TO LEAVE OCCOQUAN WORKHOUSE

When the suffragettes continued to picket, those arrested on July 14 were given the choice of a $25 fine or 60 days at the Women's Workhouse at Lorton. They refused to pay the fine and were brought down by train. They decided to cooperate but passively show their determination not to yield to coercion. The president pardoned them after three days due to political pressure from some of his supporters. (Courtesy of the Library of Congress.)

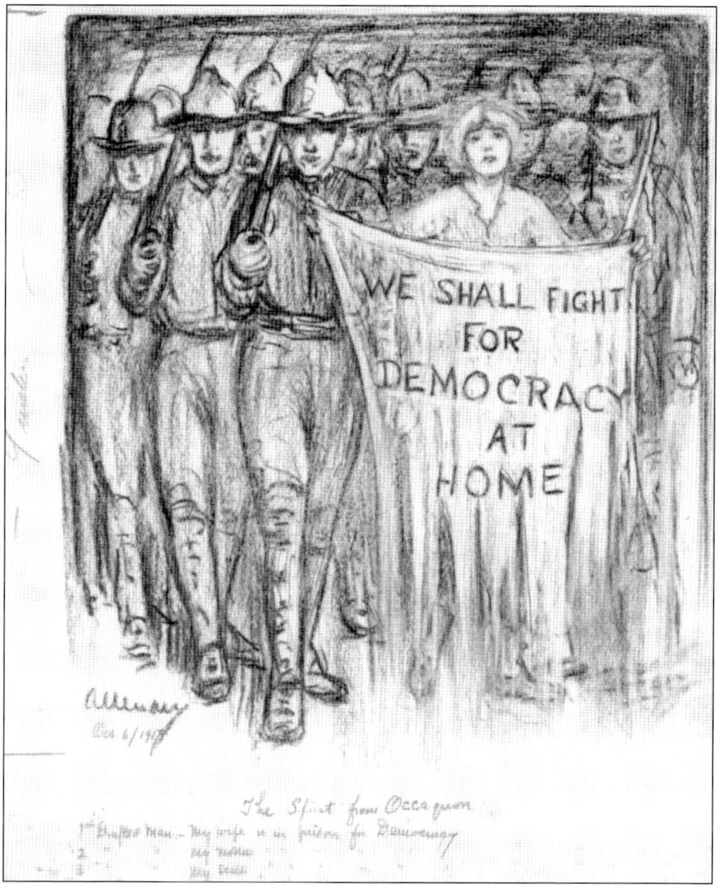

Pres. Woodrow Wilson hoped that after he pardoned the suffragettes, they would stop picketing. They did not, and their signs became more provocative. One group was sent to Occoquan in August and two more in September. They now demanded the rights of political prisoners and refused to work. With so many in Occoquan, the next group was sent to the DC Jail and three began a hunger strike. (Courtesy of the Library of Congress.)

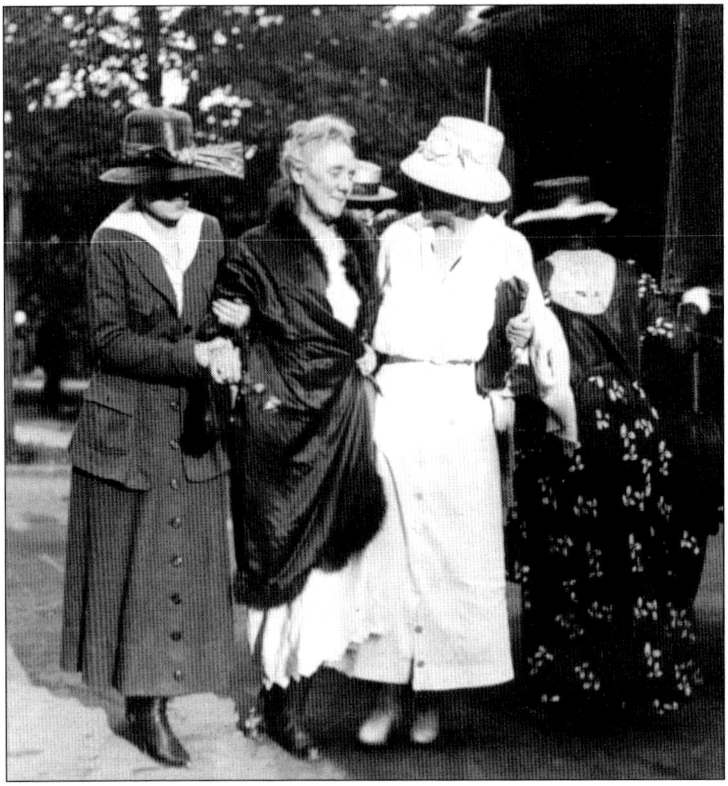

In November 1917, a total of 16 women from 14 different states, protesting the force-feeding of suffragists in the DC Jail, were arrested, brought to Occoquan, and taken to punishment cells at the Men's Workhouse. They refused to work, began a hunger strike, and two were force-fed. They sued. An order was issued for their appearance at District court. Their cruel mistreatment was evidenced by Dora Lewis and others as they testified to their experiences. (Courtesy of the Library of Congress.)

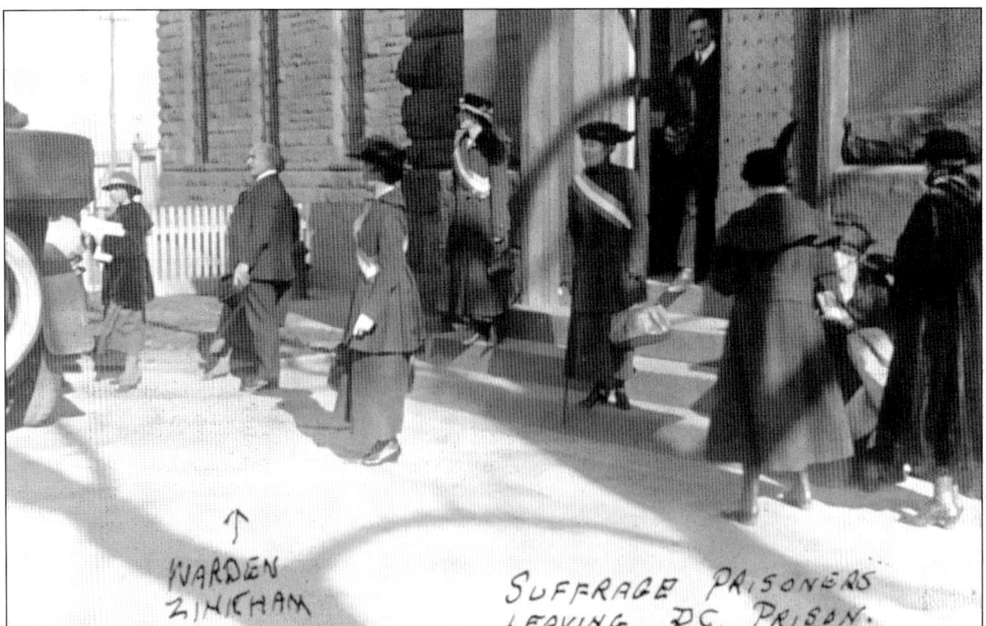

Word of their treatment horrified the nation. Woodrow Wilson sensed a change in the political wind and agreed to urge Congress to bring the 19th Amendment up for a vote in the next session. The initial battle had been won. It would take three more years of struggle, but in 1920, women could vote in every state in the union in the national election. (Courtesy of the Library of Congress.)

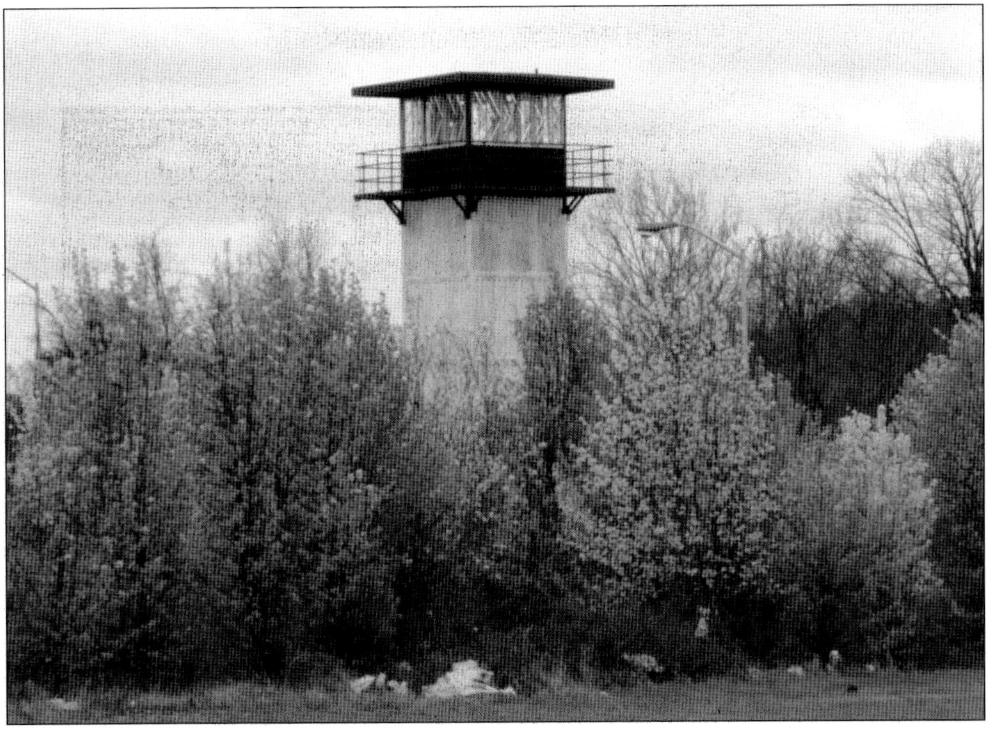

Initially, the grounds of the Workhouse were not enclosed by fences. A system of sentinel boxes was set up and manned by trustees who would alert the guards of an attempted escape. Bloodhounds were used for tracking. In this wooded, rural area with few roads, most escapees headed for the railroad tracks to follow them north. (Courtesy of Stefan Hembre.)

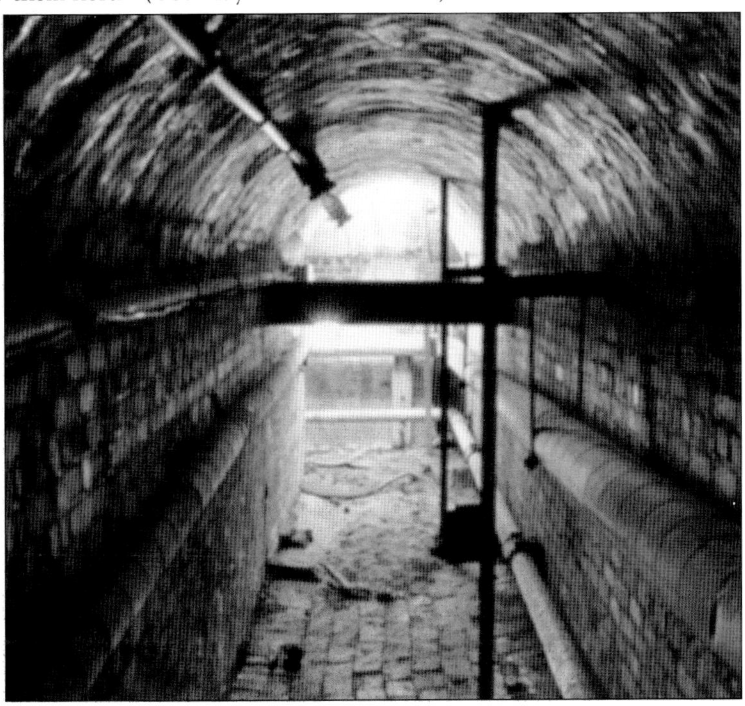

A system of brick tunnels was built to connect the buildings and house the various sewage and water pipes that served them. Guards were able to walk through them and in later years prison entrepreneurs found it a great place to hide their shoots. Entrances to them were sealed off not long after the Art Center opened for security reasons. (Courtesy of DC Archives.)

NEW TUG USED IN TRANSPORTING PRISONERS TO AND FROM WORKHOUSE AT OCCOQUAN.

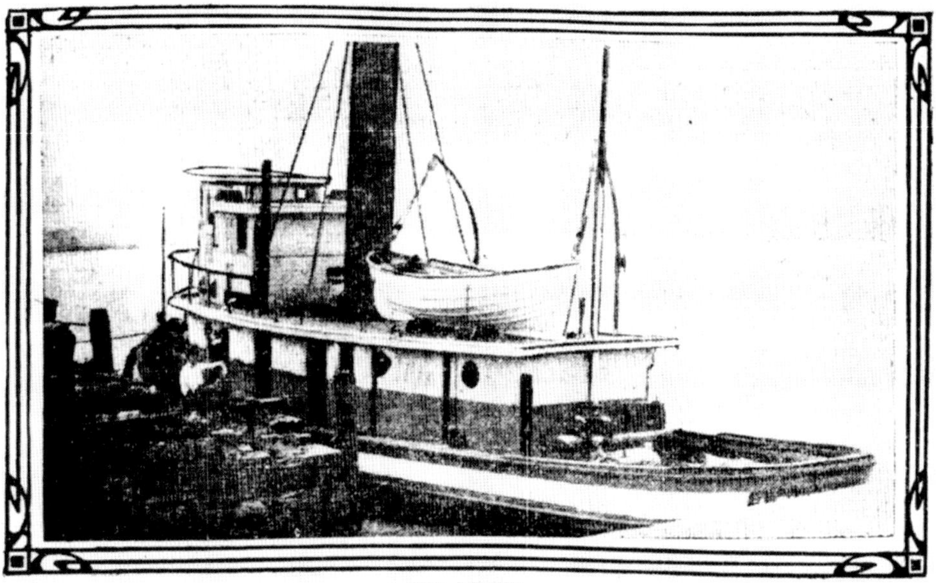

THE LOUISE.

In the summer of 1919, the District purchased a tugboat, the *Louise*, for service between the Ninth Street Wharf in DC and the new wharf at Occoquan. It ferried prisoners down to the workhouse and released men home. It towed barges carrying coal and other supplies to the prison and brought back bricks and other products from the industries in operation there. The *Louise* replaced the old Army tugboat *General Warren*. (Courtesy of the People's Archive, DC Public Library.)

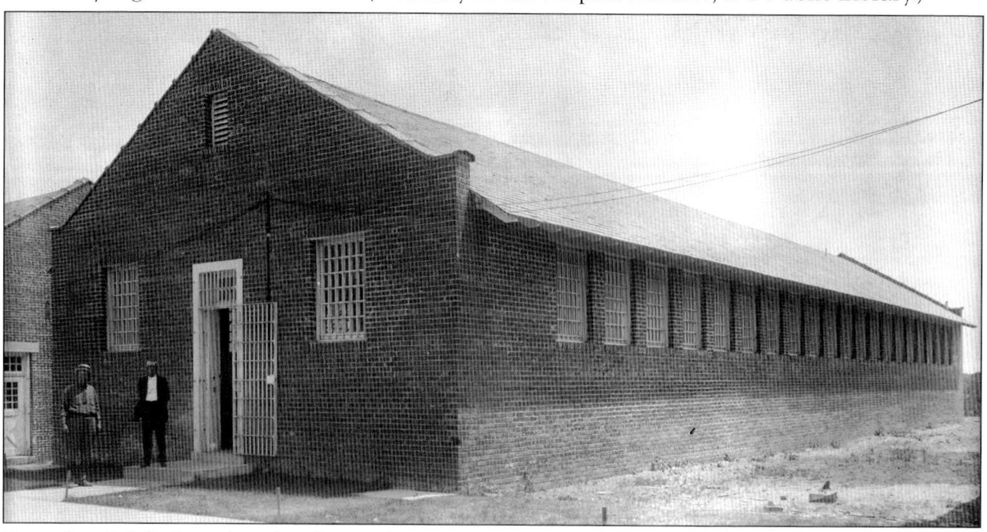

Snowden Ashford was hired to design the permanent brick buildings. Using a colonial architectural style, he purposely designed them to not look like a prison. In the fall of 1916, temporary housing for 100 inmates was opened at the Reformatory, and they were put to work building a railroad to transport construction materials and prisoners from the wharf to the Workhouse and Reformatory sites. (Courtesy of the Library of Congress.)

Two

The Expansion Years

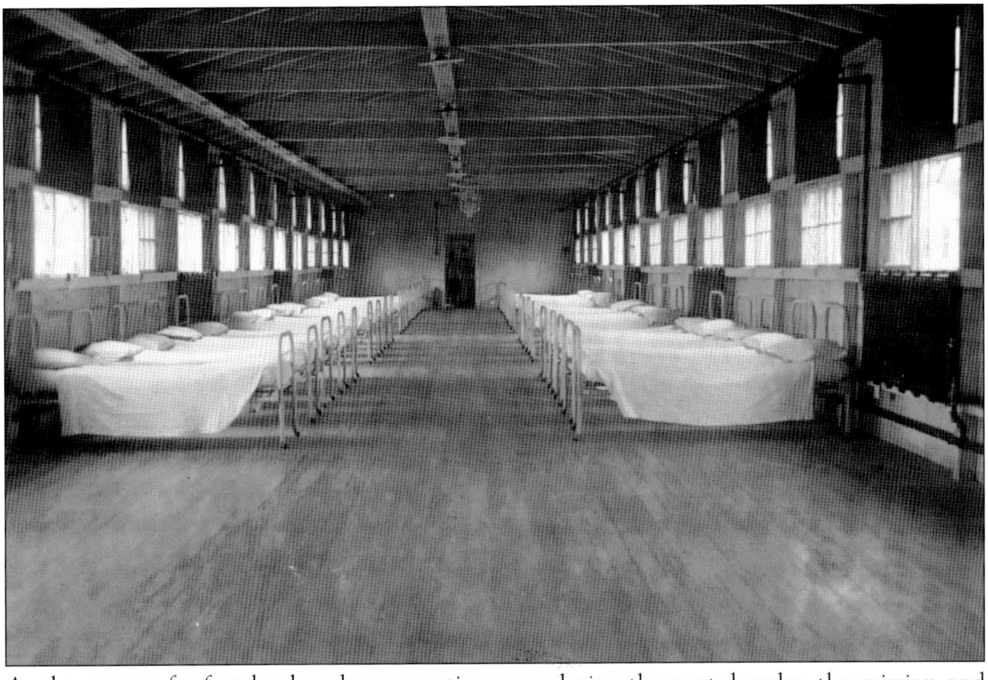

As the acreage for farmland at the reservation grew during the next decades, the mission and types of prisoners sent to Lorton also expanded. The honor system remained intact, but there was a recognition of the need, at least temporarily, for separate housing for incorrigible inmates. The Depression and World War II brought special challenges to overcome. (Courtesy of Fairfax County Department of Planning and Development.)

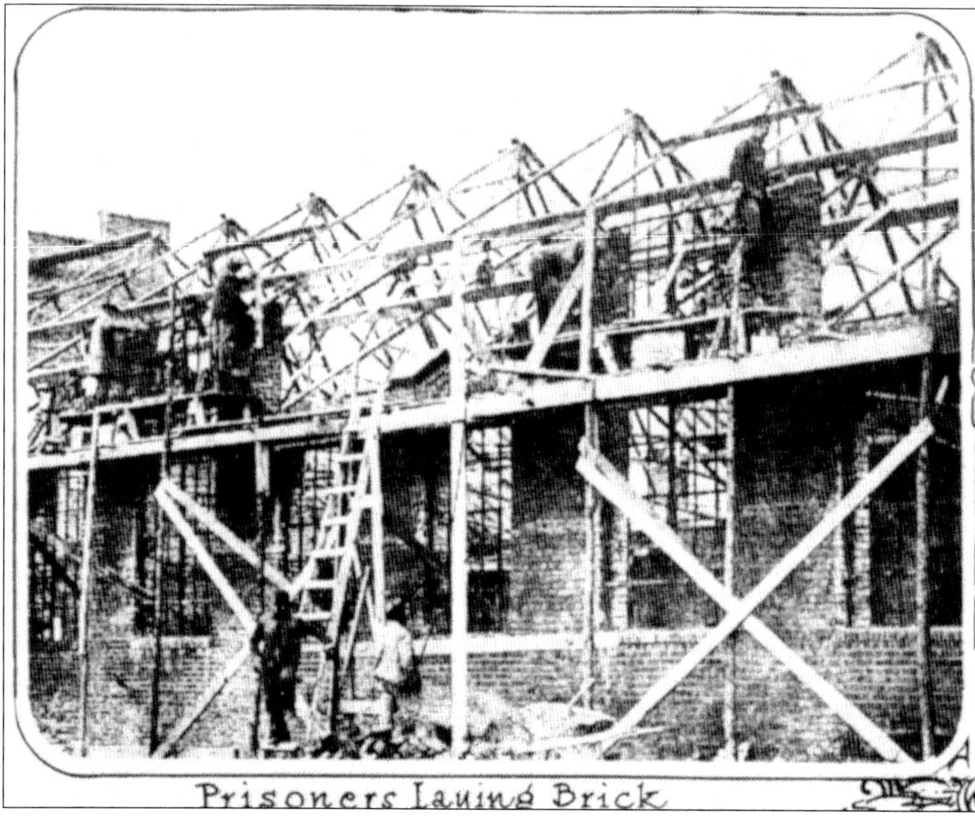

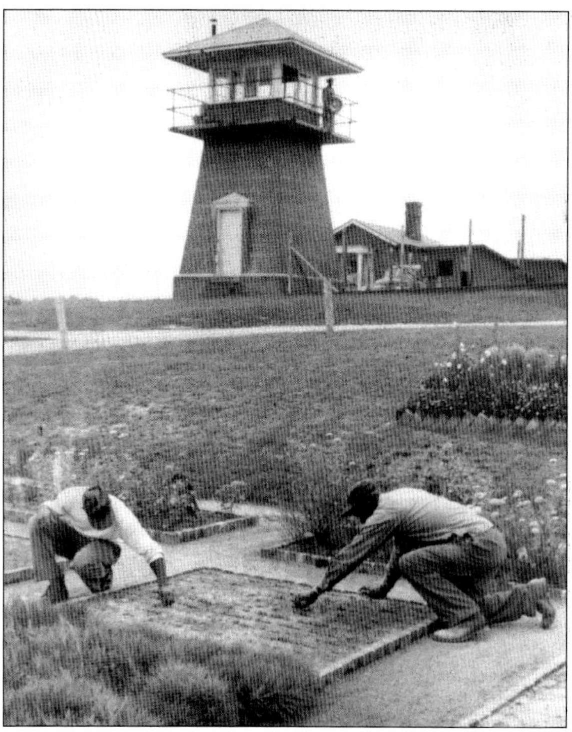

The building of the Reformatory began in 1924, and by 1928, about 75 percent of the prison population was housed. The brick manufacturing and construction work were all done by prisoners, supervised by staff. For the second time, the prisoners had to build their own prison at Lorton. (Courtesy of DC Archives.)

Inmates sent to the new Reformatory, though they had committed more serious crimes, were still considered hopefuls. If taught a trade where they could earn a good living, upon their release they would return and become productive citizens. The treatment philosophy remained the same; prisoners would be required to do a full day's work. DC prisoners with a year or longer sentences now could serve them at Lorton and not be sent to federal prison. (Courtesy of DC Archives.)

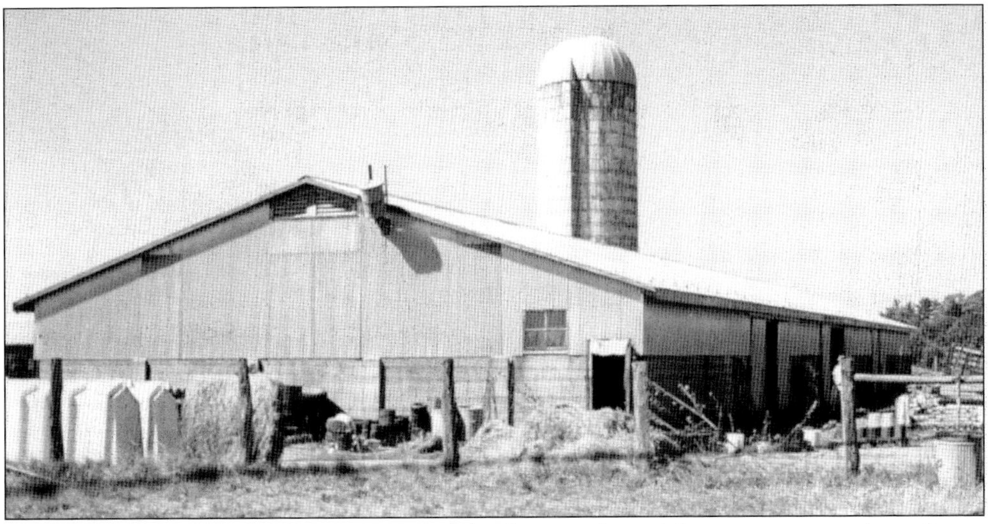

The dairy operation was a separate unit and the dairy cattle were kept in a separate barn. It was by far the longest-running agricultural operation at the prison. It was located just behind the Workhouse. Over time, three barns were built: a dairy barn, a hay barn, and the three-level barn. (Courtesy of the Library of Congress.)

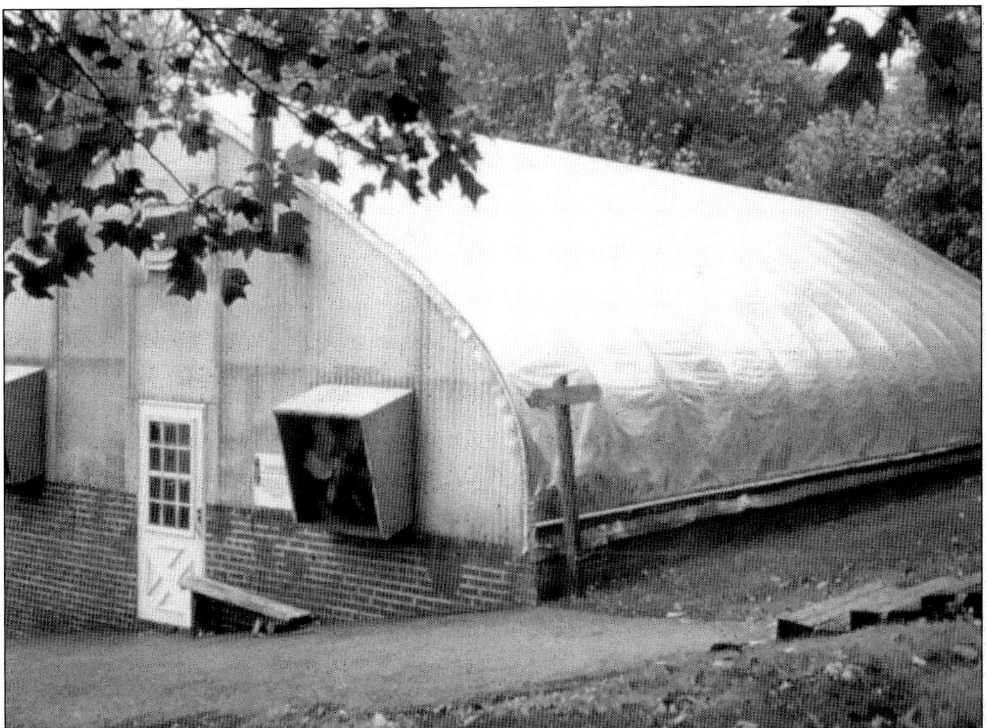

A greenhouse was built and, along with it, a series of cold frames that were used to cultivate seedlings to get a jump start on the growing season. As acreage was added to the prison, fields of vegetables were cultivated, which produced an abundant harvest; so much so that a cannery was established to preserve fruits and vegetables for use in the prison kitchens during the off-season. (Courtesy of Fairfax County Department of Planning and Development.)

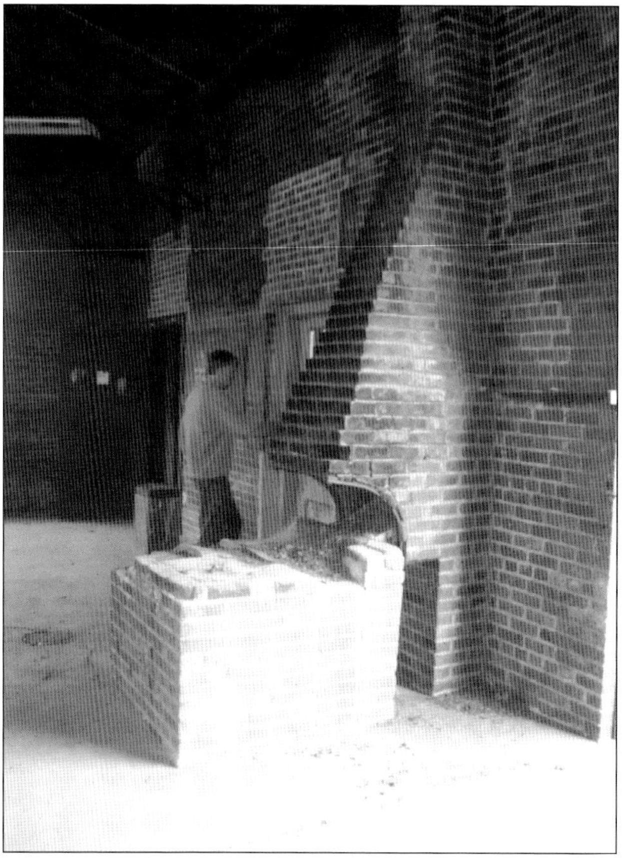

The blacksmith's forge was the center of activity at the Workhouse. On his anvil, he made the nails, shoes for the horses, chains, yoke rings, axes, augurs, bullet molds, hanging hooks, and metal parts for all the agricultural implements. He was also there to make repairs as needed. When the Reformatory was built, it included a special building for this vital work. (Courtesy of William Koch.)

The iron anvil and bellows were important parts of the blacksmith trade. Horseshoes and tools were shaped as he hammered on one and turned the handle on the other to blow air on the coals to keep the fire hot. This anvil was in use at the Workhouse from its earliest days. (Courtesy of William Koch.)

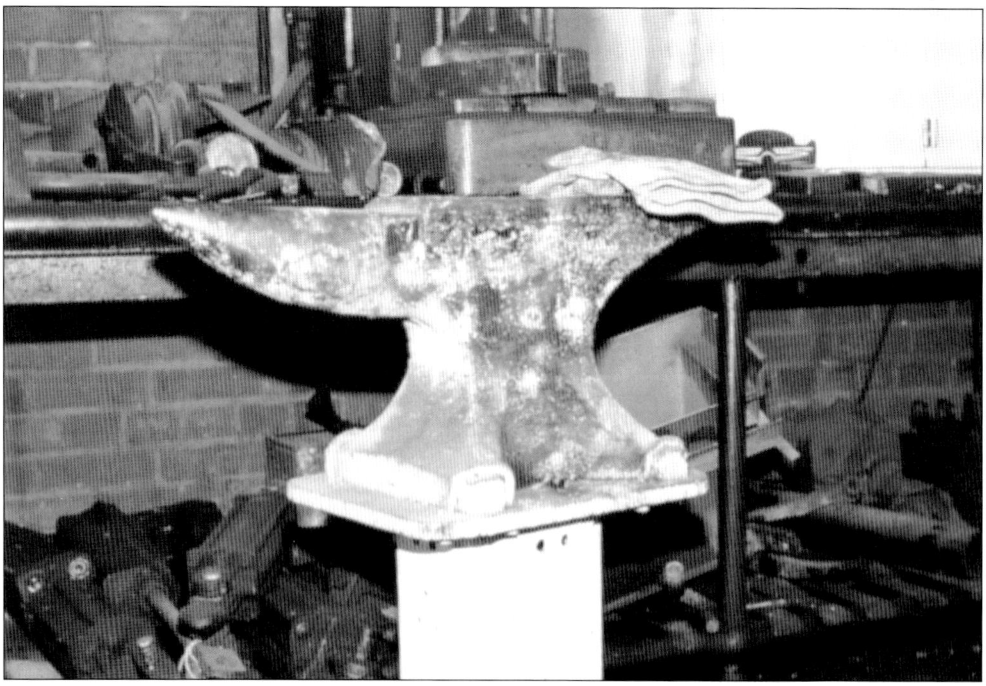

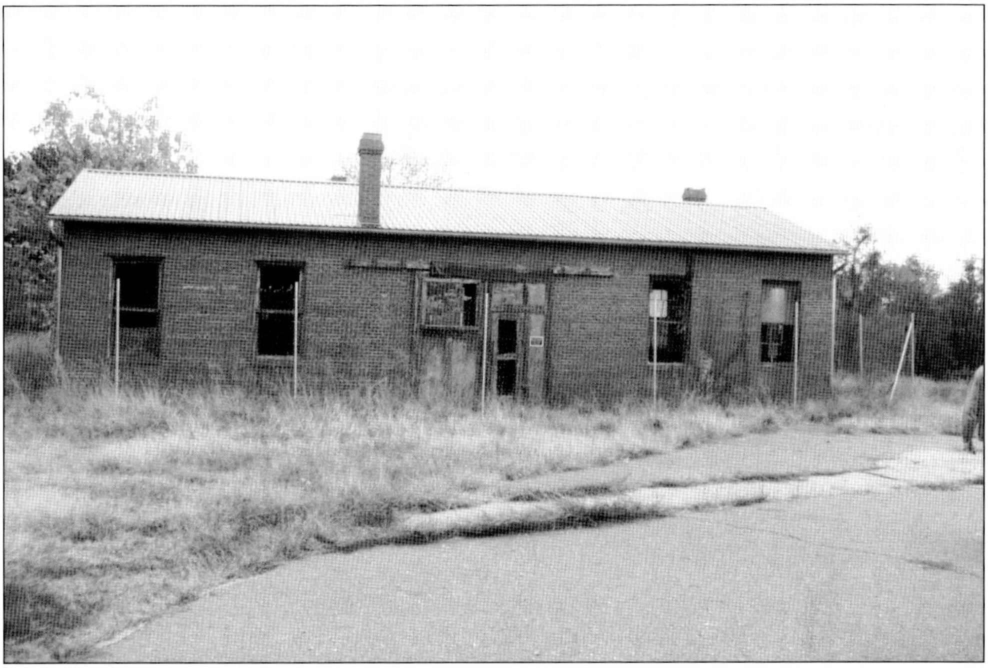

A one-story brick building housed the larger forge with its brick hearth and chimney at the Reformatory. In addition to hammering shoes for horses and repairing farm equipment, the forge could supplement the needs for small metal parts for the railroad and at the various industrial shops nearby. (Courtesy of William Koch.)

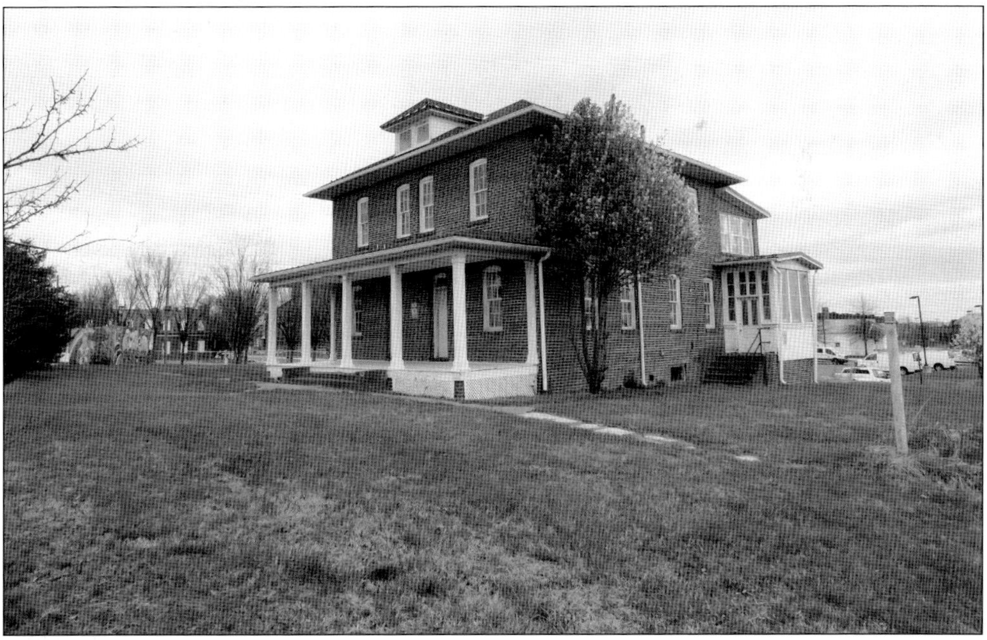

There were 13 residences built on prison property. The first superintendents occupied the Laurel Hill House. The four-square house was divided for use by multiple occupants. Senior staff and guards lived in other houses scattered throughout the complex. The doctor's house was the home of the resident physician. (Courtesy of Patrick O'Neill.)

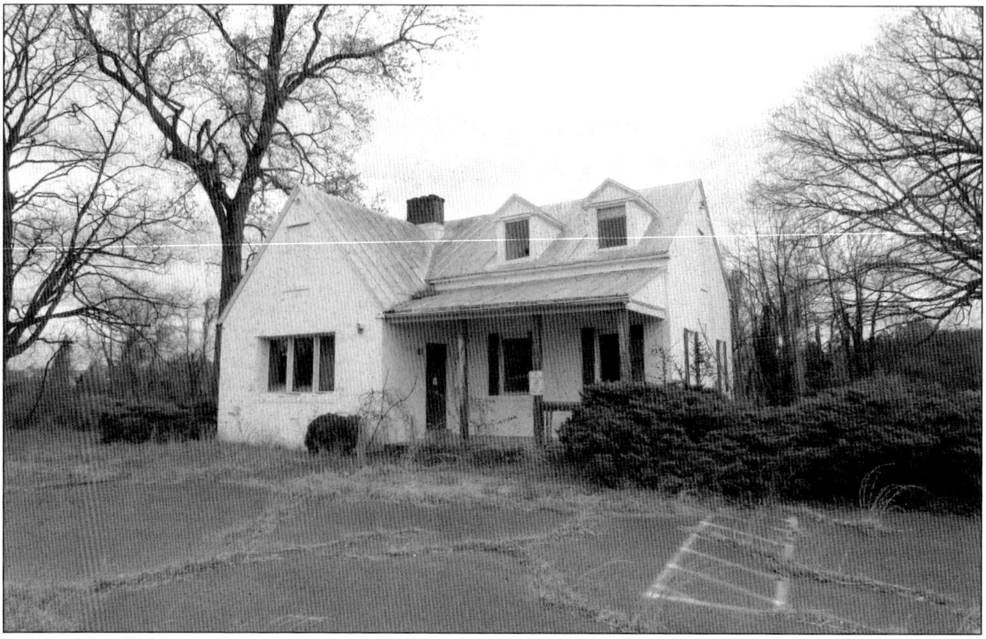

The "Doctor's House" was the residence of the prison physician, who also made house calls within the local community. In the 1950s, Dr. William Orsinger was given a movie camera for Christmas and toured the prison complex filming day-to-day activities. After his death, his family offered his home movie to the museum. Both the film and the still pictures clipped from it have been invaluable resources. (Courtesy of Patrick O'Neill.)

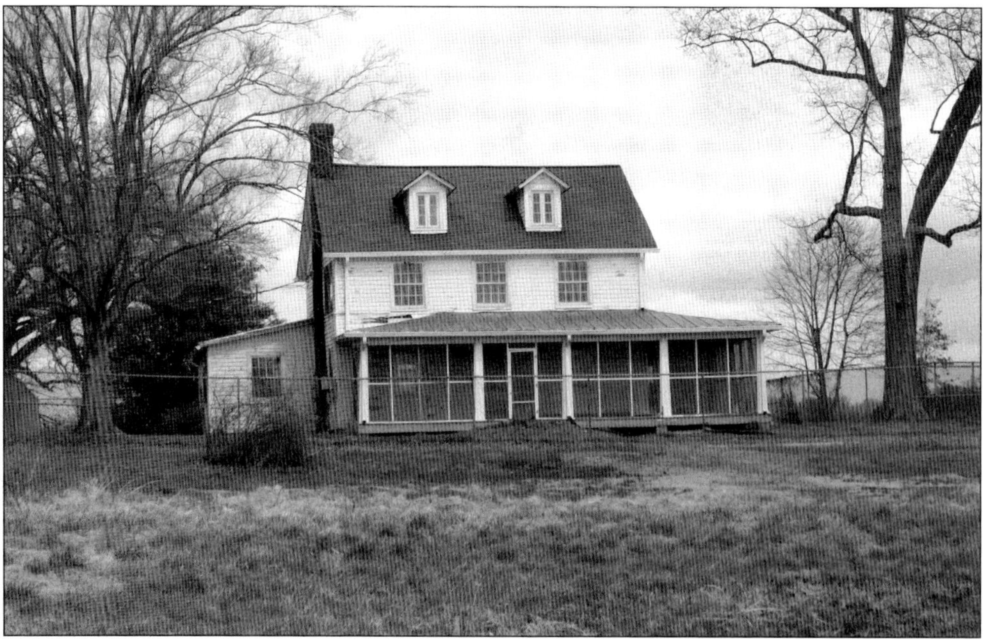

When Fairfax County was assessing the staff housing on prison grounds for condition and historical significance, the determination was made to name the house for the last family who occupied it. This became the Barrett House. Longtime Lorton citizens still refer to it as the Pegelow House as that is where Captain Pegelow lived and raised his bloodhounds. (Courtesy of Patrick O'Neill.)

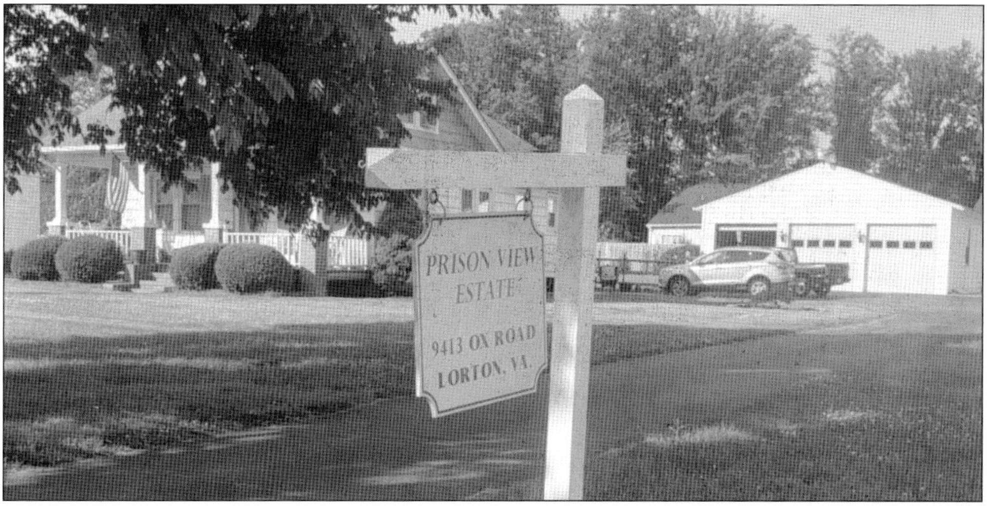

The resident houses built on prison land used prison-made materials bricks and boards and probably prison labor in their construction. A row of six mostly frame houses facing Ox Road, now a bypass after Route 123 was widened, were known by their distance from the prison, such as "the third house from the prison." It was a short walk to work for the correctional officer and a quick source of reinforcements if trouble broke out. (Courtesy of Doug Spalding.)

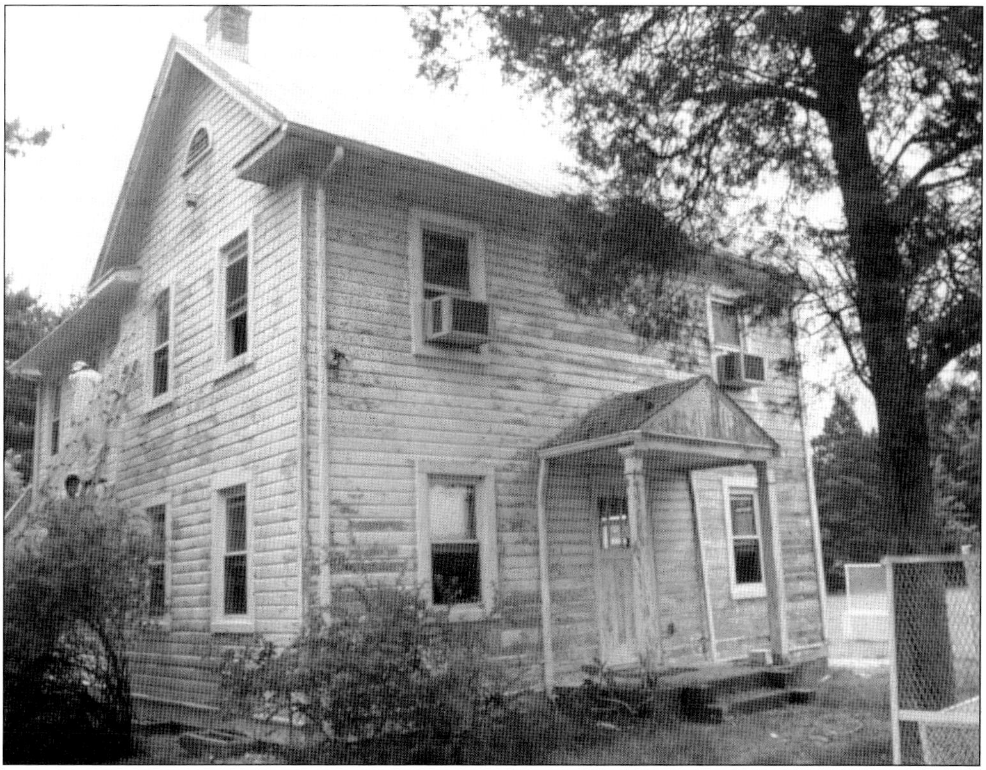

The Stempson House on Furnace Road was recently renovated as part of Fairfax County's Resident-Curator Program. Qualified residents receive long-term leases to the property and agree to rehabilitate and maintain it; The program seeks to care for the county's historic structures that might otherwise deteriorate. (Courtesy of Fairfax County Park Authority.)

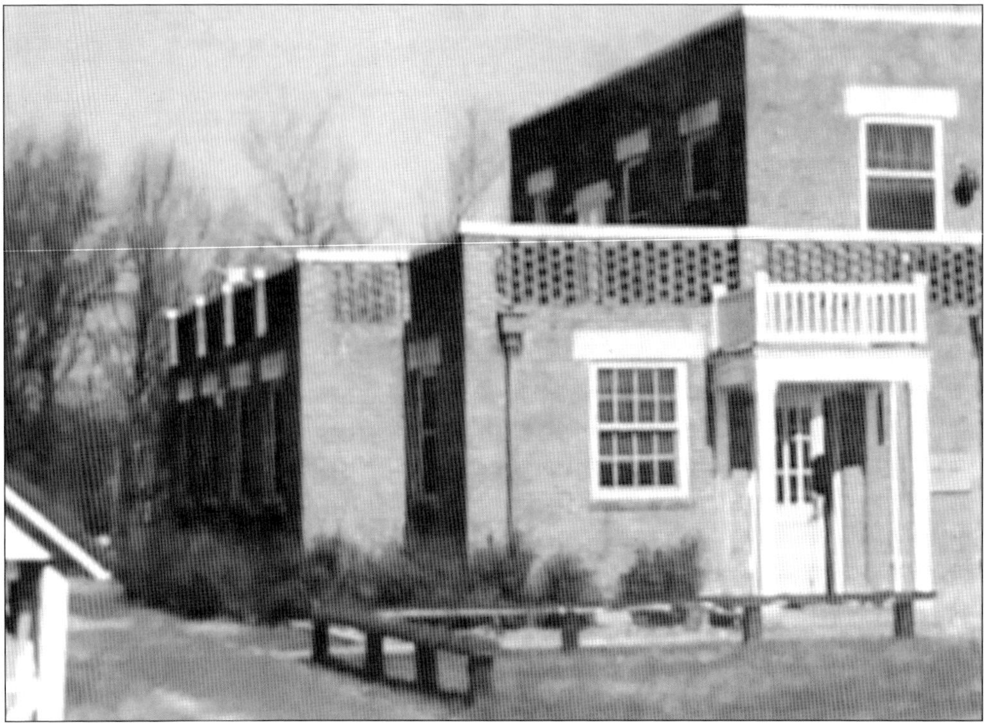

Inmates who possessed the necessary mental and physical abilities were offered vocational training as plumbers, electricians, foundry workers, and auto mechanics. Correspondence courses held in a supervised study hall provided the classroom part of the education. Often, it was taught by another inmate selected for his recognized skill and technical knowledge. The education building at the Workhouse was shared with its hospital. It is no longer there, replaced by a parking lot. In 1932, the hospital building opened at the Reformatory, staffed by a medical officer, resident physician, assistant physician, dentist, pharmacist, and graduate nurse. They were supplemented by inmate attendants and orderlies. Vocational training was offered in nursing, dental, and clinical laboratory work. Instruction in first aid, preventative medicine, and hygiene was also offered. The school and library shared the building. In later years, it was converted to a gymnasium. (Above, courtesy of DC Archives; below, courtesy of Fairfax County Department of Planning and Development.)

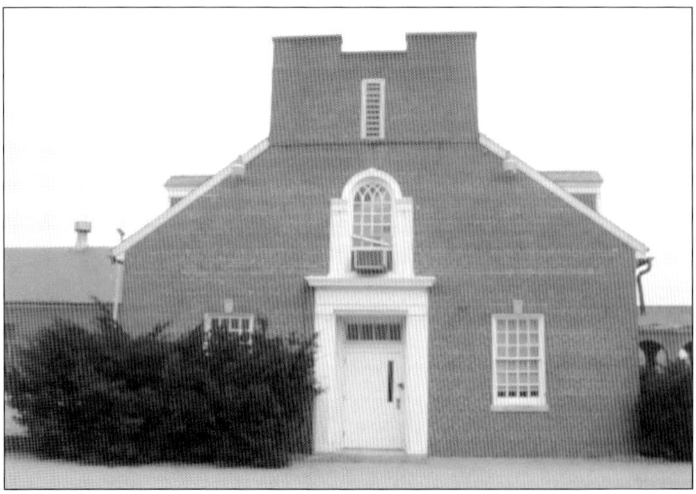

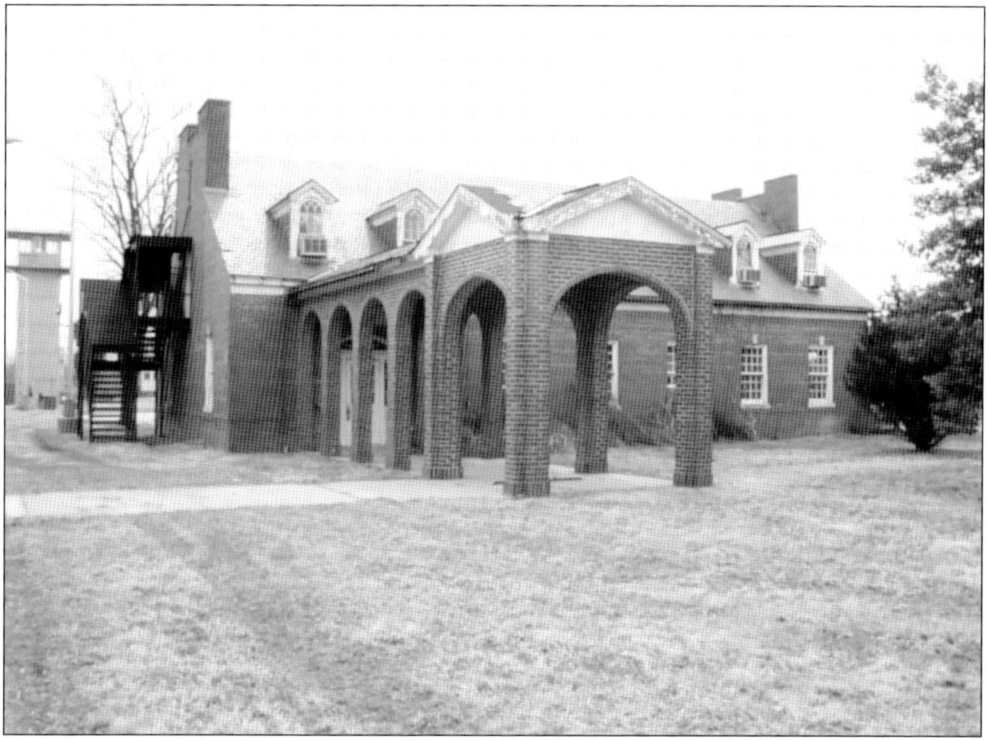

Beginning in the 1930s, men sentenced for "white collar" crimes were also sent to Lorton. These men swapped their business suits for the blue shirts and dungarees of their fellow inmates. Instead of plows and shovels, they used pencils and typewriters. The prison administration took advantage of their skills to help with the clerical work in the prison directors' offices and the upkeep of the prison records in the different industries. (Courtesy of Fairfax County Department of Planning and Development.)

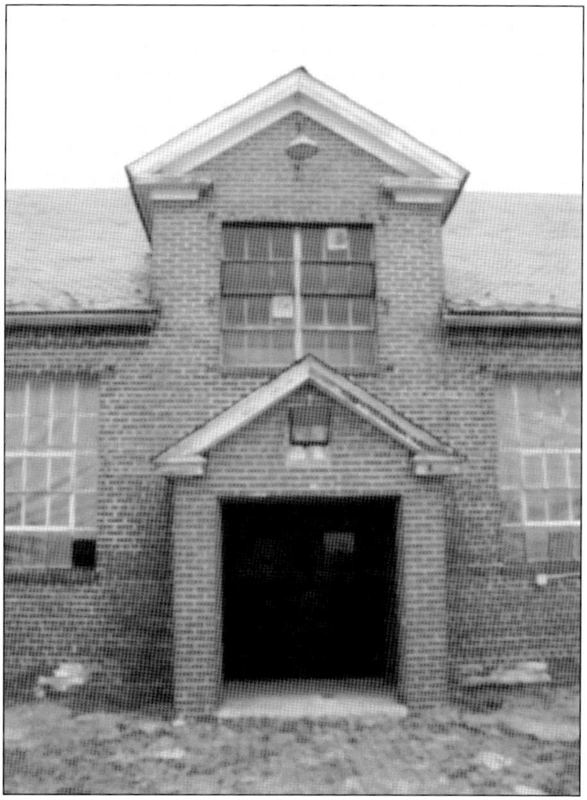

The dining hall forms the bottom of the U-shaped quad for the rows of dormitories at the Workhouse. Prisoners were fed three times a day, sitting at long tables. Meals were served on metal trays. Inmates provided the labor for cooking and cleanup, and the hogs provided garbage disposal. (Courtesy of Patrick O'Neill.)

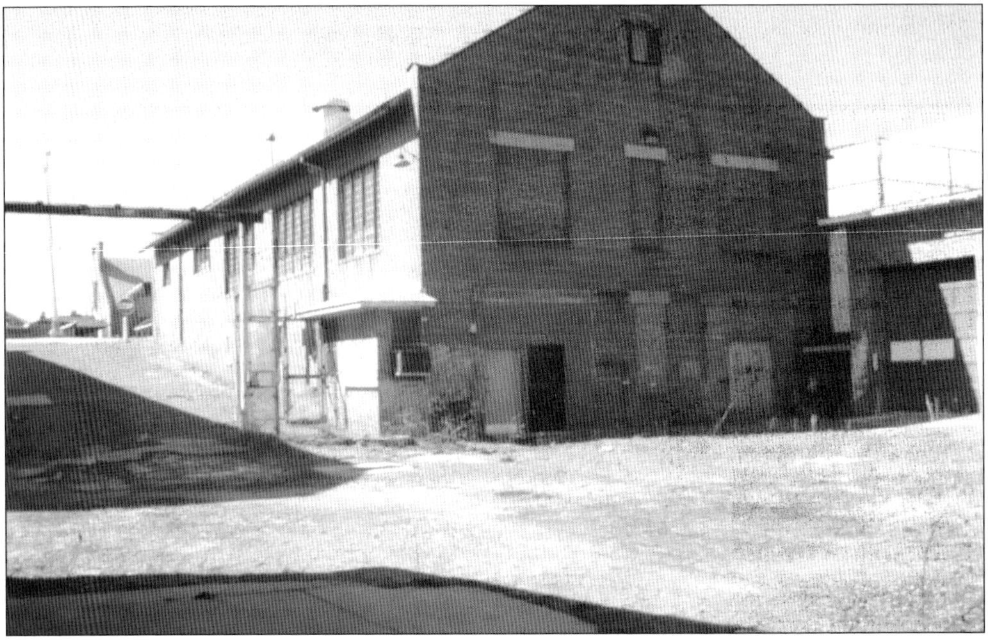

The majority of the industrial shops were lined up behind the dormitories at the Reformatory. It made a short walk to work and back. After the war as equipment was mechanized, men were taught to operate heavy equipment like bulldozers and tractors. Trustees drove prisoners back and forth to their work assignments and to bring supplies to the District. (Courtesy of Fairfax County Department of Planning and Development.)

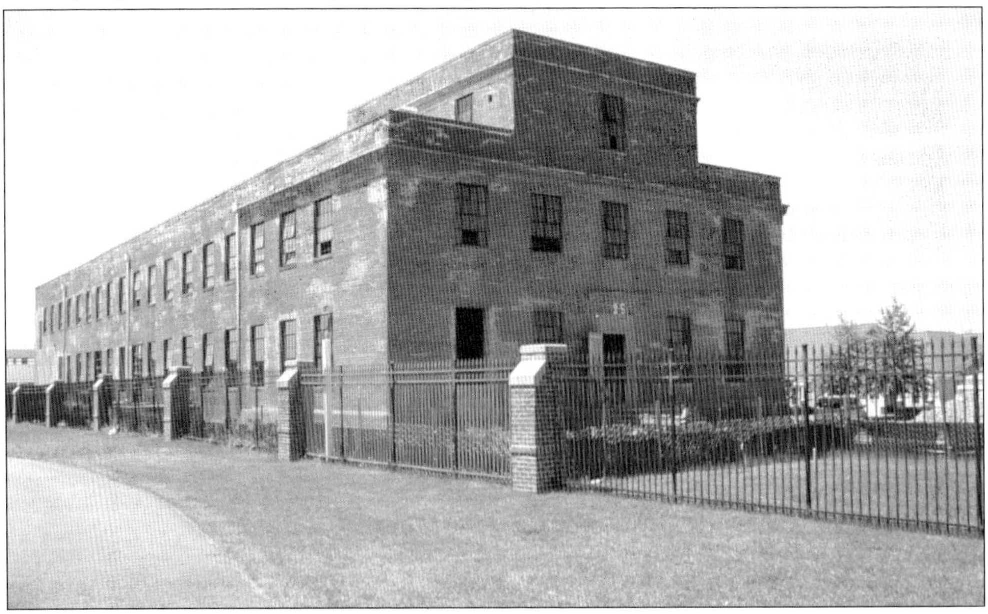

The commissary building at the Reformatory was a multiuse building situated at the end of one of the railroad spurs. It provided storage for the supplies and materials sent to the prison and its ramp provided ease for downloading. Staff responsible for receiving, distributing, and accounting for them had offices in the building. (Courtesy of Fairfax County Department of Planning and Development.)

Working at the brick kilns and the railroad was backbreaking. Coal had to be constantly shoveled into the furnaces to keep the high temperatures required for firing. Bricks had to be loaded inside the kiln just so and, when baked, had to be unloaded and placed on railway cars. Other freight had to be constantly loaded or unloaded as the train traveled back and forth between the wharf and the station at Lorton. (Courtesy of the People's Archive, DC Public Library.)

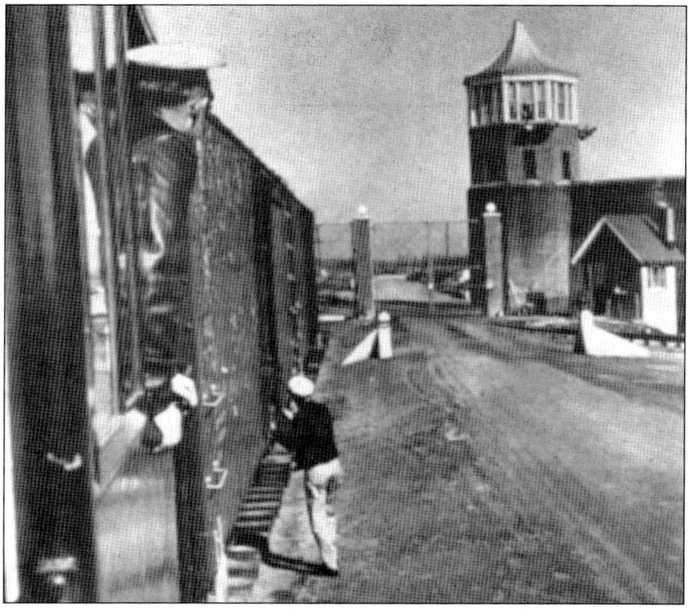

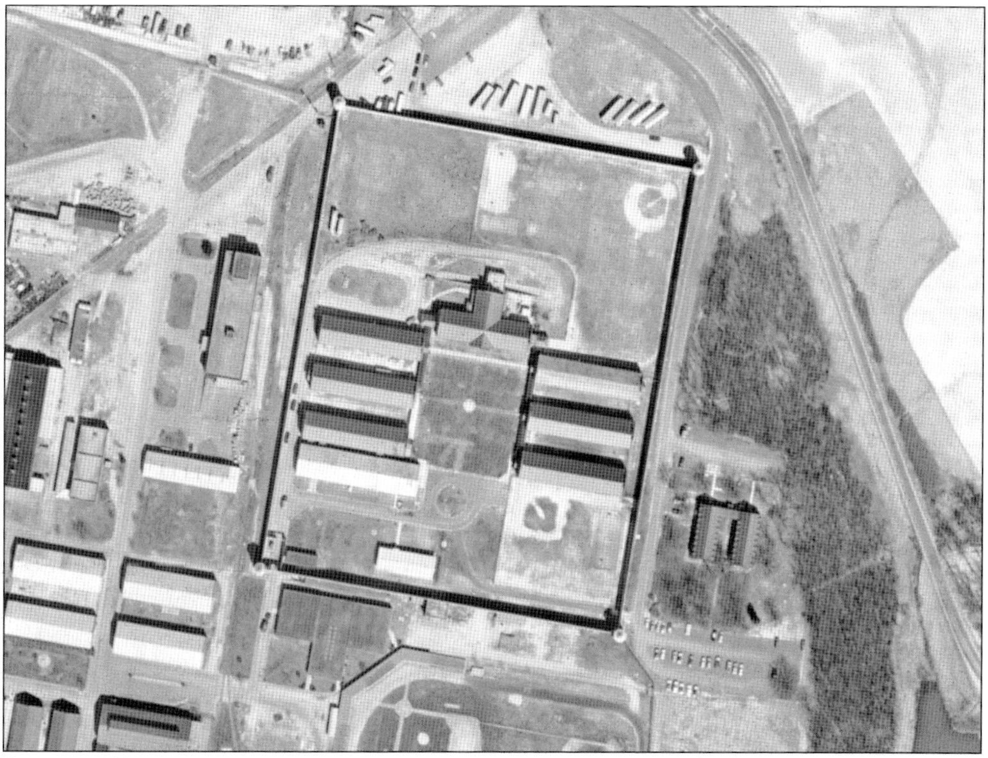

Prior to 1929, prisoners requiring maximum security were sent to federal prisons throughout the country. Overcrowded, they insisted DC take all prisoners convicted within its borders. A total of 10 acres of Reformatory land were set aside, and construction began on a Penitentiary enclosed by a 25-foot-high brick wall. Within the walls were two dormitories, a dining hall, and three shop buildings. Later, a visiting building and sally port were added outside. Work on the penitentiary was completed by 1938. (Courtesy of DC Archives.)

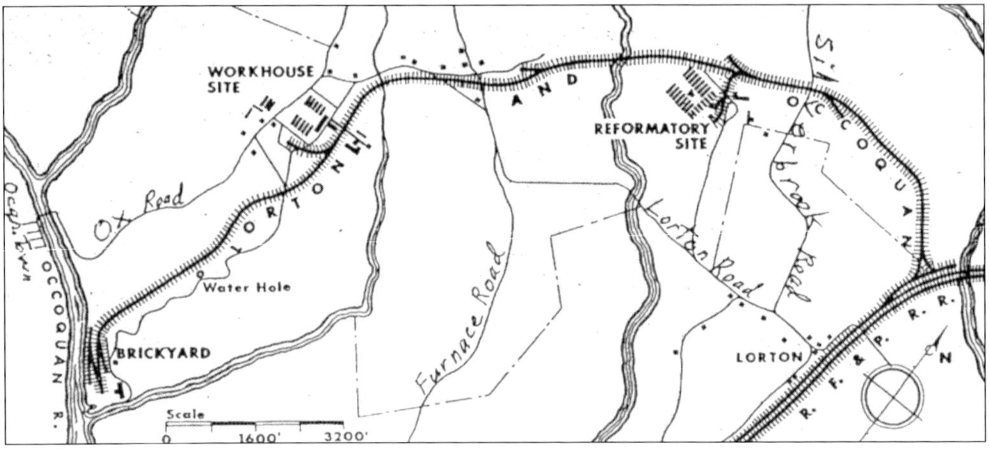

The Lorton and Occoquan Railroad (L&O) ran from the brickyard at the wharf to connect with the Richmond, Fredericksburg & Potomac Railroad (RF&P) at Lorton station—a distance of seven miles. Spurs to the commissary, foundry, and other loading points increased its total distance to nine miles. In a year, the railroad carried 20,000 tons of coal, 5,000 tons of bricks, and innumerable loads of laundry, commissary supplies, sand, cement, coke, and scrap iron. (Courtesy of National Railway Historical Society.)

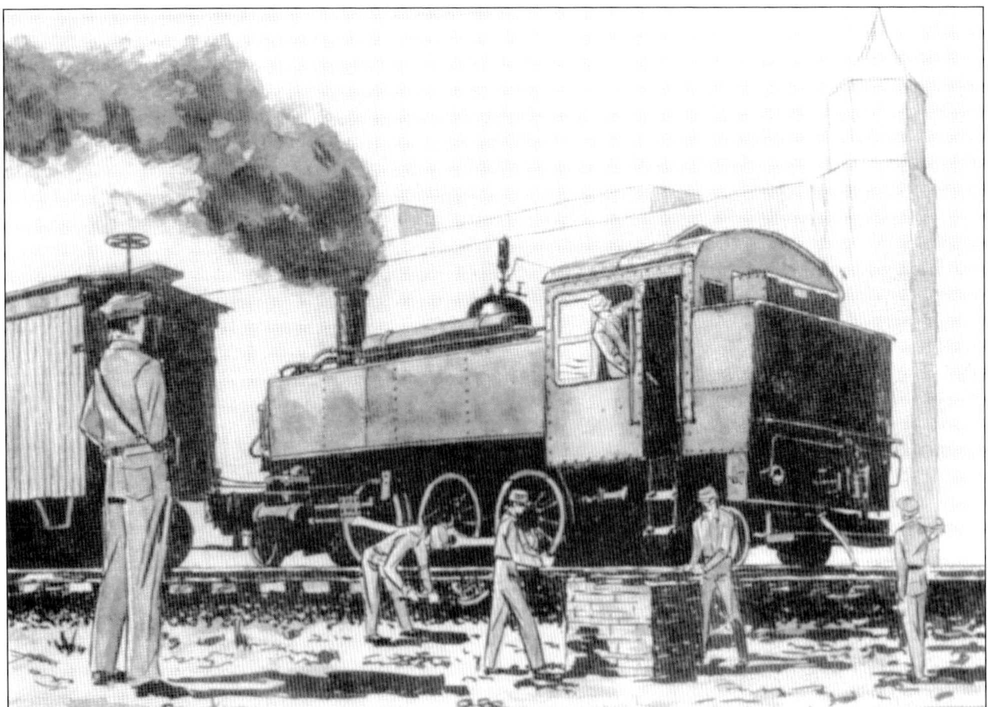

Traveling back and forth, the train had to pass through the Reformatory wall, waiting each time until the tower guard flipped an electric switch to open the gates. Derailers, designed by an inmate, were attached to the track at various points to prevent a prisoner from trying to use the train as an escape vehicle. No one ever tried. The original steam locomotive was replaced after World War II by surplus Army diesels. (Courtesy of William Koch.)

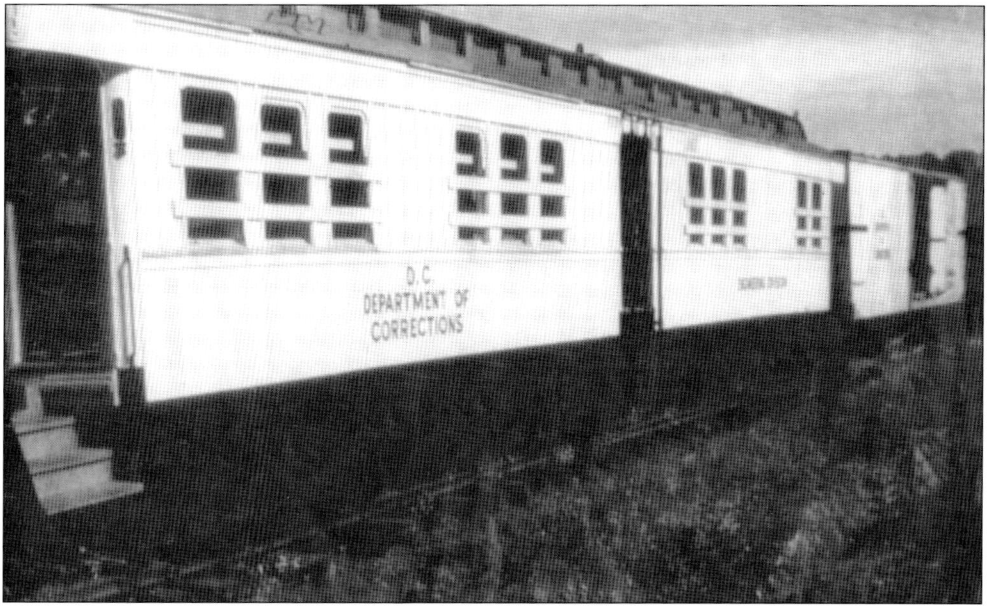

A few of the boxcars were refitted and the prisoners hopped on to ride to and from their job sites. Inmates did all railway work, except for the engineer. The rolling terrain of the countryside challenged the builders of the L&O. It needed to cross an existing road twice. They built a bridge above the road at one spot and then constructed a barrel arch bridge for the train to pass under the road at another. (Courtesy of William Koch.)

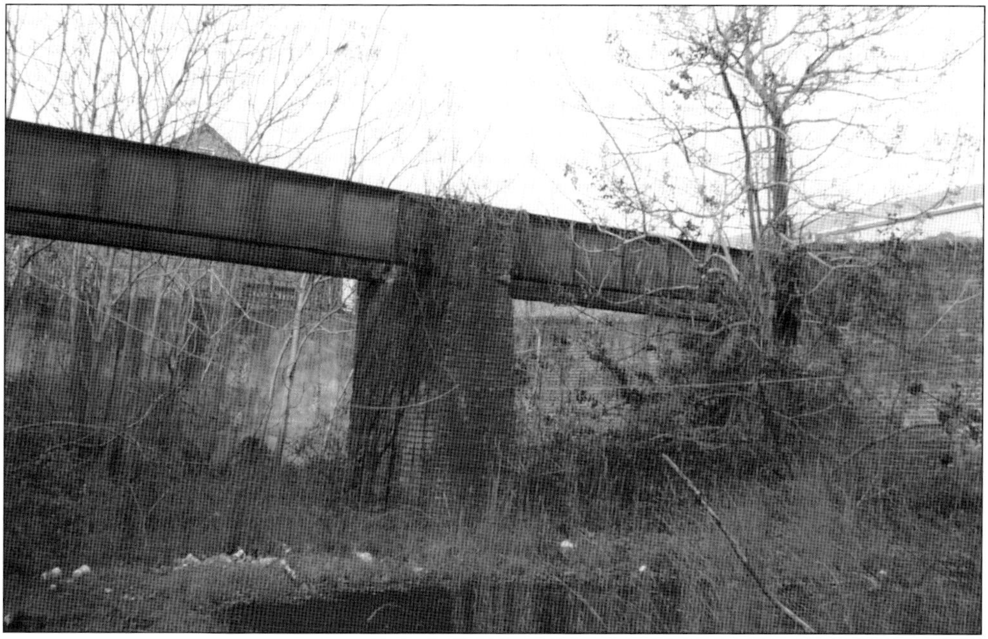

Coal was delivered to the power plants and other facilities through trestles. Coal was the primary source of fuel used at Lorton. It was loaded onto barges and floated down the Potomac River and reloaded onto cars of the prison railroad for distribution along the track and to the brick kilns to fire the furnaces. On the return trip, the tugboat and barge carried bricks for use in the construction of municipal building projects. (Courtesy of William Koch.)

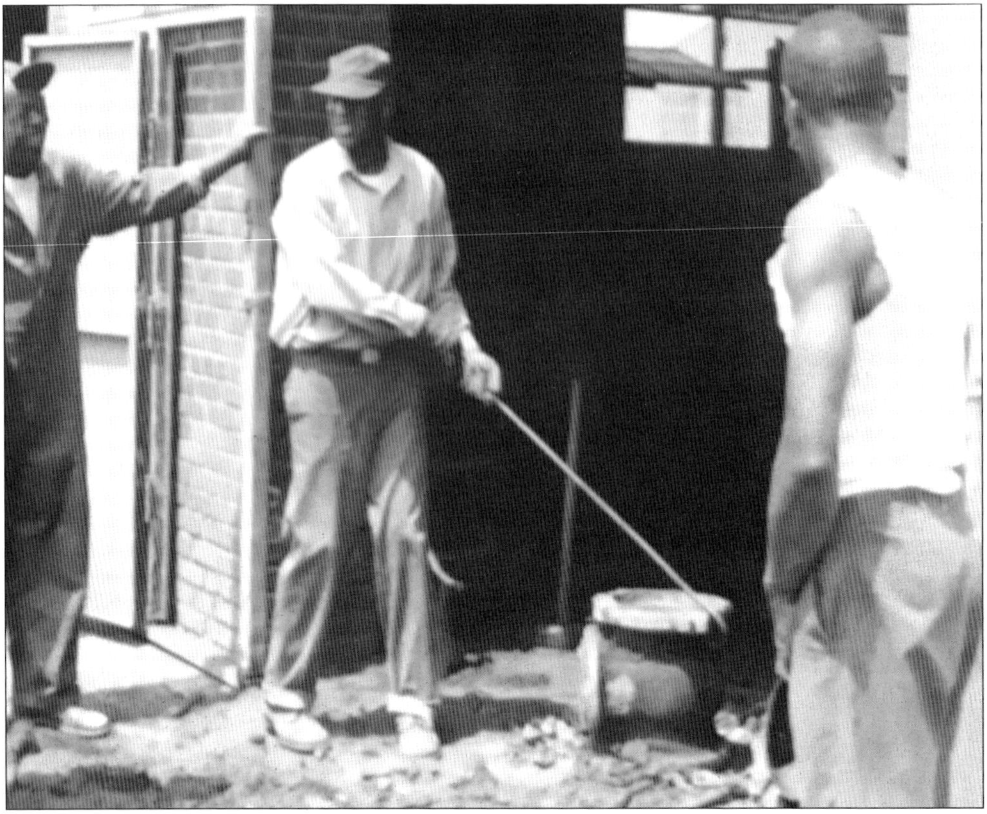

Most of the industrial shops were lined up in a row behind the dormitories at the Reformatory with a wide road between them. Developing a good work ethic was part of the program and inmates were expected to be on time and work a full eight-hour day. The wages they earned were deposited into their account at the prison or sent home to their families if specified. (Courtesy of DC Archives.)

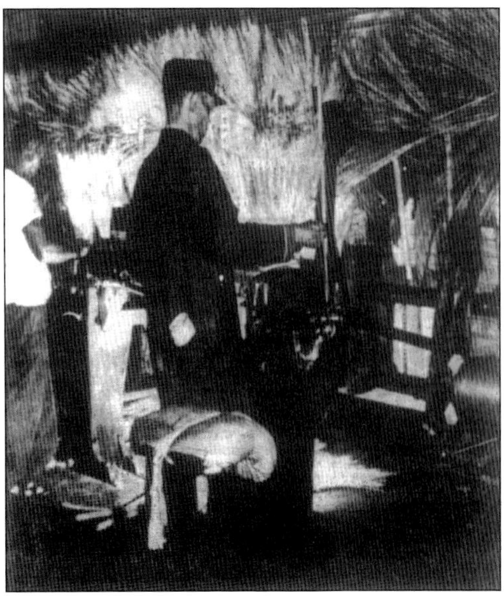

Brooms were the first item to be manufactured at the Reformatory. Under the guidance of master broom-makers, they supplied brooms of all makes and sizes to the various departments of the District government. They furnished all the mattresses used at the complex and on institutions in DC. Prisoners were taught the carpentry and plumbing trades and gained experience meeting the needs for those services on site. (Courtesy of the Library of Congress.)

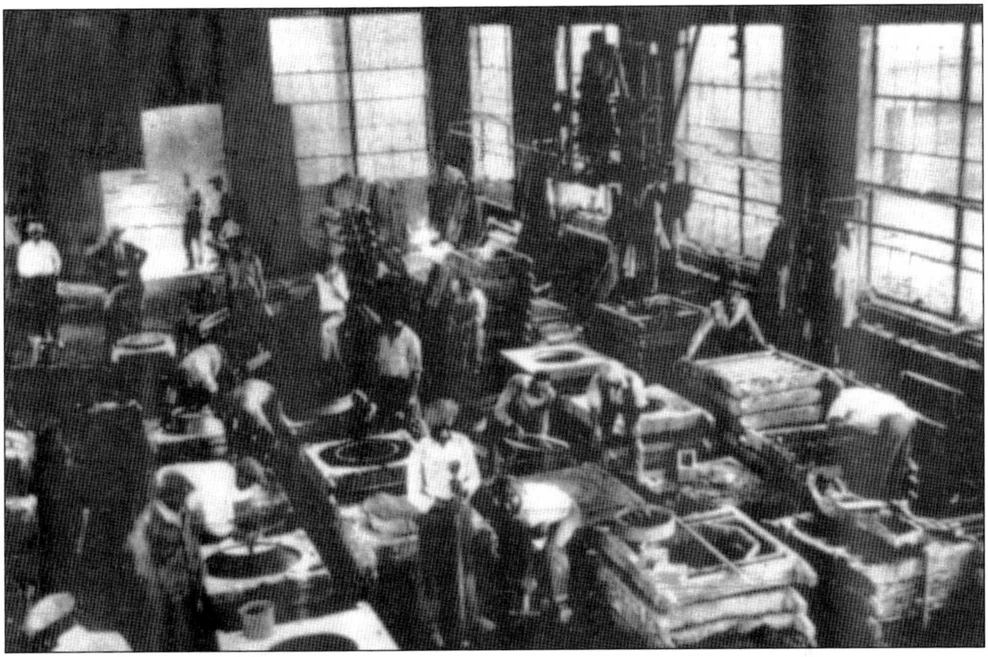

The foundry at Lorton was isolated from other buildings to protect them from its smoke and soot. It produced all the cast-iron gratings and bars used by the District Water Department as well as all the iron and steel work for projects and other industries at the prison sites. (Courtesy of the Library of Congress)

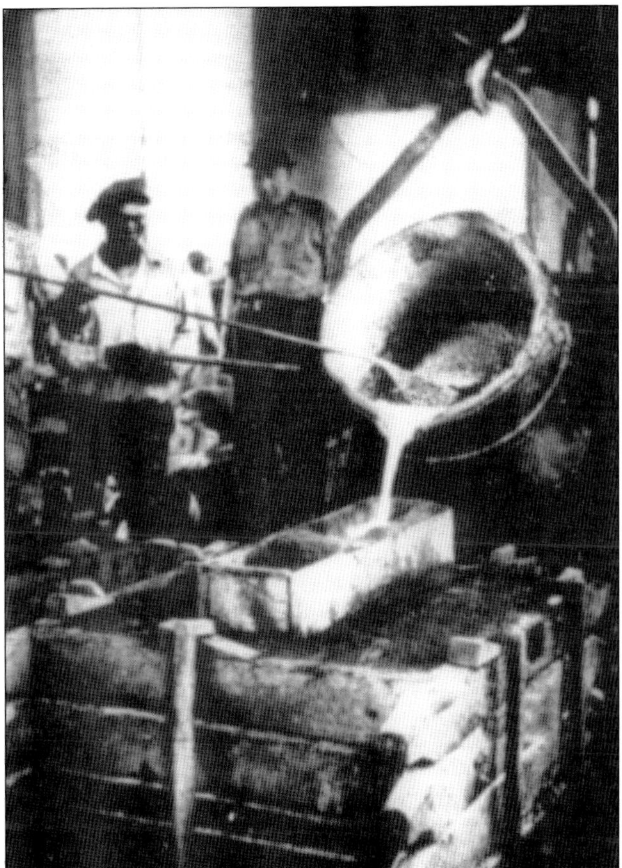

By 1930, the foundry had reached maximum production within the confines of its space and was asking for an extension to the building. The increased tonnage brought added revenue for the prison budget and decreased costs to the District departments for products they used. (Courtesy of the Library of Congress.)

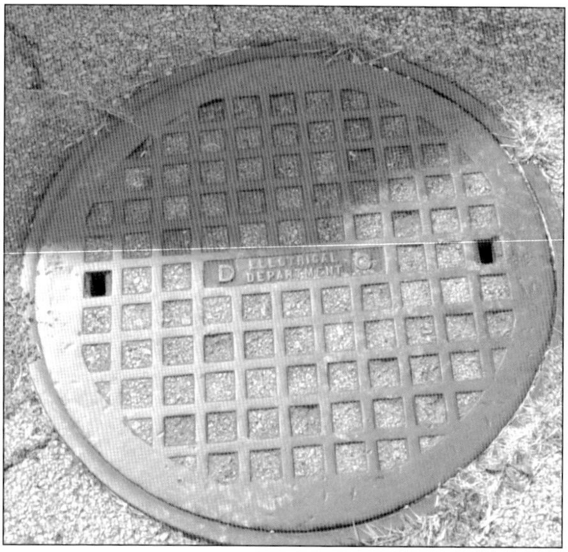

Manhole covers were another product of the foundry and can still be found today around the Workhouse Art Center campus. In 1928, a working-capital fund was authorized, which allowed prison industries to offer goods and services at fair market value to other District and federal agencies, thus enabling them to expand operations. (Courtesy of William Koch.)

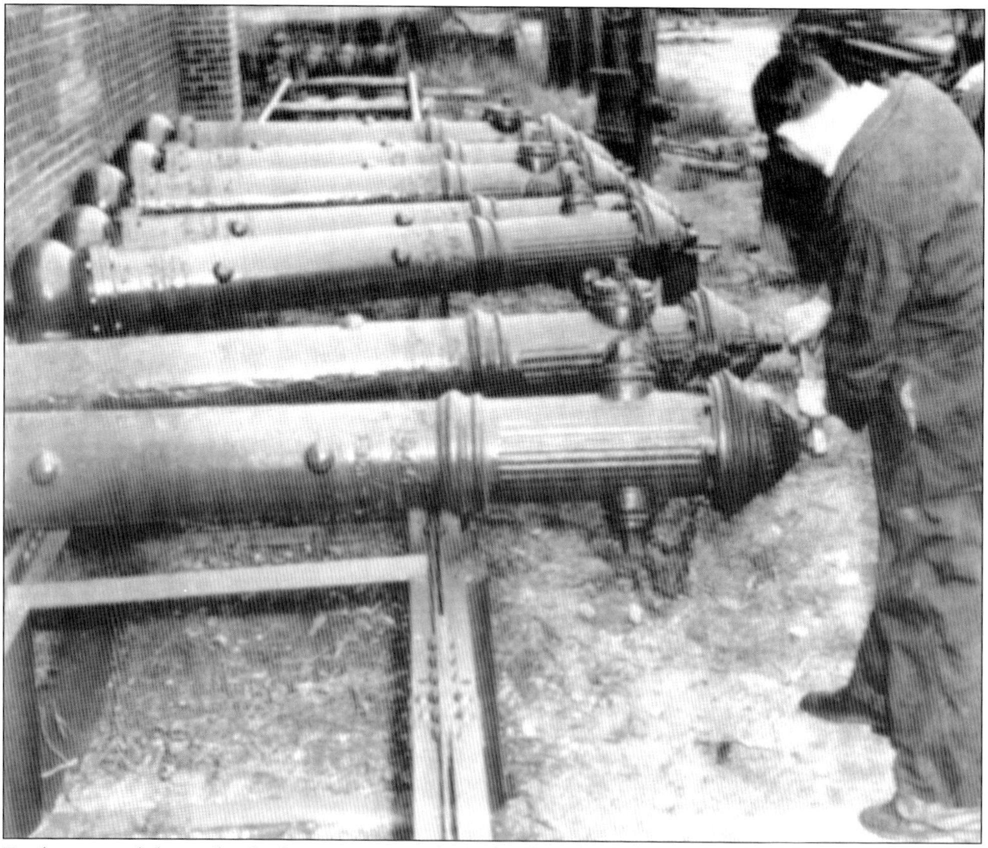

Fireboxes and, later, fire hydrants were made at the foundry. Prisoner labor kept production costs down and made it easy to obtain contracts. Soon, laws were passed that forbid Lorton products from trading on the open market. The prison could only bid on District or Federal contracts. In 1955, the industrial division grossed $964,917, out of which $54,425 went to the city's general fund. (Courtesy of DC Archives.)

Industry was the primary activity at the Reformatory from the beginning. By working in the shops, prisoners gained practical experience. Male inmates produced license plates, brooms, baskets, mattresses, fire hydrants, manhole covers, and plaques. After 1931, prisoners were able to receive a small wage based on their conduct and the amount of work accomplished. It also provided an incentive for them to do a better job. (Courtesy of the People's Archive, DC Public Library.)

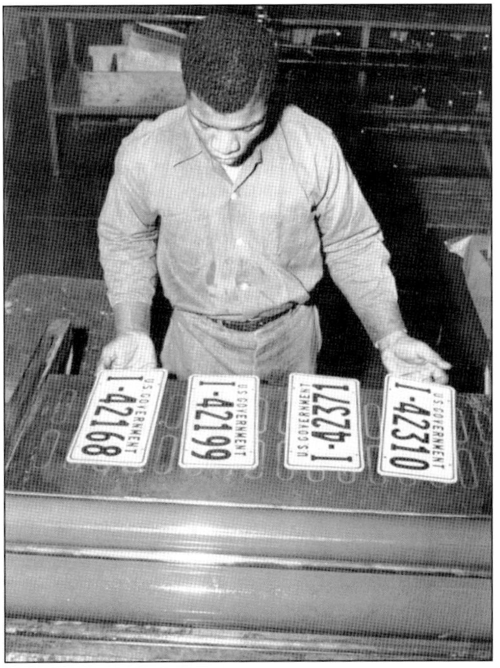

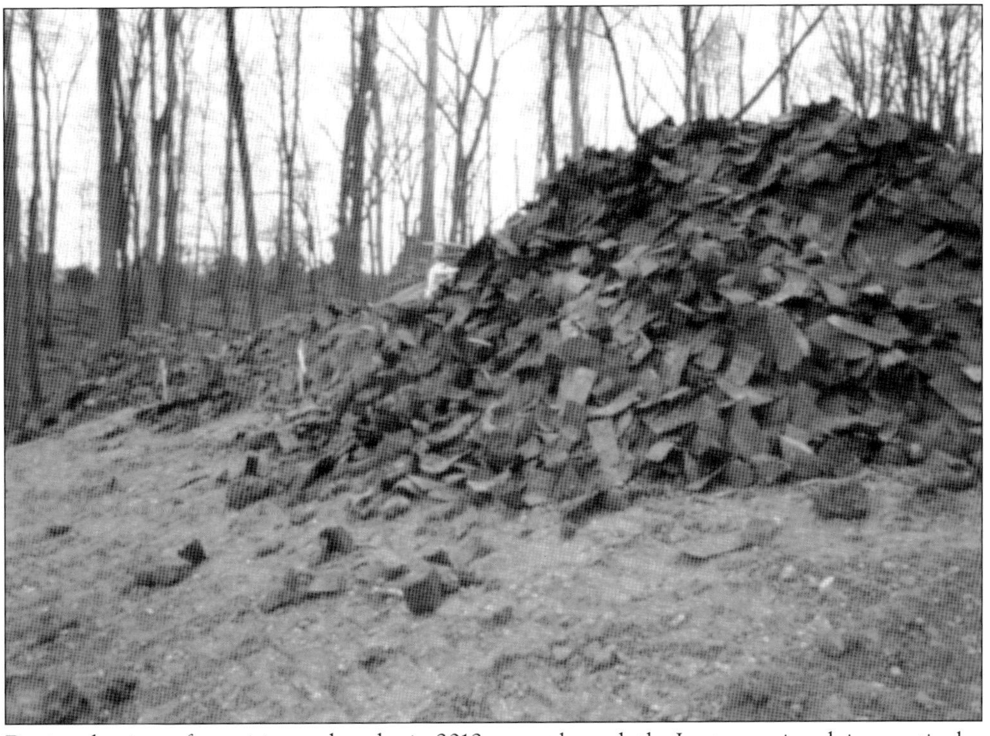

During the time of transition, a derecho in 2012 swept through the Lorton region doing particular damage to the area around the wharf and the stream beds emptying into it. Huge mounds of license plates that had been used for landfill were unearthed near the Giles Run culvert. Evidence of the storm is still visible on both sides of the road leading down to Occoquan Park. (Courtesy of William Koch.)

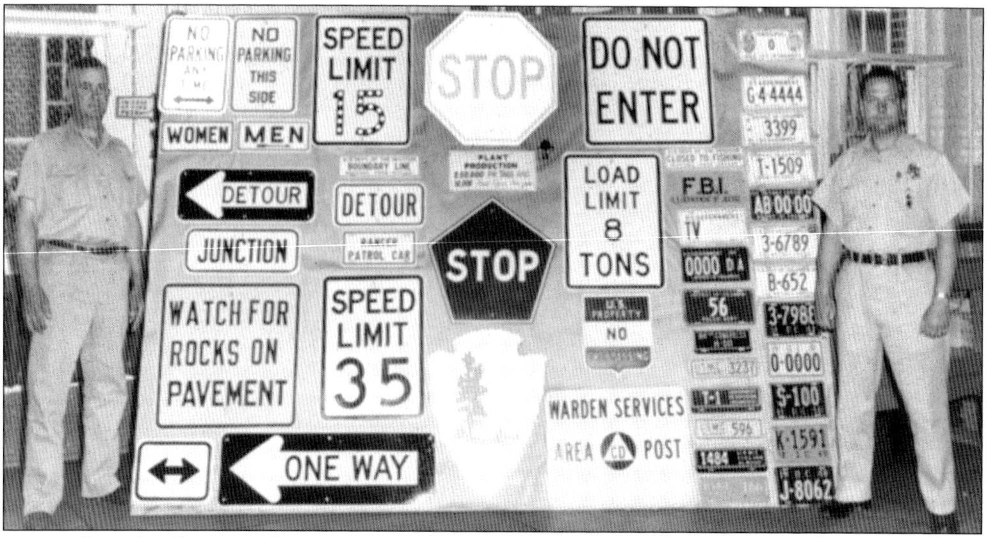

A tag plant for the manufacture of automobile license plates for the District of Columbia was established in 1927. As it became proficient, they added specialty plates and eventually made signs for the National Park Service. One former inmate remarked on a visit to the museum, "I made so many signs that I thought they had one for every tree!" (Courtesy of the People's Archive, DC Public Library.)

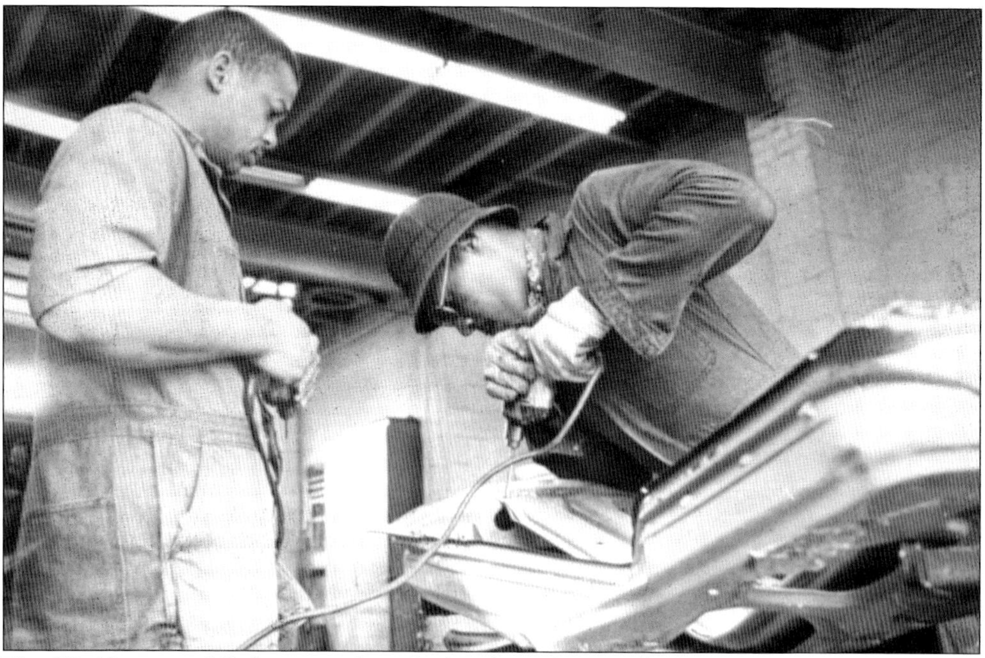

The Workhouse and Reformatory benefited and saved money by having in-house maintenance crews to handle all the necessary repairs at the complex. The automobile repair shop maintained and repaired all prison vehicles, trucks, tractors, and other farm machinery. It also took care of the equipment for the waterways and railroads operating at the Lorton complex. (Courtesy of the People's Archive, DC Public Library.)

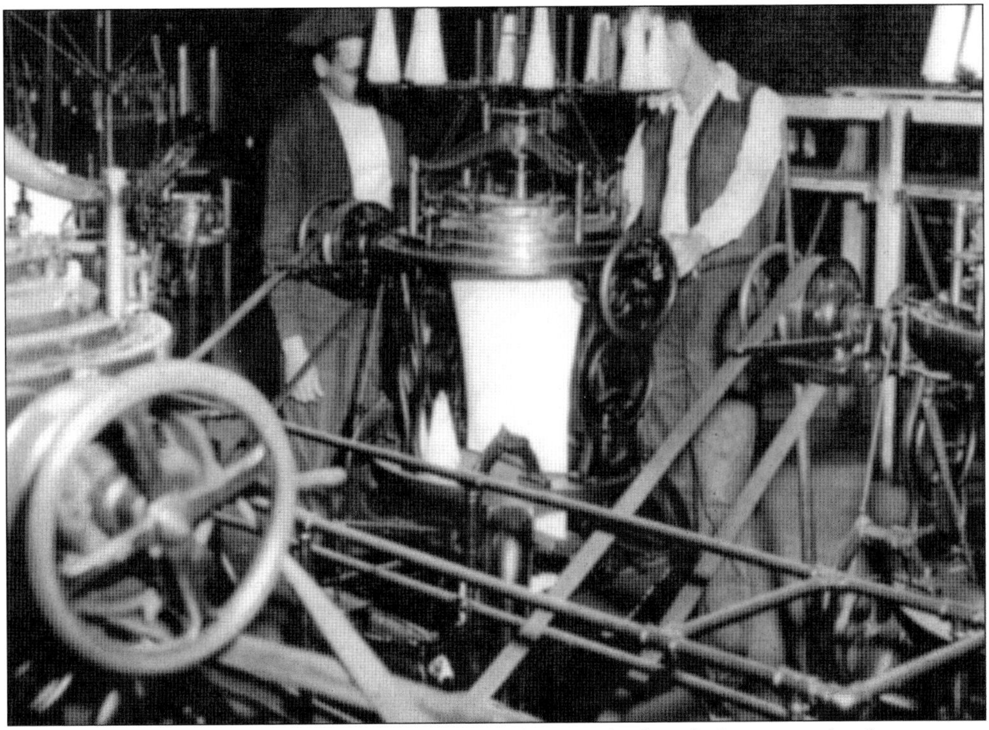

The textile factory made dungarees, shirts, blue jackets, and other clothing worn by the inmates. It produced clothing for many other departments of the DC government, including the police. They produced linens and made and repaired seat covers used in transportation vehicles. The furniture factory made desks, chairs, and cabinetry for use in the prison and did custom work and repairs. (Courtesy of the People's Archive, DC Public Library.)

The well-equipped printing plant reproduced a variety of publications and documents for the Lorton complex. The use of prison labor reduced the cost of publication and it was used by other departments of the DC and federal governments. The inmates developed a marketable skill. (Courtesy of the People's Archive, DC Public Library.)

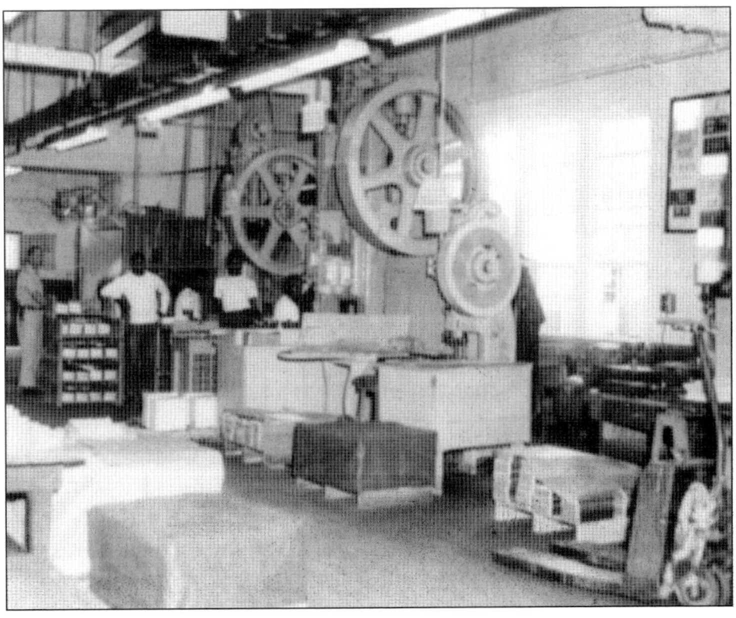

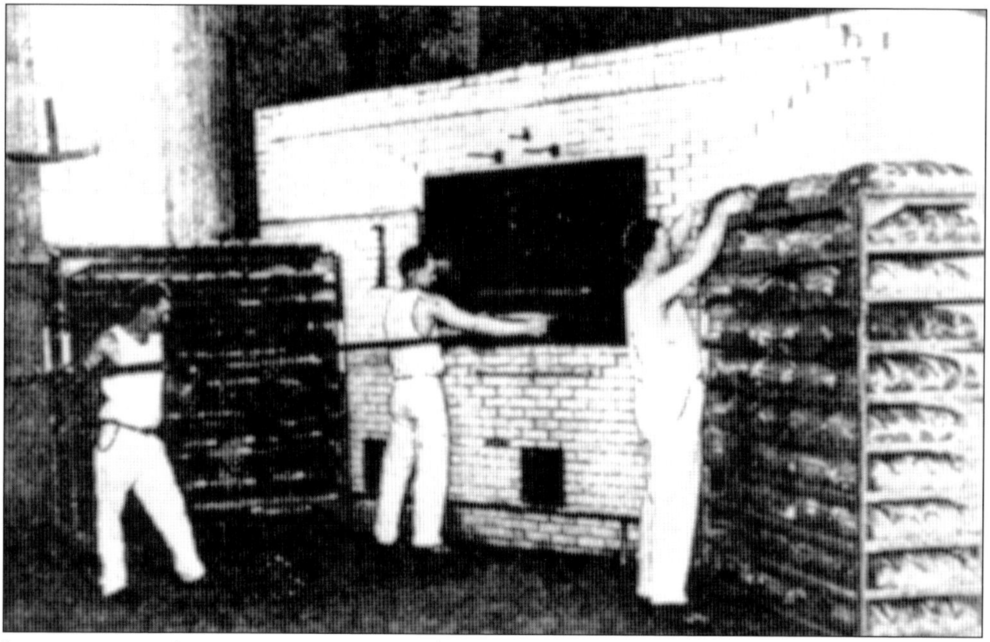

Inmates received apprentice training working in the fully equipped bake shop. It had electric mixers and an oven where 600 pounds of bread could be baked at a time. According to a 1928 article in the *Washington Star*, "Some of the District's best bakers are men who learned their trade at Lorton." (Courtesy of the People's Archive, DC Public Library.)

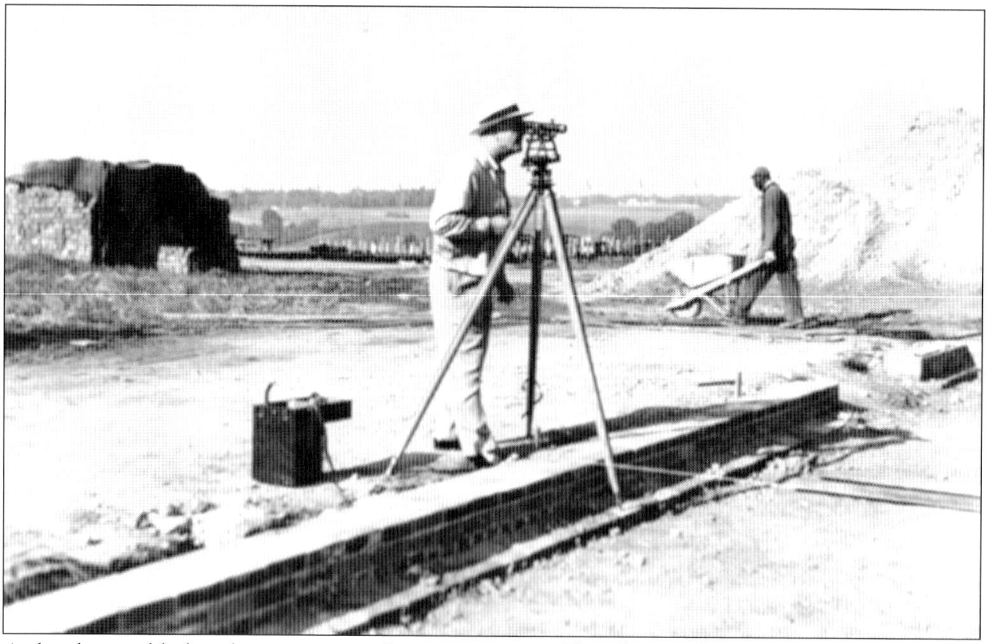

As land was added to the prison complex, it was mapped by a licensed surveyor assisted by inmate labor. Many prisoners became adept at the job and could work on their own, but always under the supervision of a professional. In addition to the small wage earned at the prison, the prisoner developed a marketable skill as he sought employment upon release from the prison. (Courtesy of DC Archives.)

Ray Huff was Superintendent of the Lorton Prisons in the mid to late 1930s. He sought to implement strategies for discipline that would replace punishment with policies designed to construct self-respect in the individual, He and his family were the first to reside in the Widow Violet House at the corner of Lorton and Furnace Roads. He left to become the first general superintendent of DC penal institutions. (Courtesy of the Huff family.)

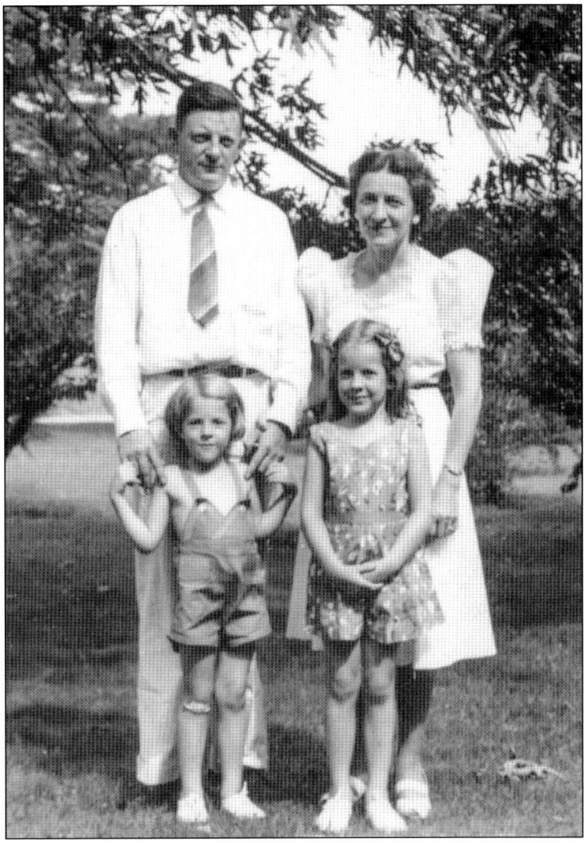

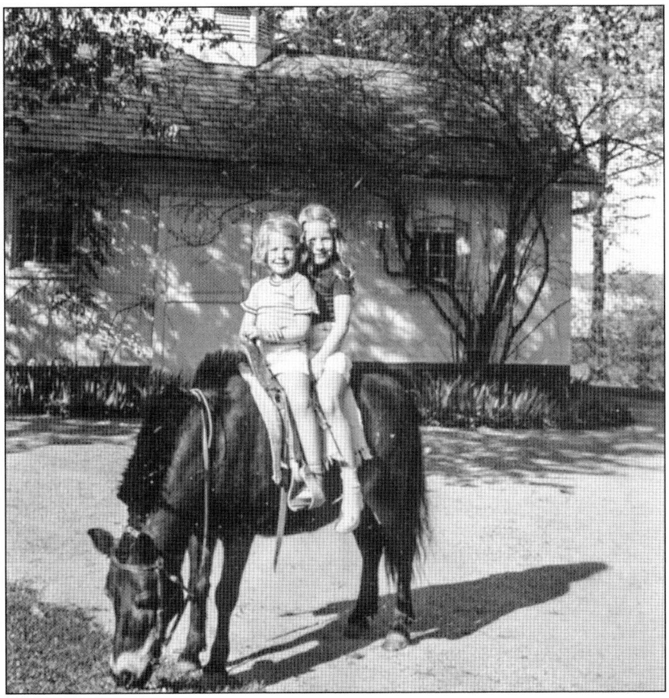

The Huff daughters remember going with their dad when he visited different parts of the prison farm, including the slaughterhouse. He introduced a parole system, and two parolees lived and worked in their house. The girls helped train new bloodhound puppies by hiding deep in the cornfields for the dogs to find. The girls "rode to school in the paddy wagon" and had permission to ride some of the mules and horses. (Courtesy of the Huff family.)

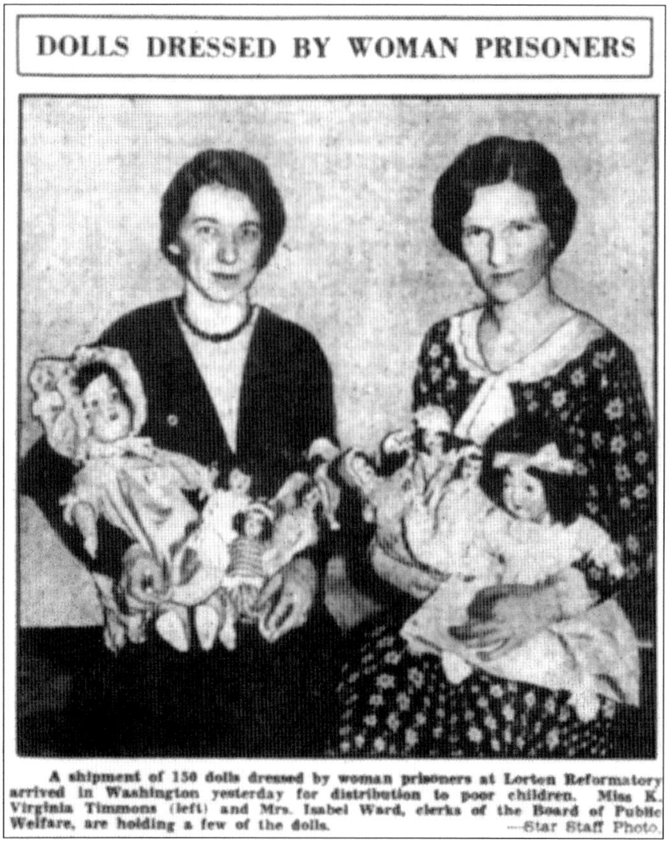

DOLLS DRESSED BY WOMAN PRISONERS

A shipment of 150 dolls dressed by woman prisoners at Lorton Reformatory arrived in Washington yesterday for distribution to poor children. Miss K. Virginia Timmons (left) and Mrs. Isabel Ward, clerks of the Board of Public Welfare, are holding a few of the dolls. —Star Staff Photo.

Sewing was one of the jobs always available for women inmates. In the early years, they made the clothes worn at the prison. Socialization skills were stressed and positive contributions to the community were encouraged. Women at the workhouse dressed 156 dolls for distribution to poor children by the Board of Public Welfare. Two clerks of the board hold some of the dolls. (Courtesy of the Library of Congress)

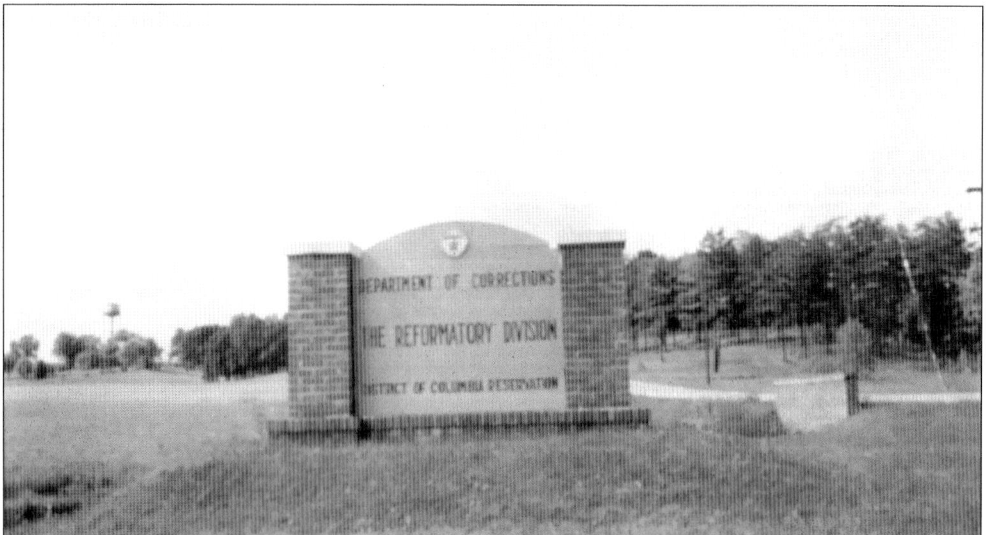

The grounds at the prisons that were not under cultivation by the industrial farm were always carefully maintained by the inmates. Bricks from the kiln sit atop a mound and hold the sign denoting the area of the Reformatory Division. A brick culvert for drainage is visible at left. In the early days, the entire campus was referred to as the reservation, as shown on the sign. (Courtesy of Irma Clifton.)

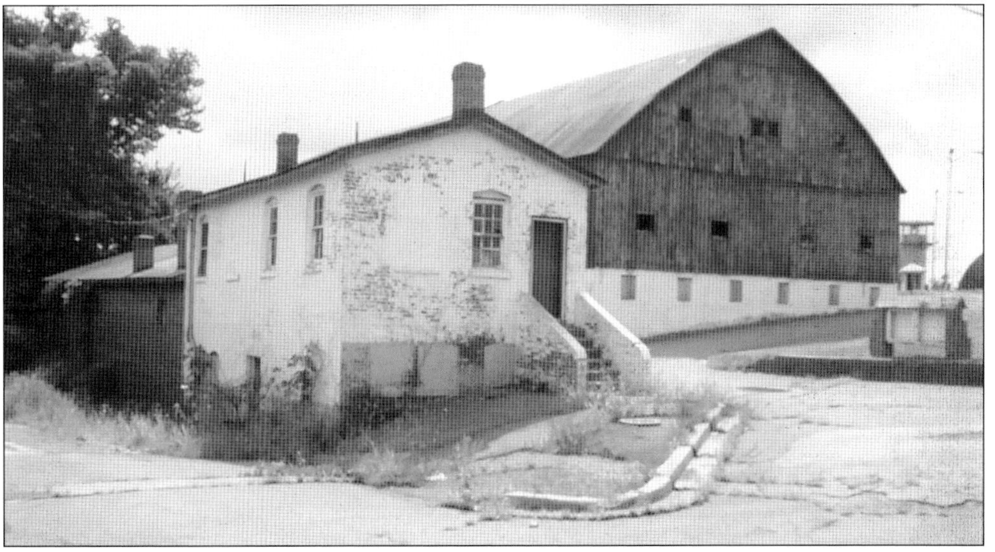

The economic depression of the 1930s increased the population of the Workhouses and Reformatory dramatically. By 1937, tents were needed at the Men's Workhouse to deal with the overflow. The medical staff was overwhelmed as it tried to meet major and minor demands for services. The Reformatory struggled to maintain sufficient staff to handle the numbers and assure a full day's work for each inmate. On-site projects for additional buildings helped. (Courtesy of William Koch.)

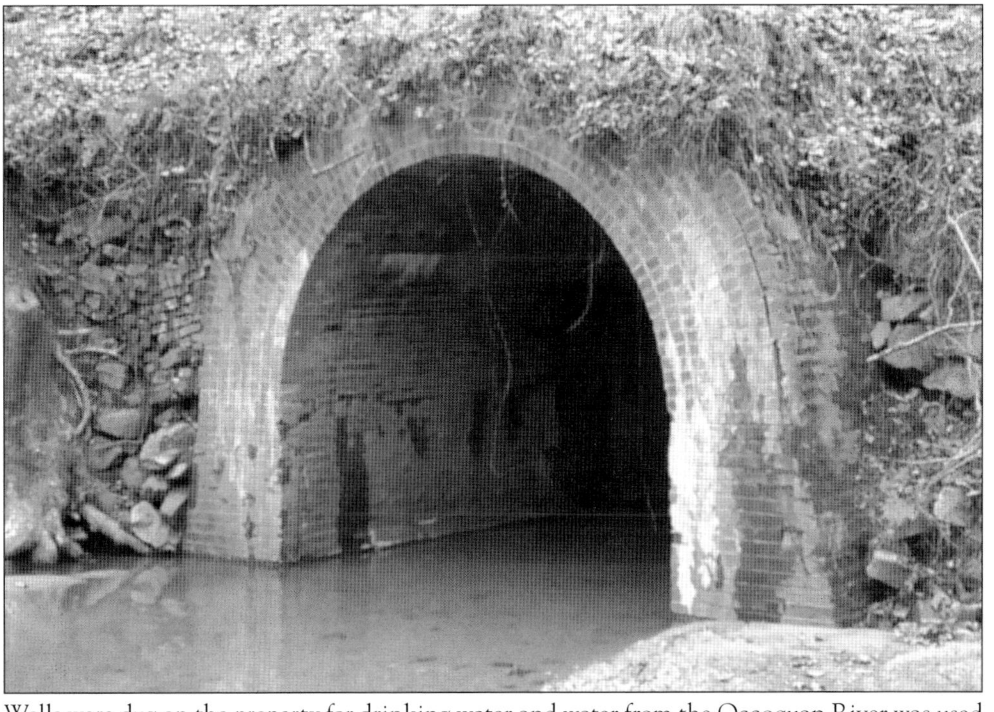

Wells were dug on the property for drinking water and water from the Occoquan River was used for other purposes. In 1935, work began on a small dam at the junction of Elkhorn Run and Occoquan River and used inmates for labor. Prison superintendent Arthur Petitt supervised the project. After completion in 1936, water was pumped through a system of pumps and raised to elevated steel tanks supplying 1.25 million gallons daily. (Courtesy of William Koch.)

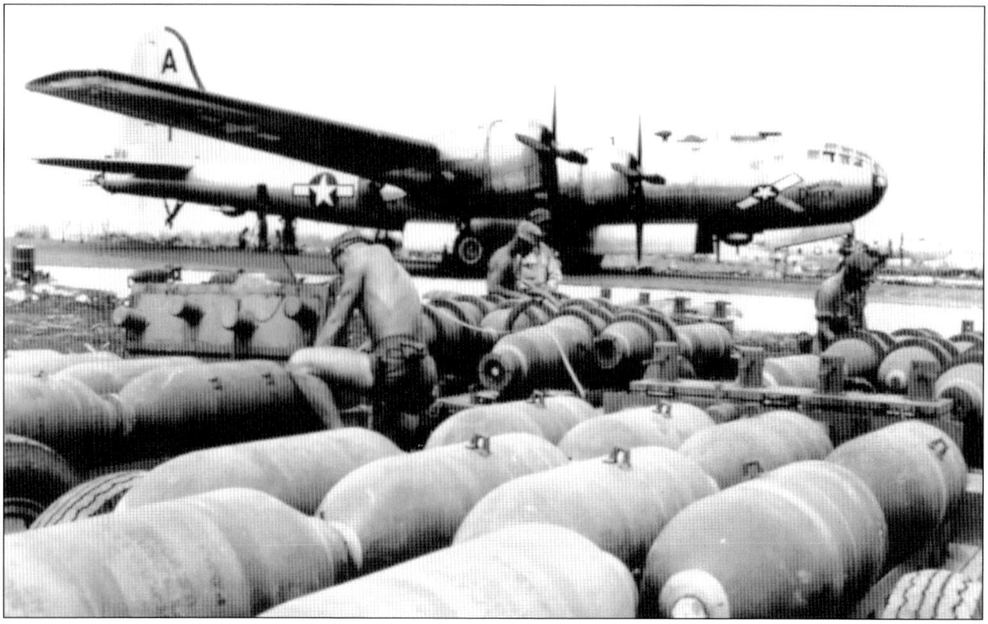

During World War II, the industries division of the Reformatory made 350,000 bomb noses for the War Department. They also provided the Navy with shirts, mattresses, deck brushes, and furniture. Parole boards allowed inmates with good prison records to enlist in military services. Production during the war years was hampered by the scarcity of raw materials and trained supervisory personnel as many of the guards had joined the military services. (Courtesy of William Koch.)

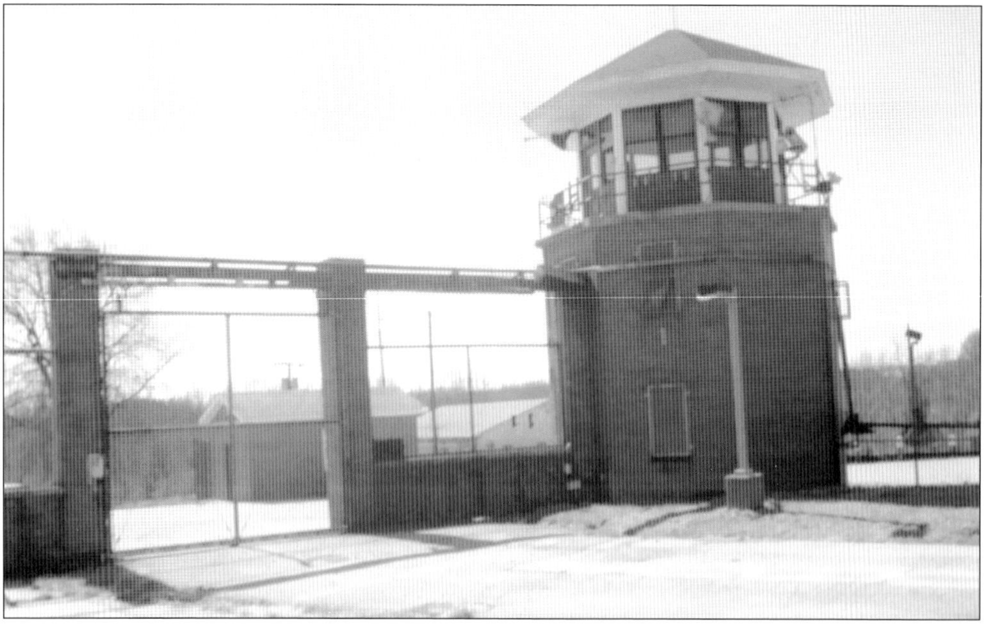

During World War II, a 24-hour plane-spotting post was maintained on Wall Tower I at the Reformatory. Six men were selected from volunteers by their good prison records. Two at a time, they worked eight-hour shifts. More than 200 inmates at the Reformatory volunteered to participate in an agricultural department experiment on the use of a blister agent (mustard gas) antidote. An additional 100 took part in a study on penicillin. (Courtesy of DC Archives.)

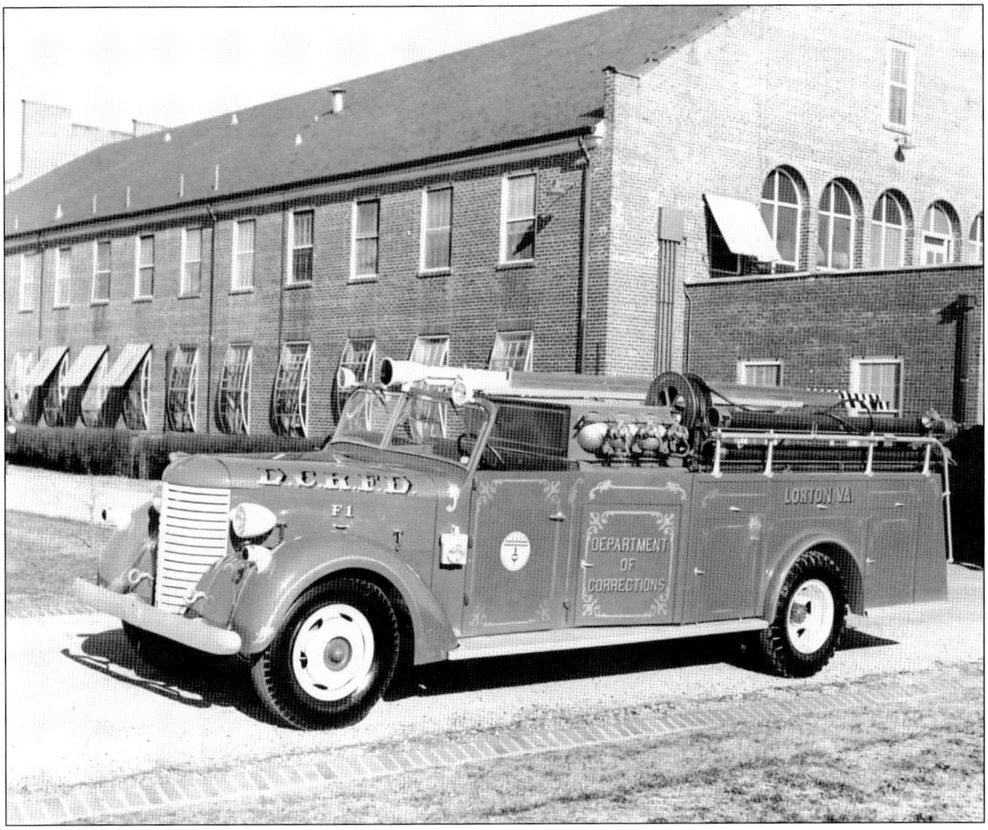

There was no organized fire department in Lorton, Virginia, when the prison was first established nearby. Some inmates received training as firefighters and were used within the prison complex and also assisted in putting out fires in the local community. During World War II and the early postwar years, they again responded to calls for help from outside the reservation. (Courtesy of DC Archives.)

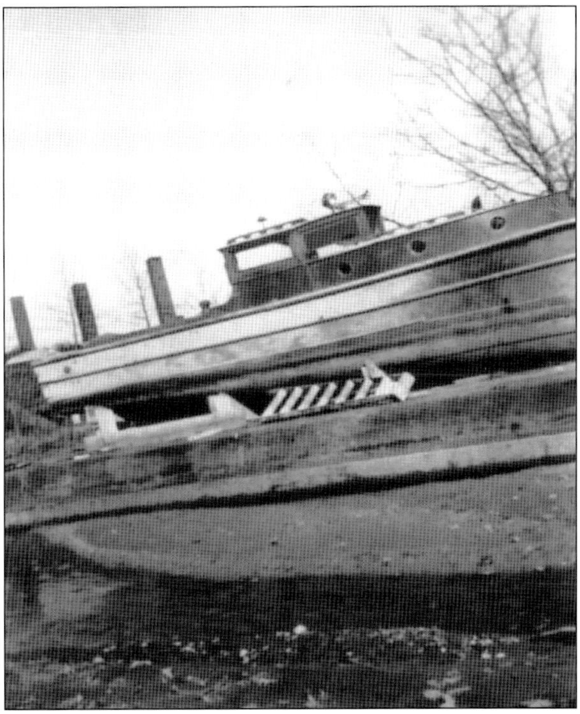

In the autumn of 1947, using two 22-foot power skiffs towed by a 25-foot powerboat, the Reformatory added a fishing industry. Five trustees, under the direct supervision of a professional fisherman, fished the Potomac tributaries and river near Lorton for rockfish, herring, shad, and perch. Nets for the operation were made at the prison. (Courtesy of DC Archives.)

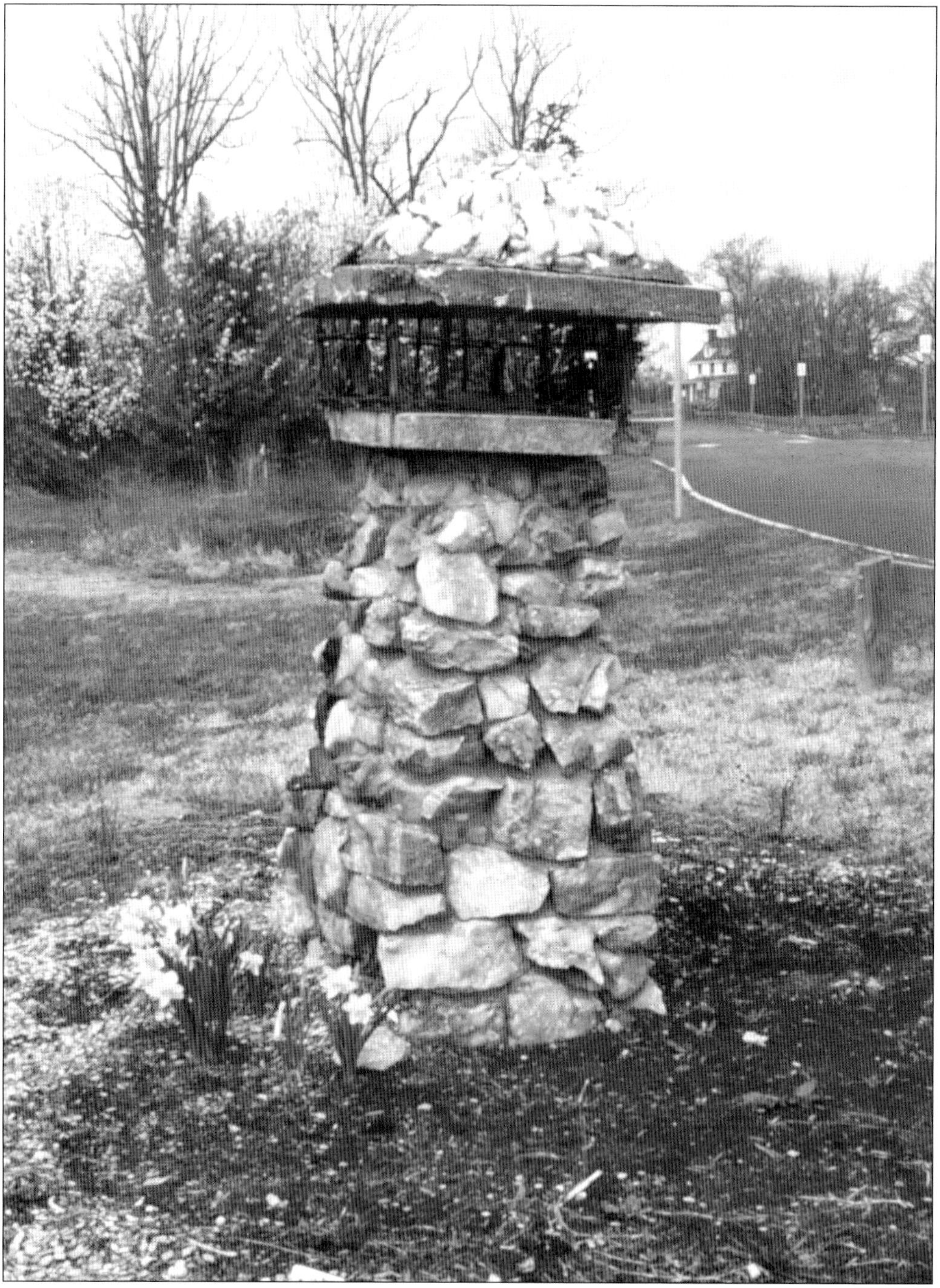

On the other side of the old Lorton Road (now Workhouse Way), there were two stone towers at the entrance to the superintendent's house. One of the towers was lost in road construction, and one was saved. They were likely built by prisoner masons, as similar stonework is found in the picnic area and gardens they built across the road from the house. (Courtesy of Patrick O'Neill.)

Three

THE YEARS OF CHANGE AND REORGANIZATION

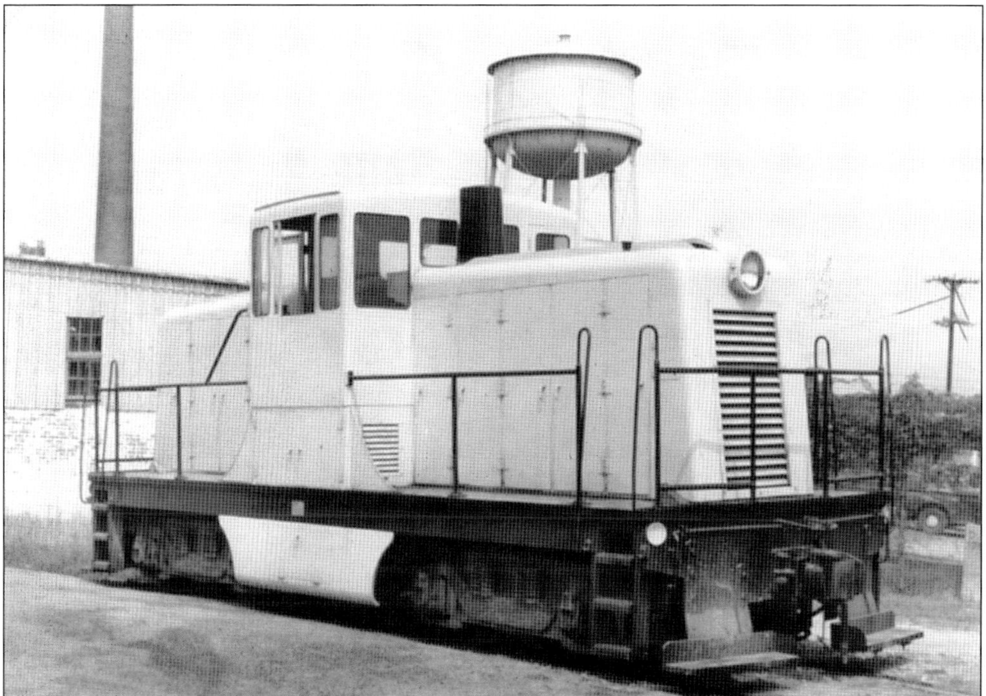

The United States became a more mobile and less rural society during and after World War II. Technologies developed during those years were applied to peaceful pursuits in industry, transportation, and daily living. The prisons took advantage of the opportunities to modernize. In addition, a new penal philosophy and new laws enacted by congress challenged the status quo. (Courtesy of William Koch.)

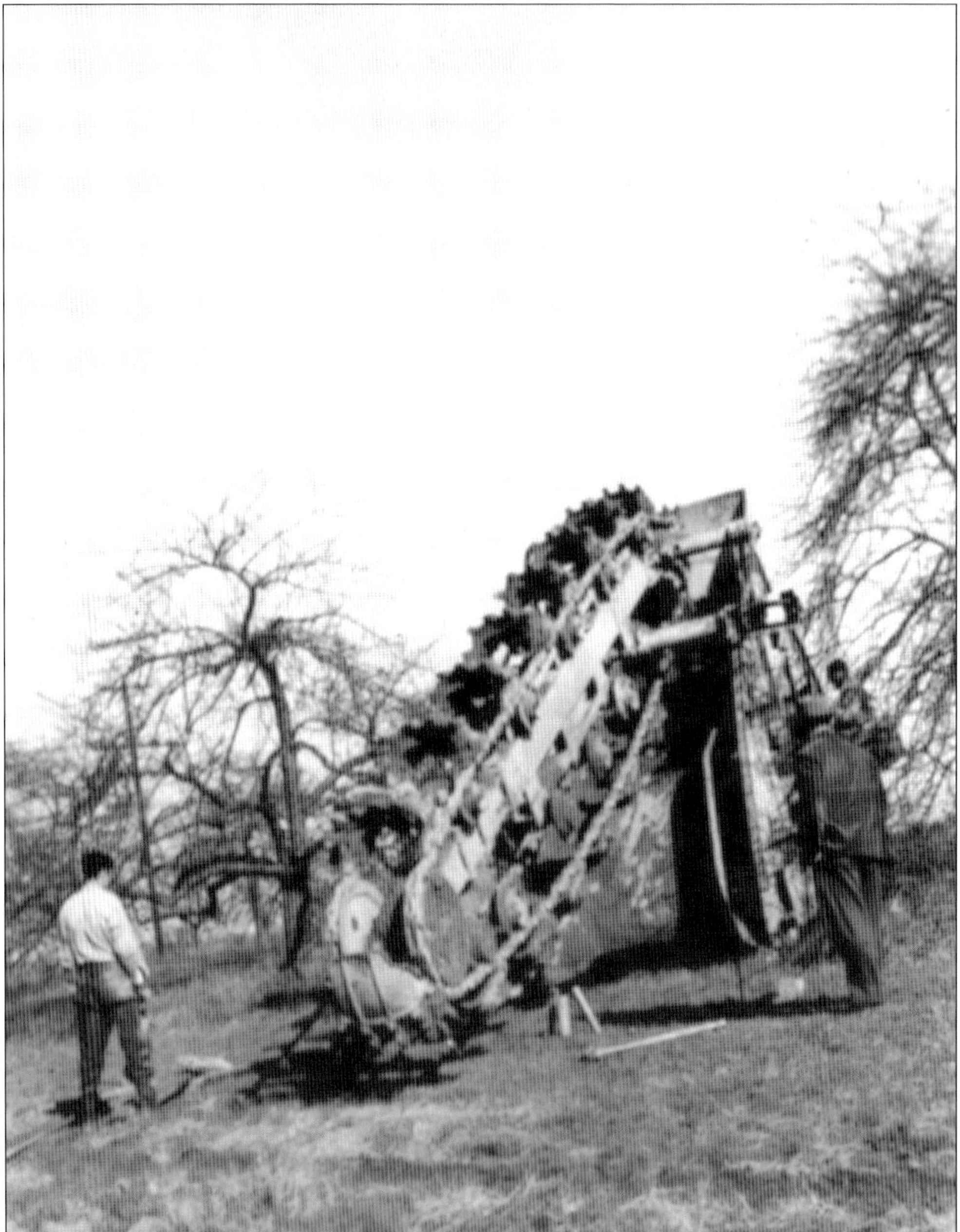

Something was always under construction or needed to be repurposed at the Lorton complex. By 1950, the prison was 90 percent mechanized. The prisoners assigned to the Engineering Division no longer had to dig ditches by hand and were taught to use this machine under the supervision of staff. (Courtesy of Irma Clifton.)

In 1946, Pres. Harry Truman signed a law creating the District of Columbia Department of Corrections and transferred the management and regulations of the district's penal system from the Board of Public Welfare to it. He appointed three commissioners to oversee the new department. It was given the ability to submit its own budget directly to the commissioners. Donald Clemmer, who was serving as the superintendent at Lorton, became its first director. (Courtesy of Irma Clifton.)

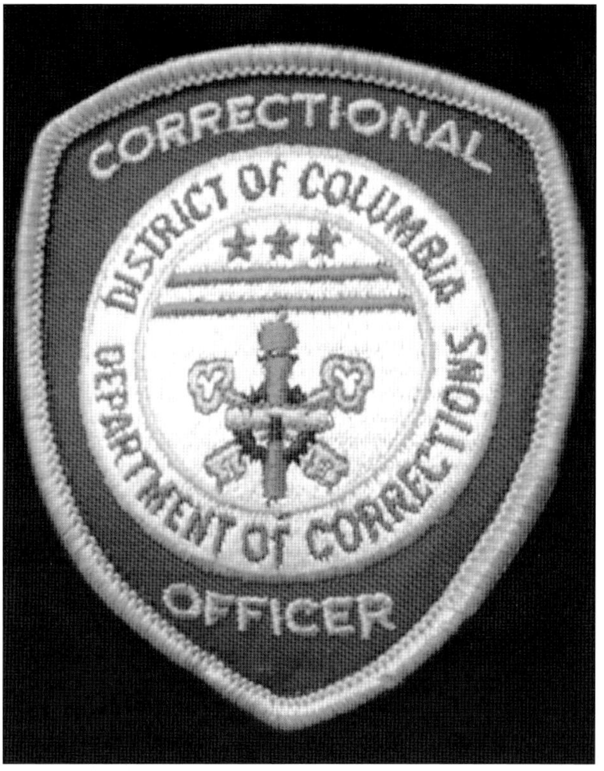

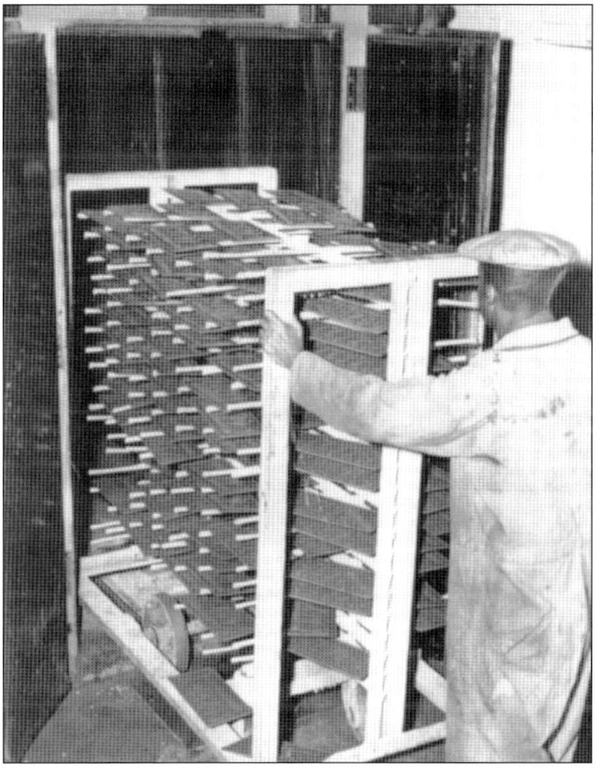

Clemmer's appointment ushered in a new era and Rehabilitation replaced Progressive as the dominant philosophy. It stressed improvements in policy that affected both inmates and employees. Maintaining close custody and the work requirement were still important and now opportunities for varied forms of education and improvement of skills were added. The goal was to ensure that upon their release, as many inmates as possible would return to society and become good, productive citizens. (Courtesy of DC Archives.)

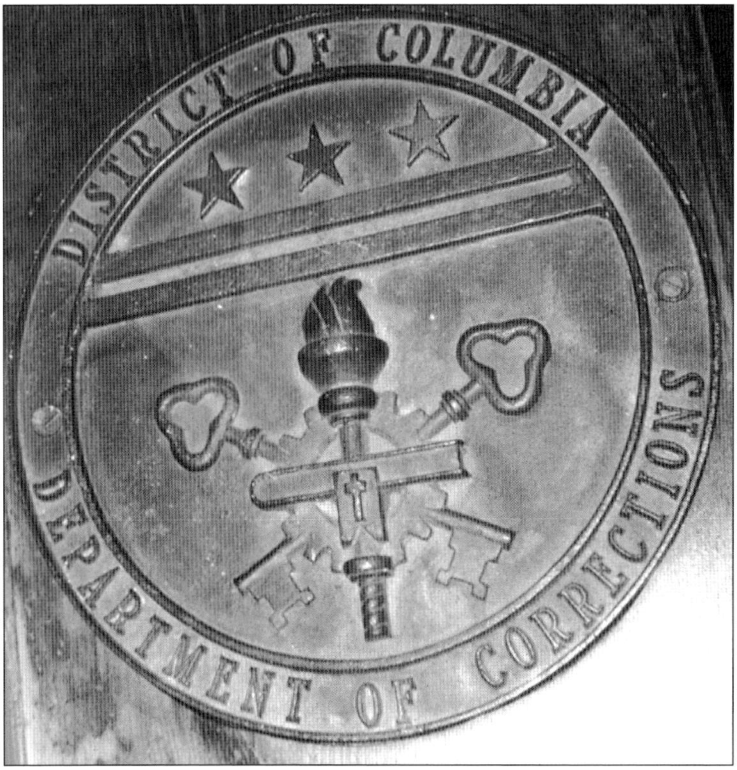

Clemmer's challenge was to develop a staff that would work in unity to accomplish these goals. He invited employee participation in developing a seal for the new department. Sixty-seven employees submitted drawings. A committee of employees helped choose the winner. The seal was used on all letterheads and a bronze plaque of the seal was made in the foundry. The three stars stood for the three commissioners. The two bars for the House and Senate. (Courtesy of William Koch.)

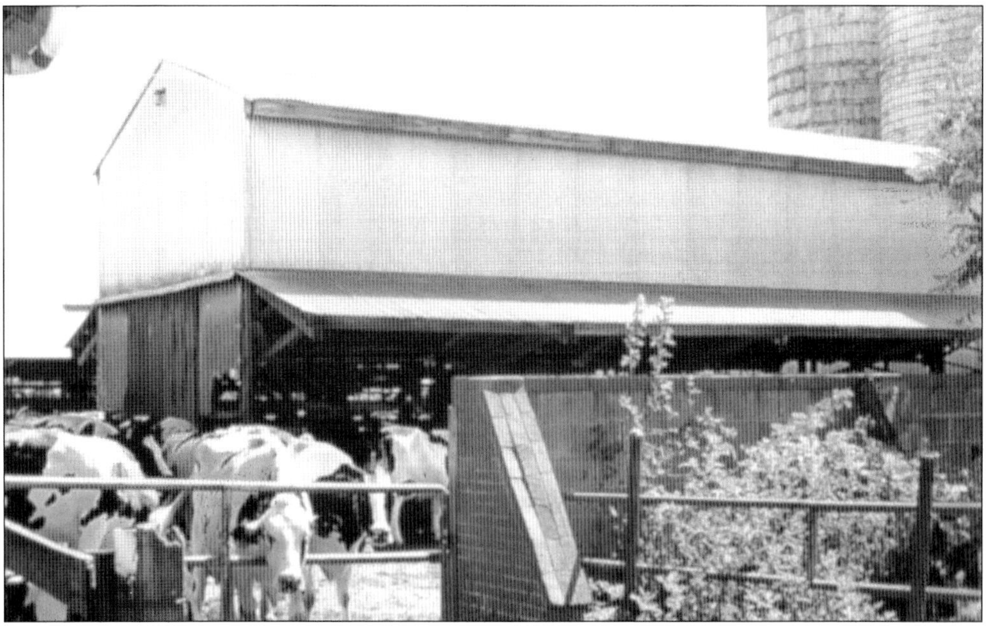

Agricultural acreage was extended as the complex grew. Inmates raised swine, poultry, and beef and dairy cattle. A swine ranch housed thousands of hogs raised for consumption by the inmates. In the 1950s, disaster struck in the form of hog cholera, which led to the destruction of over three thousand hogs to prevent the spread of the disease. The swine ranch was on property now part of the Occoquan Regional Park. (Courtesy of Laura McKie.)

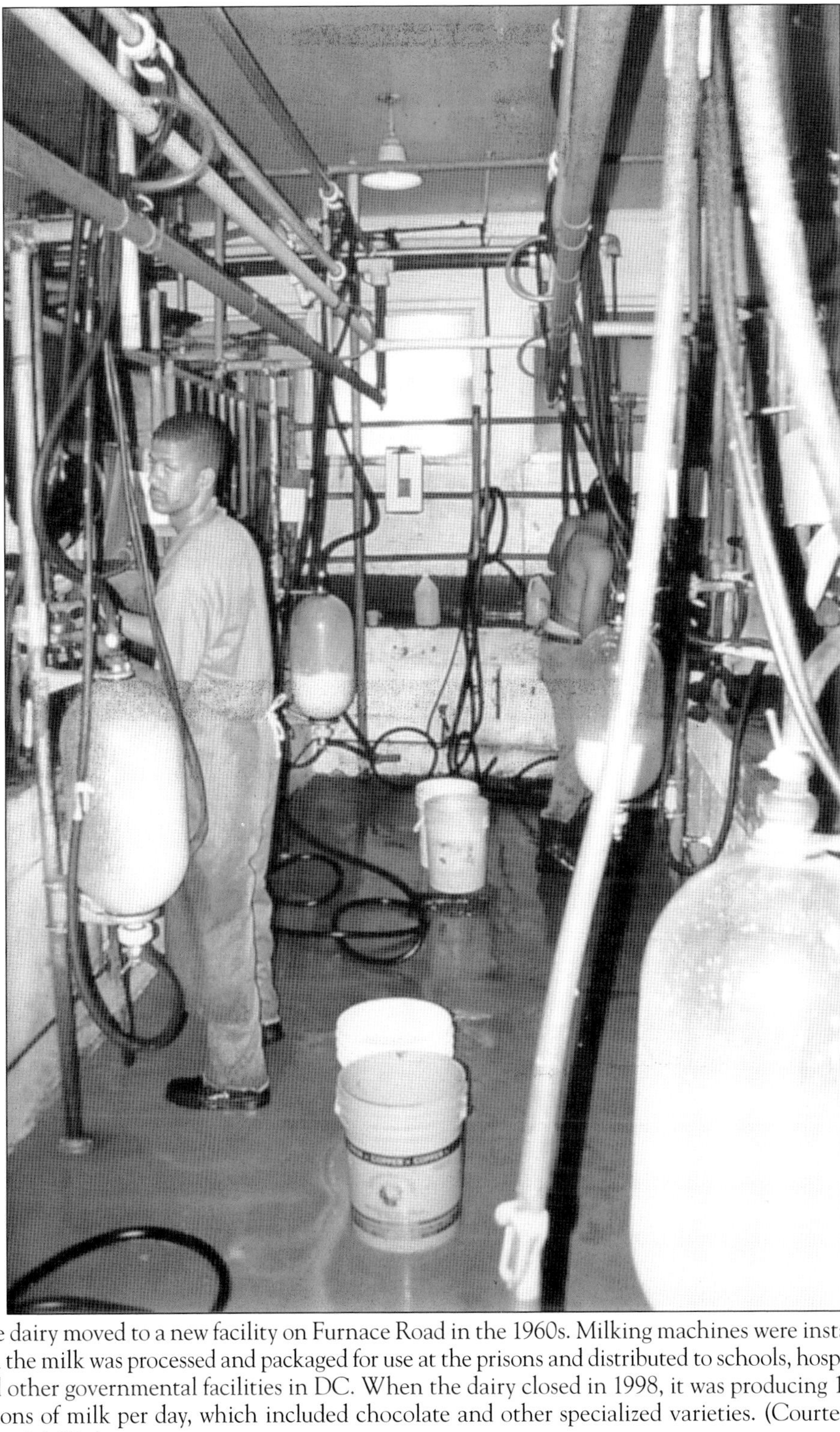

The dairy moved to a new facility on Furnace Road in the 1960s. Milking machines were installed and the milk was processed and packaged for use at the prisons and distributed to schools, hospitals, and other governmental facilities in DC. When the dairy closed in 1998, it was producing 1,850 gallons of milk per day, which included chocolate and other specialized varieties. (Courtesy of Laura McKie.)

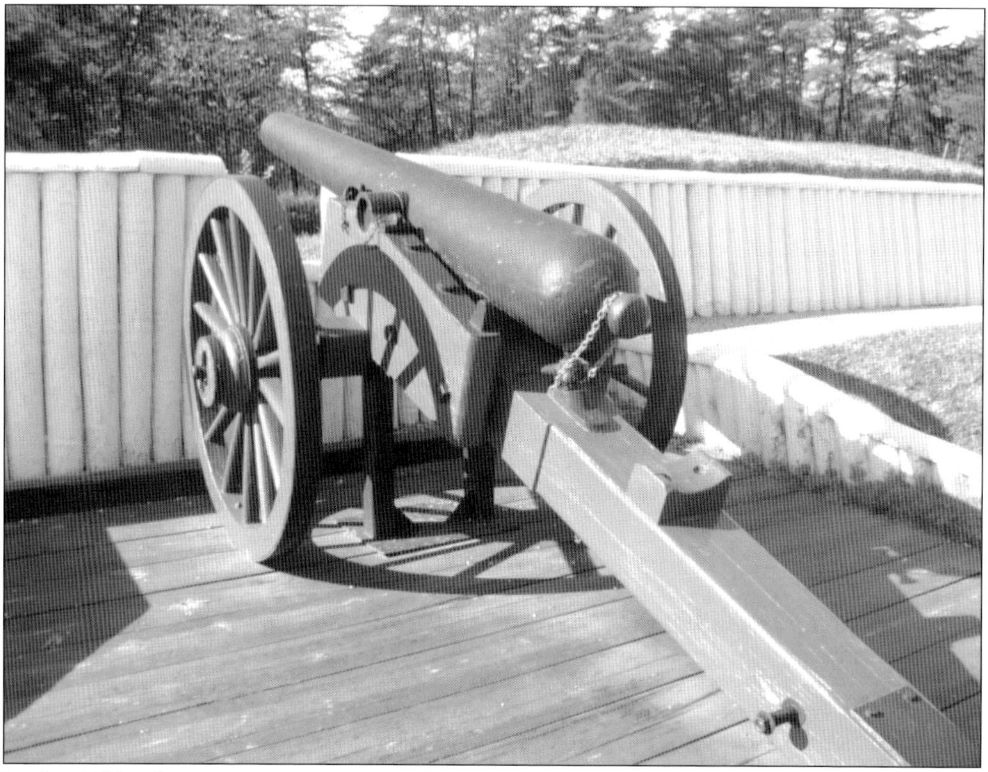

In the 1950s, the nation was preparing for the centennial commemoration of the Civil War. Cannons were needed for the national and state parks. The foundry at Lorton contracted to produce some. When no original plans could be found, a skillful inmate drew up new ones after carefully studying a vintage cannon made at the Torpedo Factory in Alexandria. The wooden carriages for the cannon were made at the prison furniture shop and the metal parts were supplied by the foundry. Lorton cannons remain in several parks in the local area, including Fort Ward Park in Alexandria and Manassas Battlefield. The Lorton-made cannon can be identified by the lack of a foundry mark designating the maker. (Both, courtesy of William Koch.)

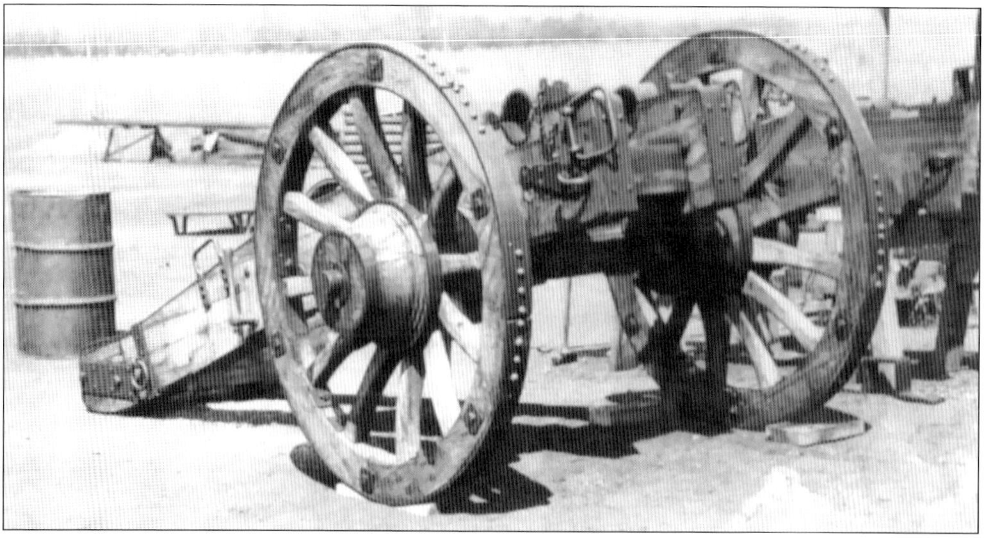

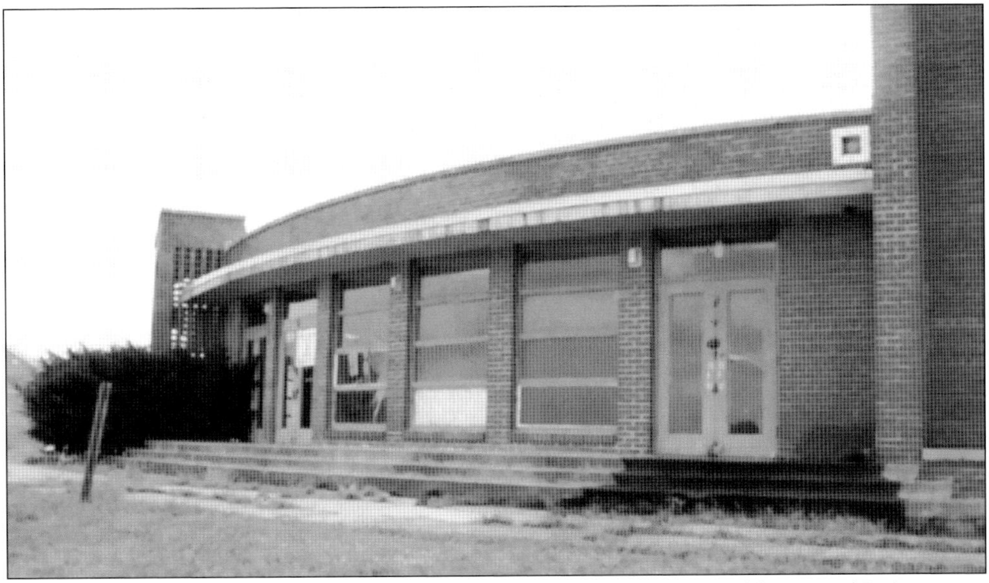

Religious services for prisoners were first held in the auditoriums at the Workhouse and Reformatory and led by visiting pastors from DC or the local community. Full-time prison chaplains were appointed around the middle of the 20th century. They convinced the DC Department of Corrections and Congress that there was an urgent need by the inmates for a chapel. Money was appropriated, and the site was selected by the chaplains and the superintendent of the Reformatory. (Courtesy of Fairfax County Department of Planning and Development.)

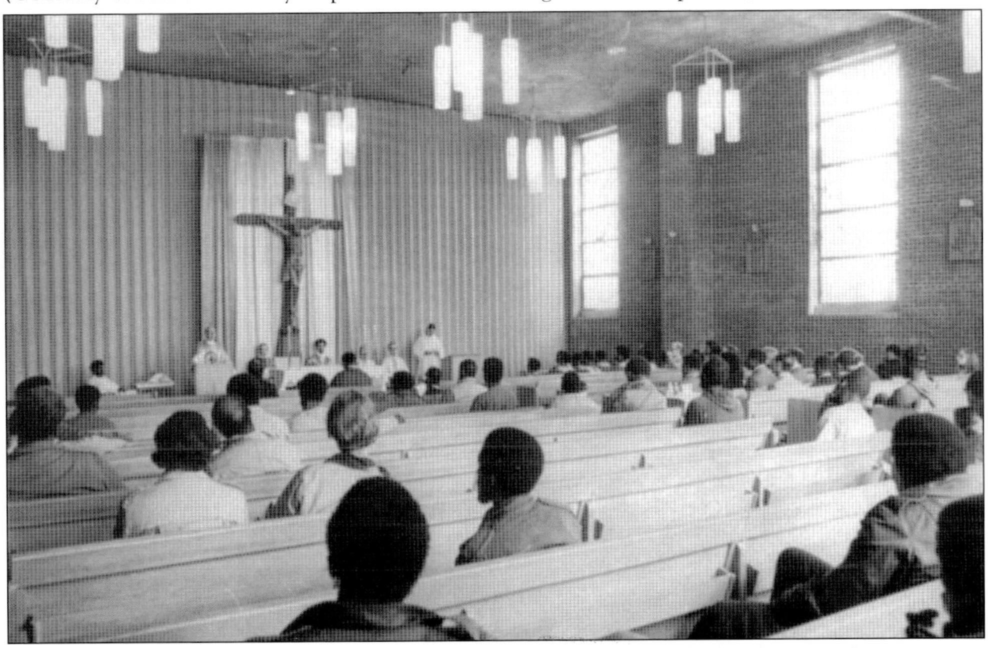

The blueprints for the chapel were drawn by a prisoner who had studied architectural engineering while incarcerated at San Quentin. His design provided that three religious services could be held simultaneously with a capacity of 400 to 500 or opened up for one gathering of 800 or more. All the excavation, making and laying of bricks, and other tasks needed for its construction were done by volunteer inmates. (Courtesy of DC Archives.)

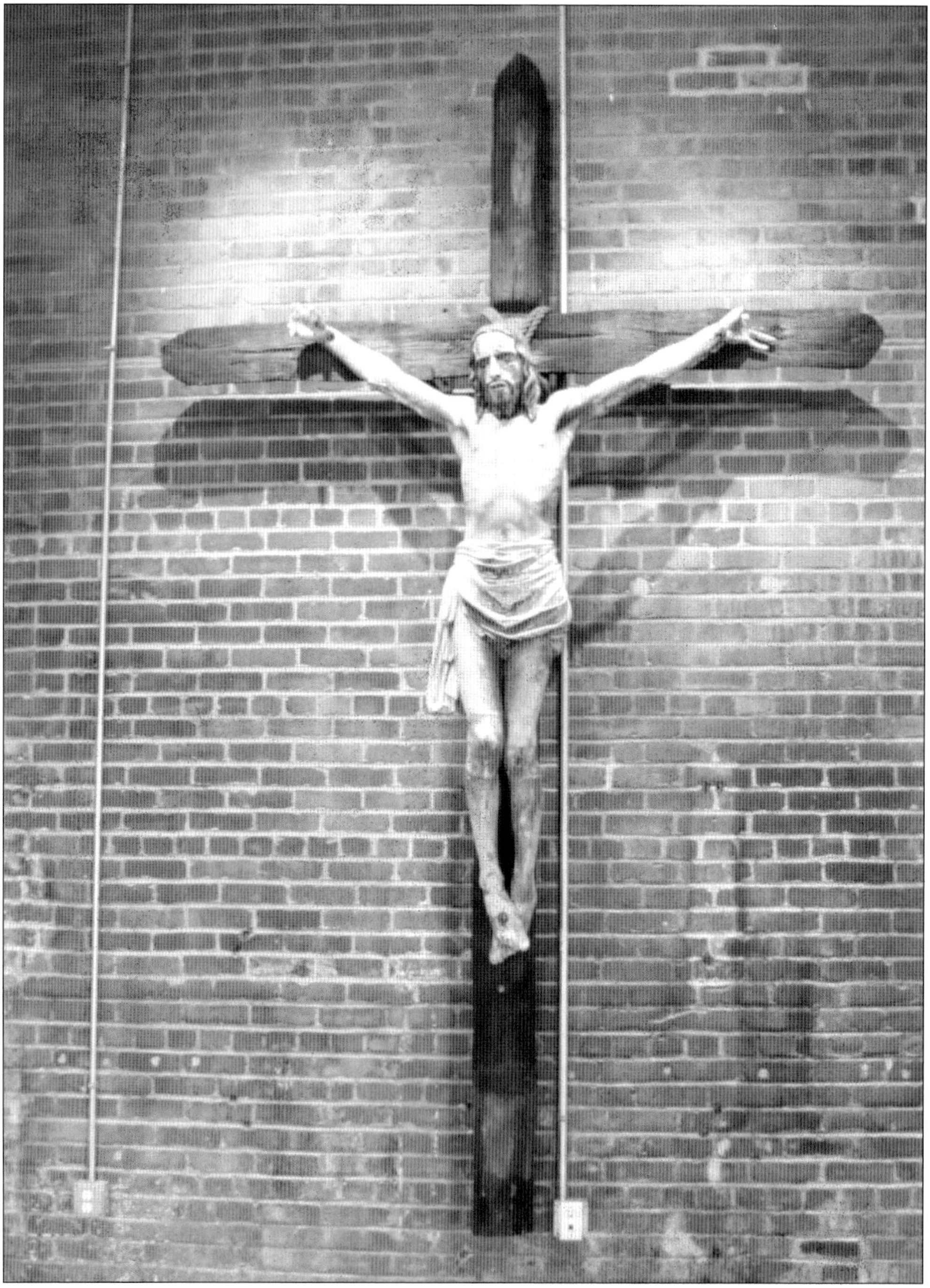

Prisoners also furnished the inside of the chapel. Sketches for the 10 tall stained-glass windows depicting the Ten Commandments were drawn by two inmates. One developed the process of staining the glass by trial and error. The life-size Catholic crucifix dominating the Catholic chapel was sculpted by an inmate using another prisoner as his model. The Christ figure is attached to a large wooden cross carved by a third prisoner. (Courtesy of Fairfax County Department of Planning and Development.)

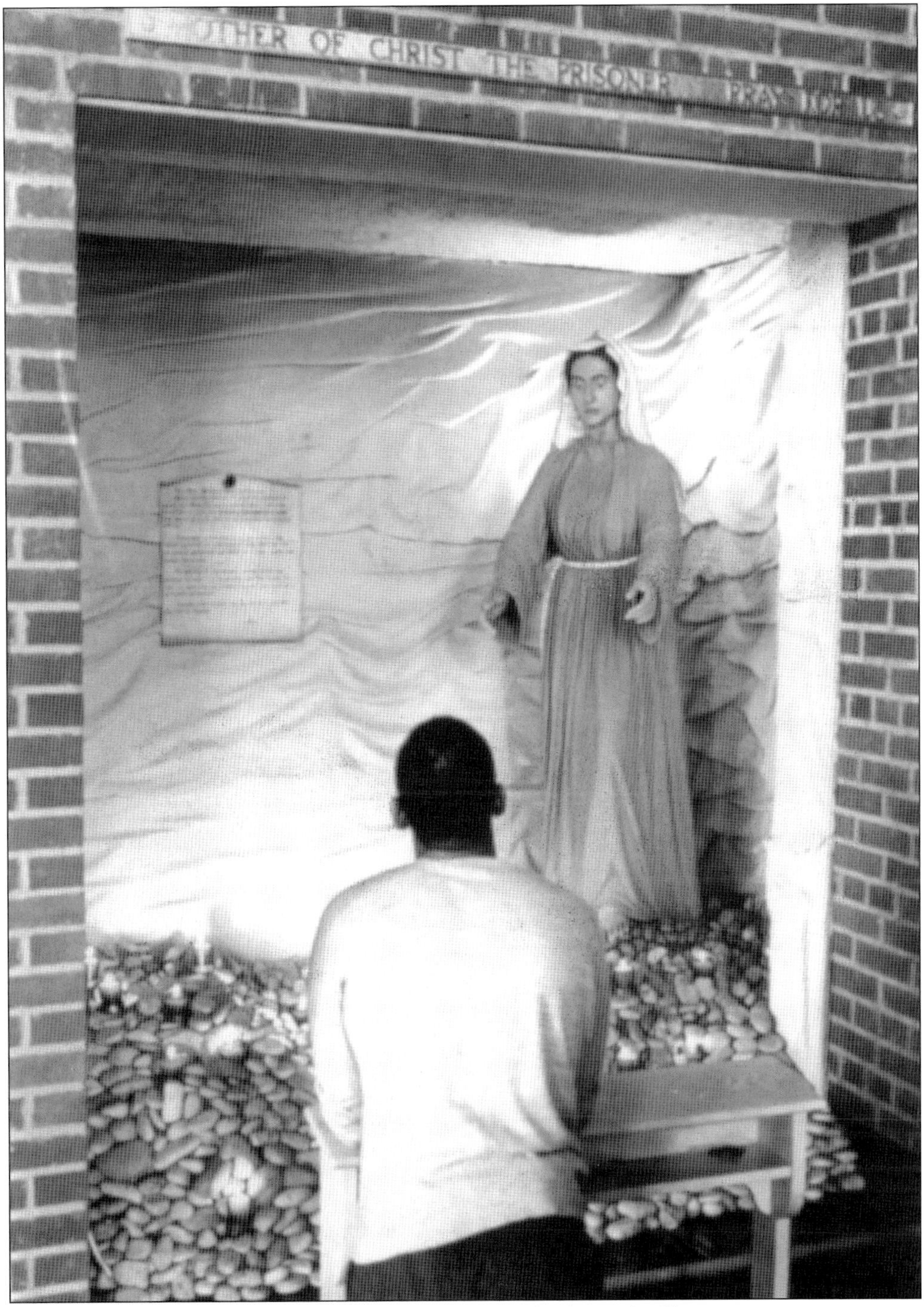

The chapel was named for Saints Peter and Paul because both men had been prisoners at one time. The first service was held on July 1, 1961. Attorney General Robert Kennedy was in attendance. Choirs for men were formed for the Protestant chapel. They entertained with concerts, both alone and together. They also performed for groups outside the prison including at the Summer Watergate Concerts in DC. (Courtesy of DC Archives.)

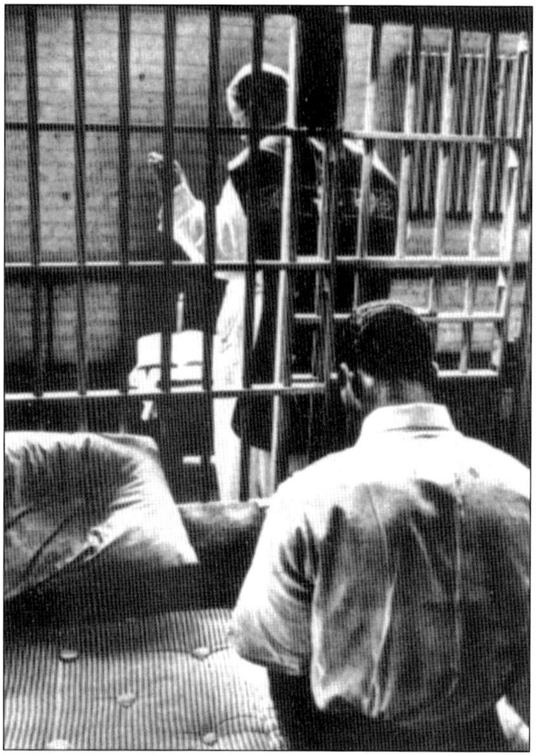

Three Protestant chaplains and three Catholic chaplains together laid the groundwork for the religious programs at Lorton and found ways to integrate them into the penal system. Muslim chaplains were added and shared the facilities as the Islamic faith took hold. Interfaith connections secured the services of a rabbi should one be needed. (Courtesy of the Library of Congress.)

In addition to the work of the chaplains, men's and women's groups from local churches were checked in through the prison gates for weekly bible studies and fellowship. They also sponsored tutorial programs that included basic reading and math skills, preparing for the GED exam, or introductory computer courses. (Courtesy of DC Archives.)

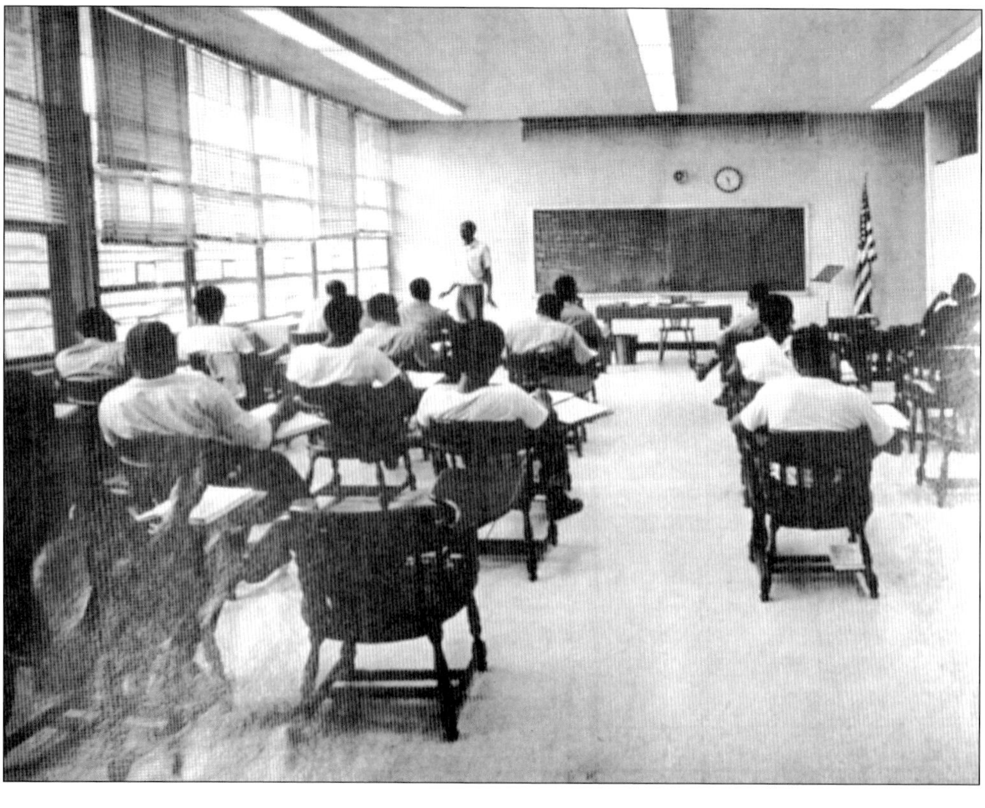

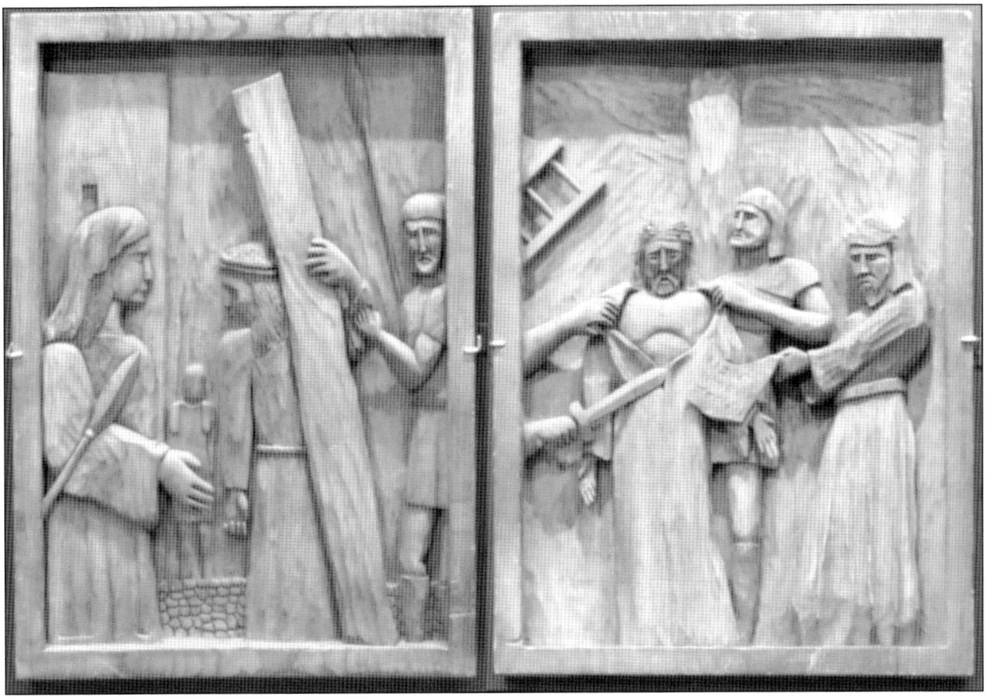

Trees grew in abundance on the prison property and were logged for use in building and at the furniture factory. The wood was also used as a creative outlet. The Stations of the Cross for the chapel were carved by a prisoner. Their uniqueness suggests they may be reflecting the prison experience as well, and this is being explored. (Courtesy of Patrick O'Neill.)

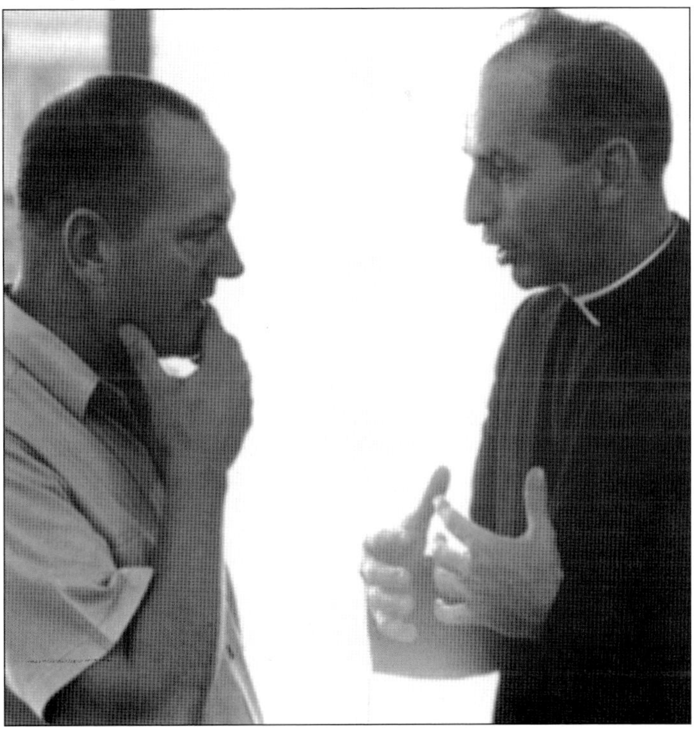

Fr. Carl Breitfeller (right) talks with Capt. Paul Pegelow. A charismatic personality, Father Breitfeller commanded the respect and admiration of inmates, correctional officers, and administrators alike. With his casual manner, friendly smile, offbeat sense of humor, and good listening skills, he offered a safe place to discuss problems large and small. The inmates trusted him with their confidences, and the administration gave him leeway with the knowledge that he knew the prisoners in ways they never would. (Courtesy of the Library of Congress.)

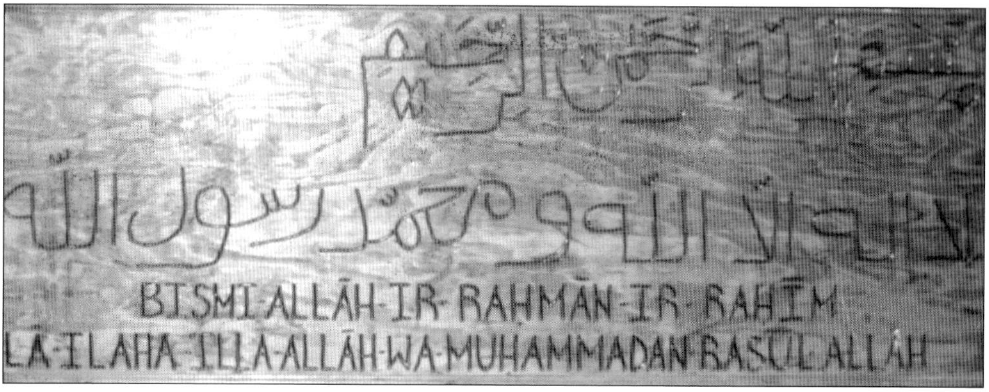

Religion and faith inspired many of the artists. The Arabic words carved into this beautiful wooden block translate: "In the name of Allah the all-merciful; I declare that there is no God but Allah and Muhammad is his prophet." It is a common and traditional start to Muslim prayer and must have been very important to the Lorton artist during the long hours of the plaque's creation. (Courtesy of DC Archives.)

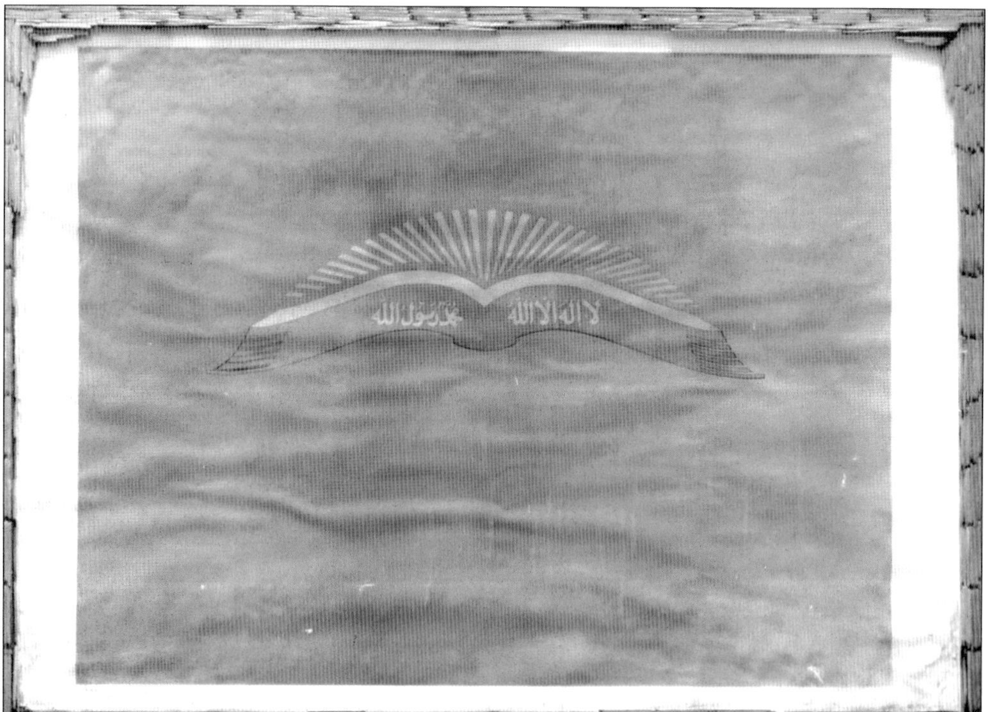

In the 1960s, Muslims increased their successful outreach in the nation's prisons. At Lorton, their largest numbers were in the Youth Center. This affected the complex in many ways. Pigs had been the major meat source, but pork products were forbidden to Muslims. They sued the prison and won the right to have a halal diet. They also sued and won the rights to have prison chaplains, hold services, and observe their holidays. (Courtesy of Patrick O'Neill.)

In July and August 1963, serious disturbances at the Youth Center caused $7,000 in property damages before order was regained over the riotous behavior. The Annual Report for 1963 recorded that "throughout the year the agitation of Muslim inmates tended to upset the good order of not only the Youth Center, but also the Reformatory Division." (Courtesy of DC Archives.)

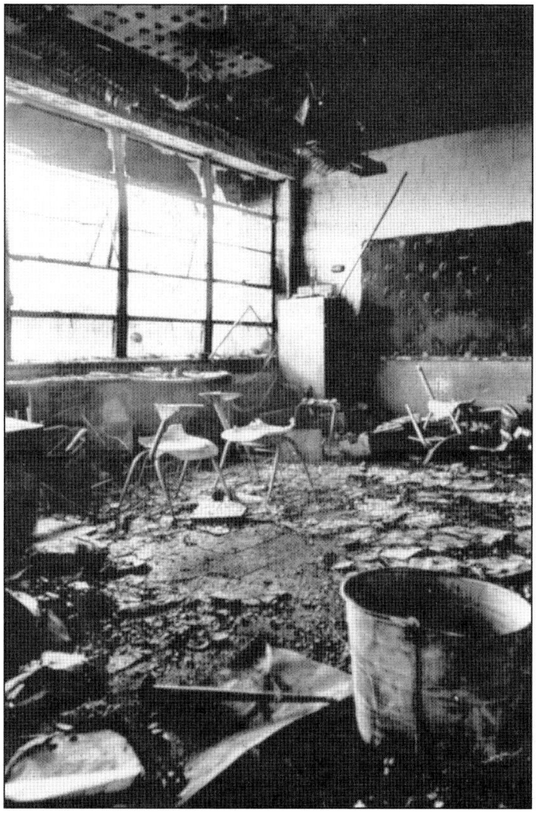

Cassius Clay, later known as Muhammad Ali, spent a day at the Youth Center in April 1967. He addressed a group in the morning, gave the sermon at the afternoon mosque service, and addressed another large group in the evening. His messages were preaching and proselytizing for the Nation of Islam Muslim faith. To the delight of the crowd, and at their request, he sparred briefly with the center's 1966 heavyweight champion. (Courtesy of the Library of Congress.)

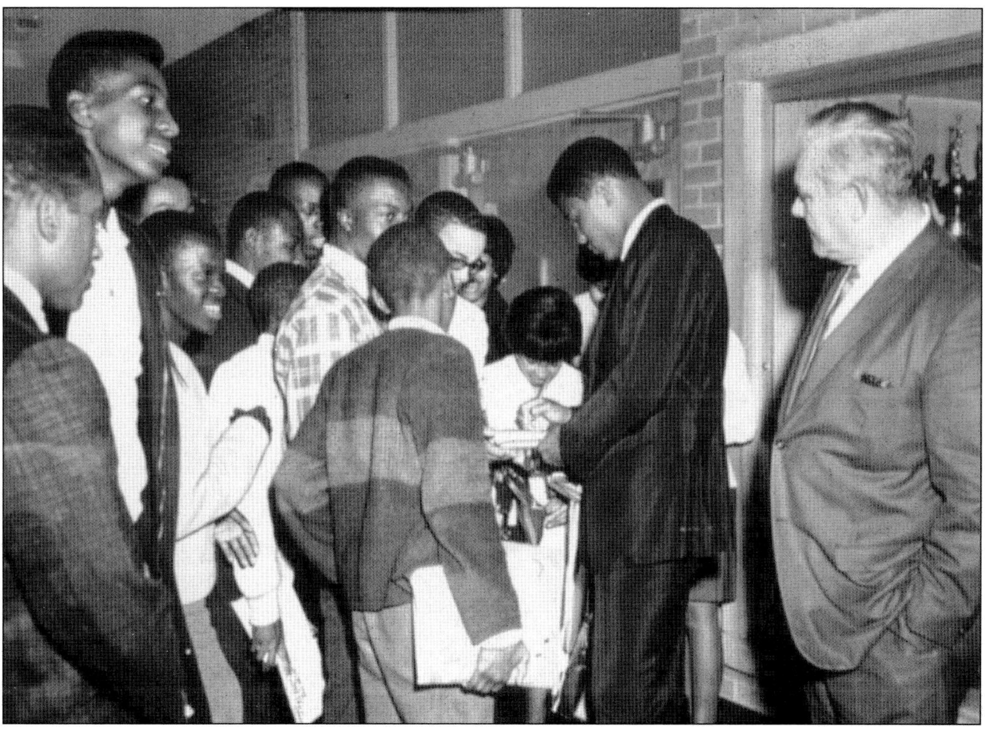

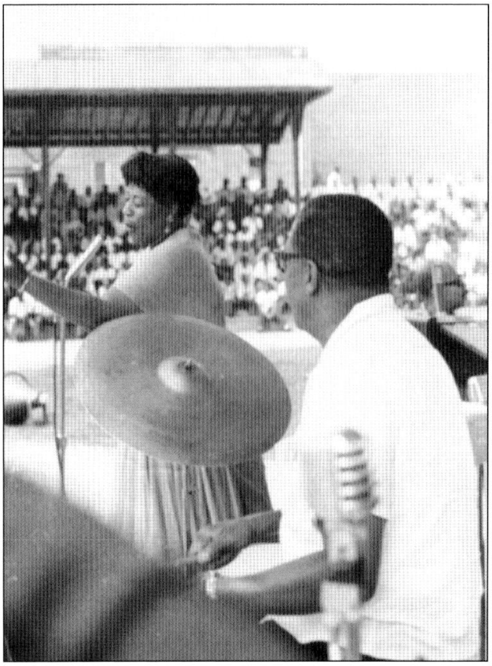

Father Breitfeller, so instrumental in building the chapel, also instigated the Annual Jazz Festivals in 1955; they continued until the mid-1960s. Felix Grant from radio station WMAL emceed the programs. They featured local artists like Nancy Wilson and nationally known entertainers that included Duke Ellington, Ella Fitzgerald, Frank Sinatra, Count Basie, and Louis Armstrong. (Courtesy of DC Archives.)

The concerts were held on the Reformatory ball field and a stage was erected near the pitcher's mound. The prisoners sat in the brick bleachers and correctional officers and guests sat in chairs near first base. In 1968, the cover of the program featured all the artists that had donated their talent to the jazz festivals. (Courtesy of DC Archives.)

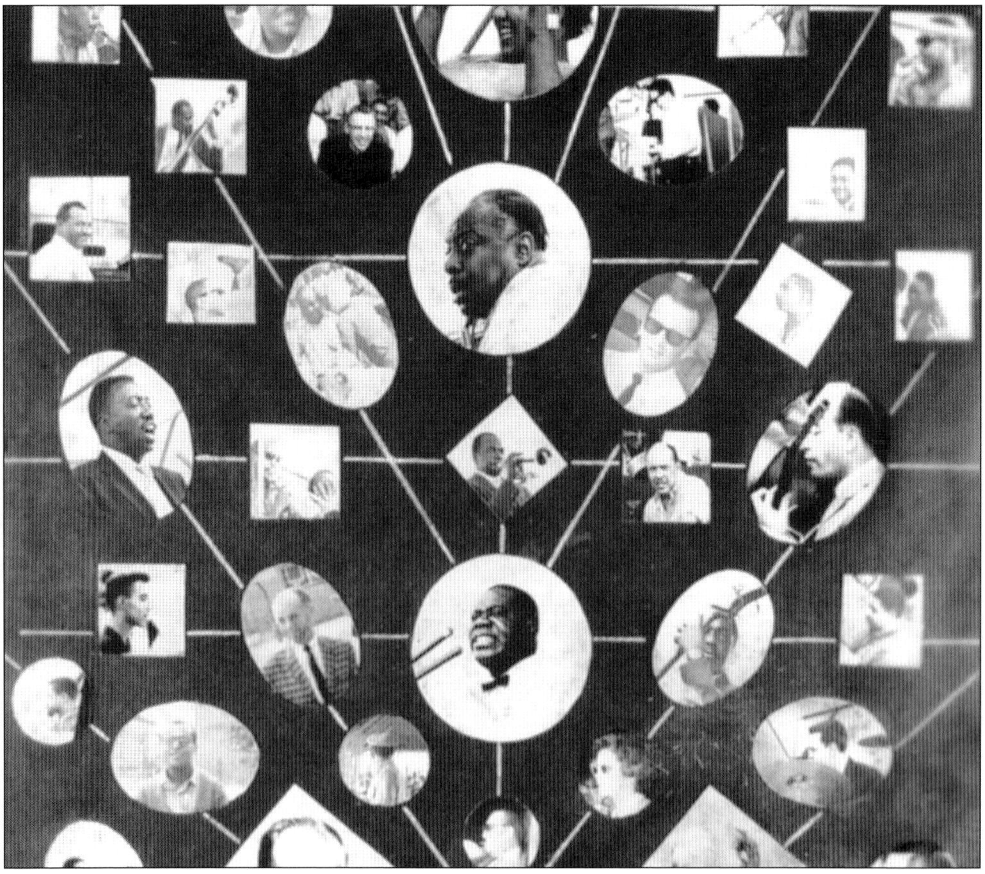

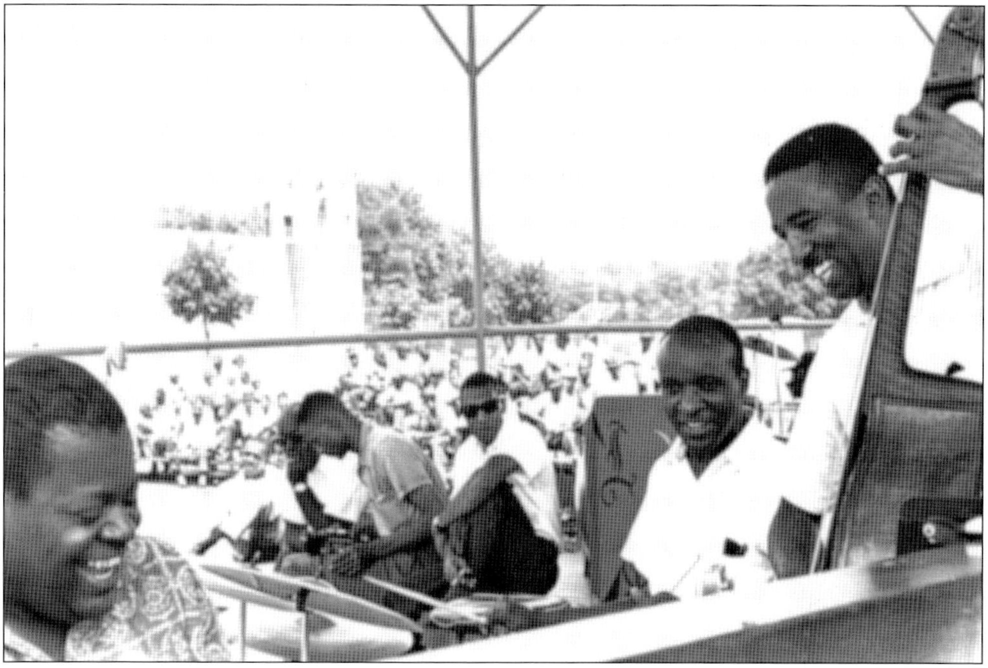

When there was a need in the prisoner bands for an instrument, the Army and the other military bands were often able to help. A correctional officer would contact a source in the service band and ask if a trumpet or tuba were available. Among the five military units, a used one could usually be found and sent down to Lorton. Musicians among the inmates taught others how to play them. (Courtesy of DC Archives.)

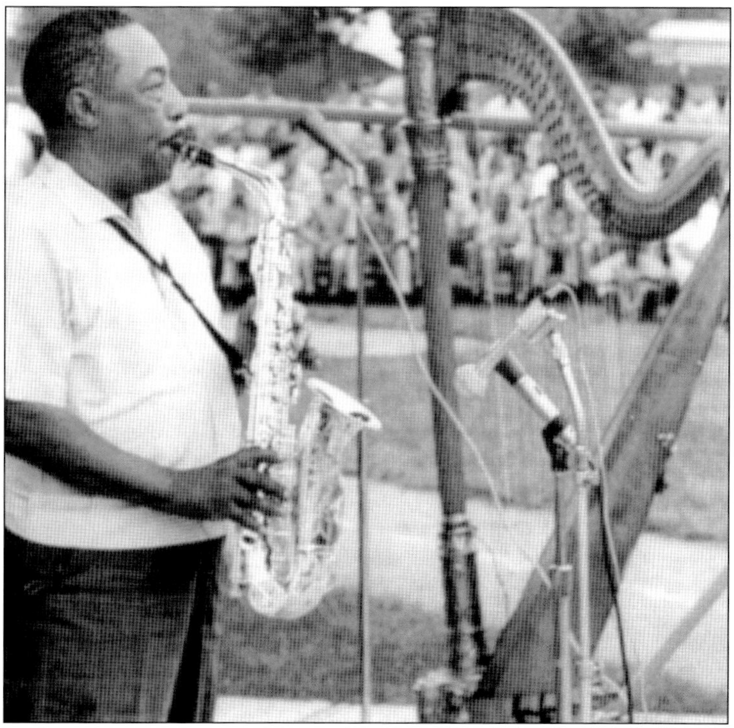

Inmate bands played as backup or warm-up acts for visiting artists. They provided dance music for staff parties and affairs. They also performed at prison talent shows. Another popular performer at the shows was Chuck Brown, the "Godfather of Go-Go." He bought his first prison-made guitar at Lorton and developed his signature sound that invited audience participation with calls and responses and a heavy drumbeat. (Courtesy of DC Archives.)

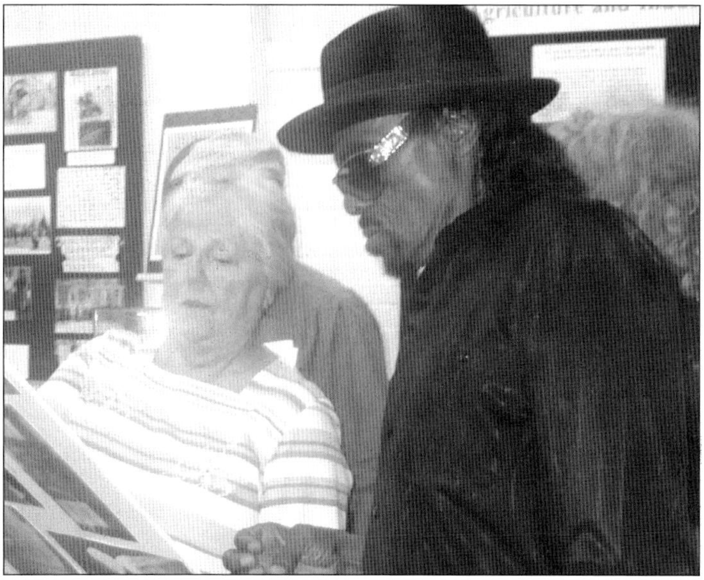

Chuck Brown returned to visit Lorton and sat for an oral history about his imprisonment. He said if a person accepted the help that was offered, he left with three things: an education (he earned a GED), a skill to help earn a good living, and self-respect (his debt to society was paid and he could start anew). He returned later with his band for a concert on the quad. (Courtesy of Kenena Spalding.)

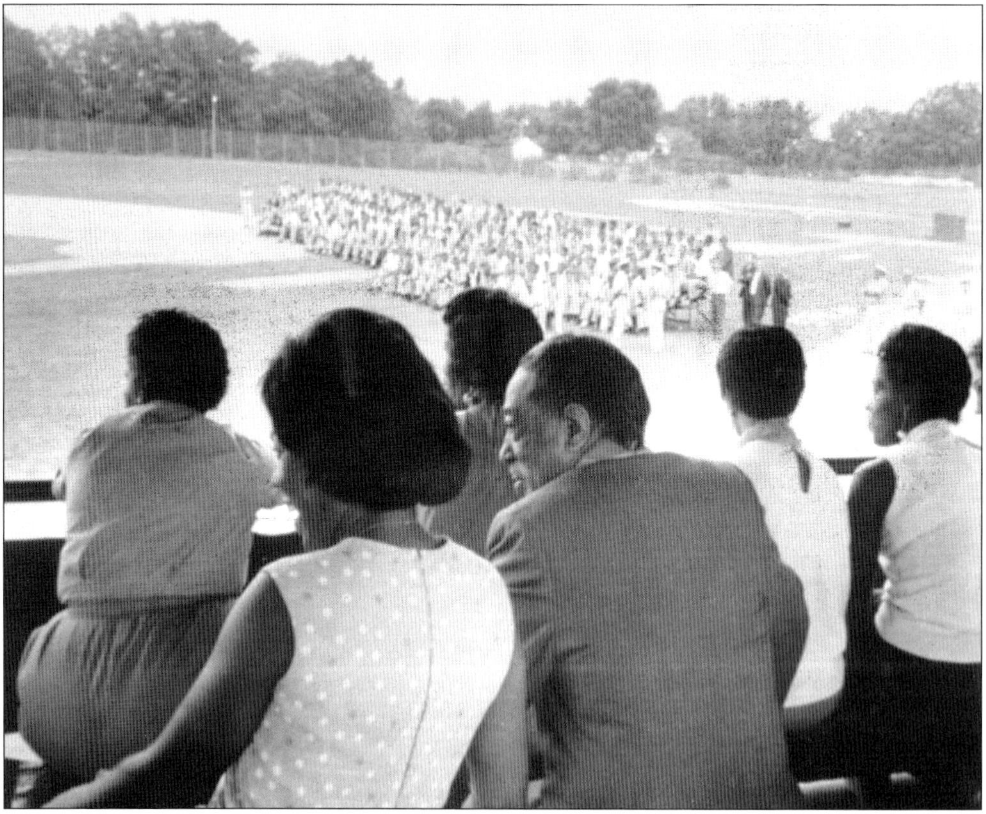

Duke Ellington grew up in Washington, DC, so it was not hard to persuade him to be part of the jazz festivals. One hot summer's day, he was in the stands with Ella Fitzgerald at Lorton, watching others perform on the bandstand. He returned again with Frank Sinatra and brought his whole orchestra with him to entertain the inmates with songs from his hit recordings and his signature jazz. (Courtesy of DC Archives.)

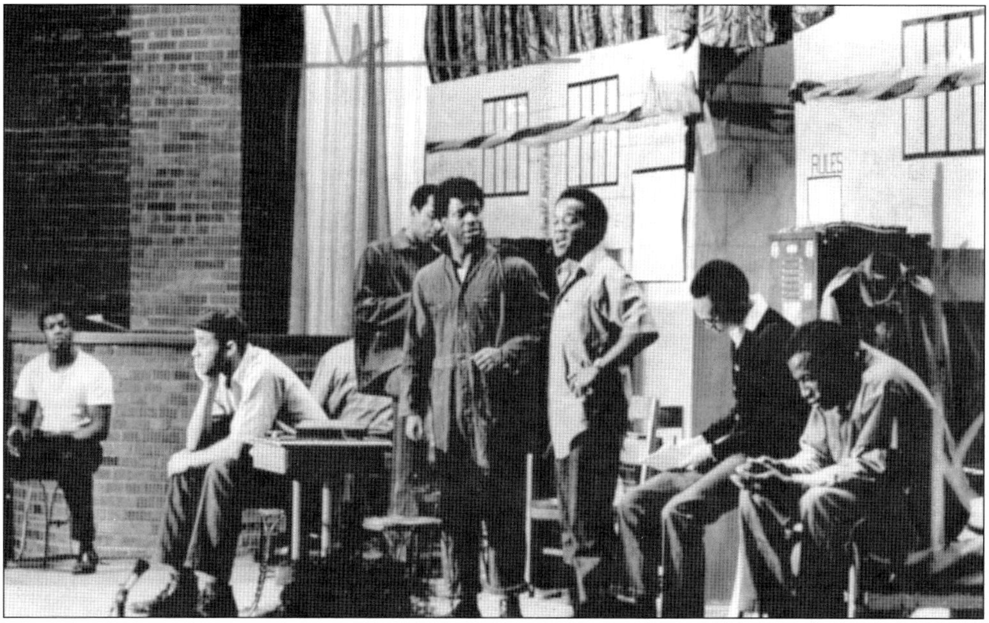

Inner Voices, a prison drama group created by Rhozier "Roach" Brown, was geared to the particular lifestyle of the cast members. His first play, *Christmas in Time*, was an overwhelming success at the Reformatory in 1969. Brown was granted extended furloughs to work for National Public Television. Rewritten and renamed *Holidays/Hollow-days*, his play won an award at the New York Film Festival. Metro Media TV hired Brown upon his release. (Courtesy of Irma Clifton.)

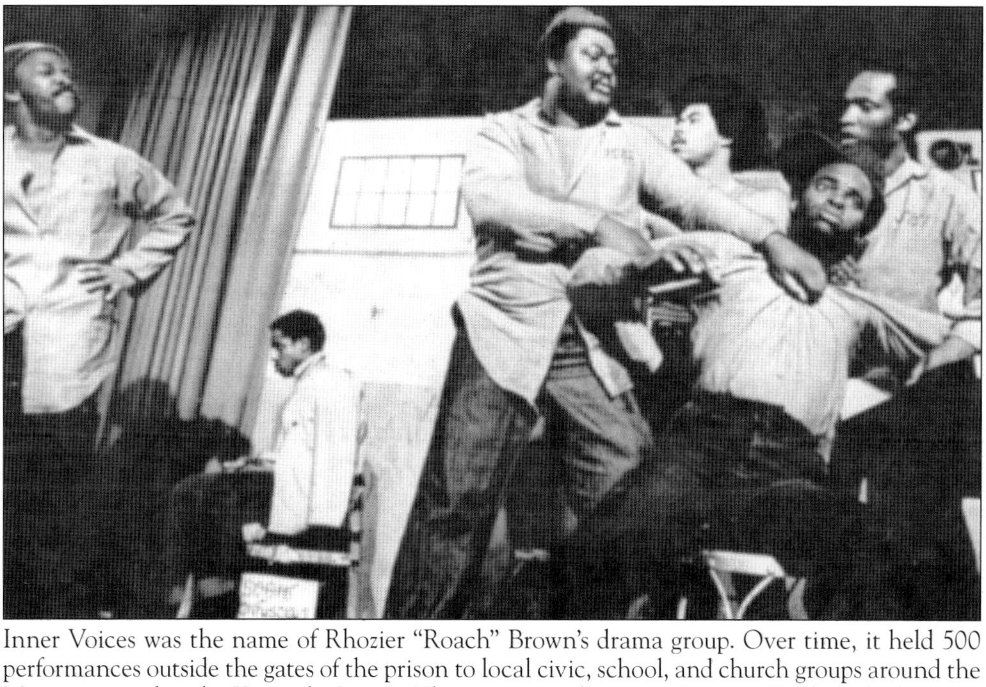

Inner Voices was the name of Rhozier "Roach" Brown's drama group. Over time, it held 500 performances outside the gates of the prison to local civic, school, and church groups around the Metro area and at the Kennedy Center. The group members were accompanied on the bus by a lone correctional officer who checked them out and back in. The fact that no one ever attempted an escape attests to the dedication of the cast. (Courtesy of Irma Clifton.)

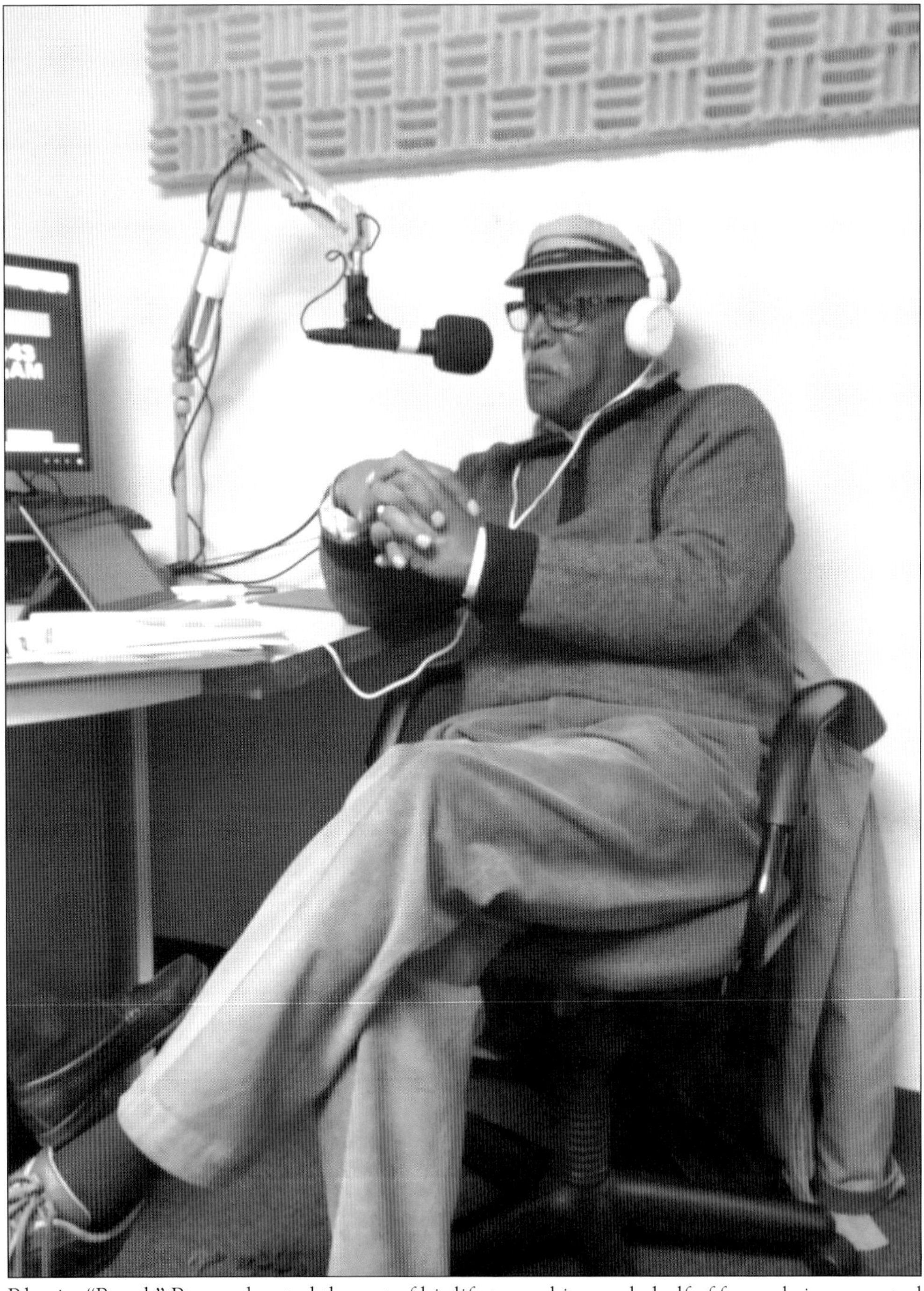

Rhozier "Roach" Brown devoted the rest of his life to working on behalf of formerly incarcerated people, or his preferred term, "returned citizens." He was appointed to both city and congressional committees working on their behalf. He has been chairman of the Coalition of the National Association of Ex-offenders and is a sought-after speaker. The troupe he formed to present his plays raises funds and an awareness of the needs of his returned citizens. (Courtesy of Laura McKie.)

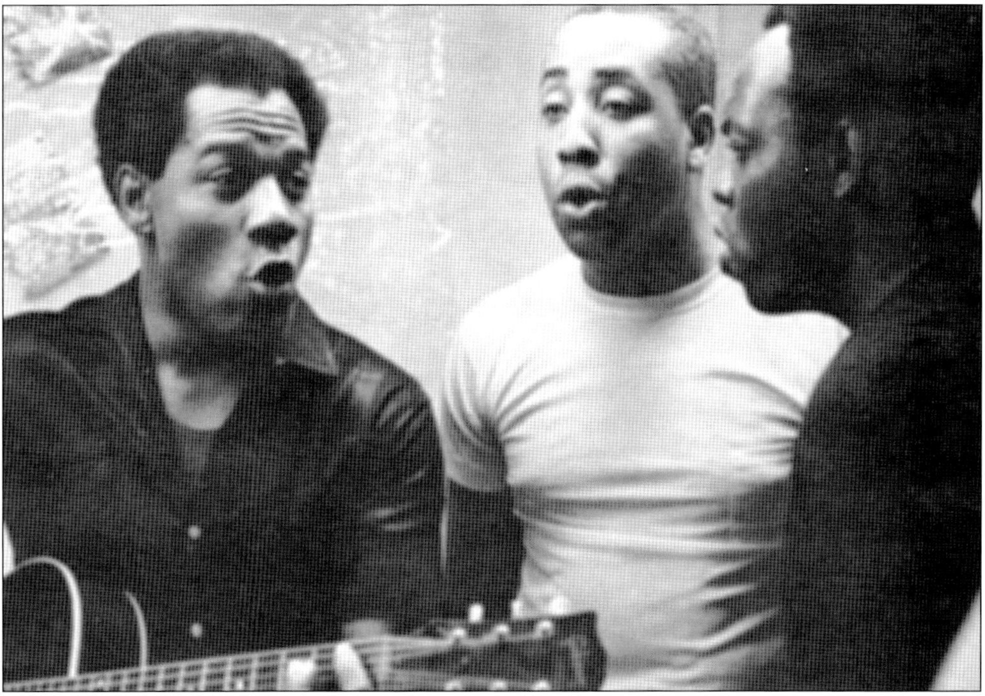

The Amazing Gospel Souls band was formed inside Lorton prison in the 1980s, and all members are returned citizens. Their original intent was to bring hope to other inmates. Now with their concerts, mentoring, testimonies, and examples, they try to save today's young people from incarceration. As one band member put it, "We can't tell them what not to do, but we can tell them what will happen to them if they do." (Courtesy of Irma Clifton.)

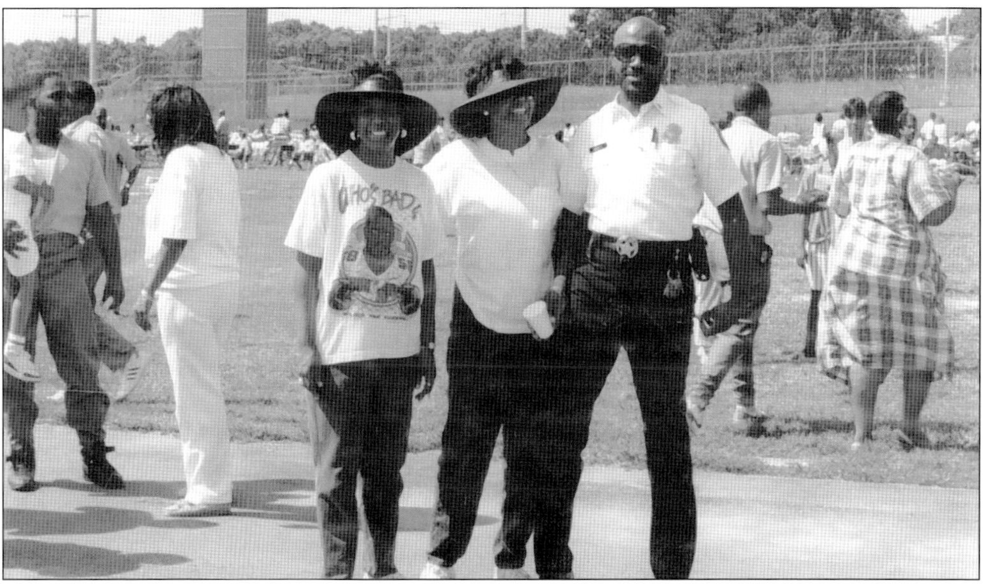

With the focus on rehabilitation, prison officials thought a system of rewards for positive behavior would give inmates something to look forward to, work toward, and could be reflected in improved behavior. They also recognized the need to channel their physical energy in positive directions. Yearly summertime Family Days were organized. (Courtesy of DC Archives.)

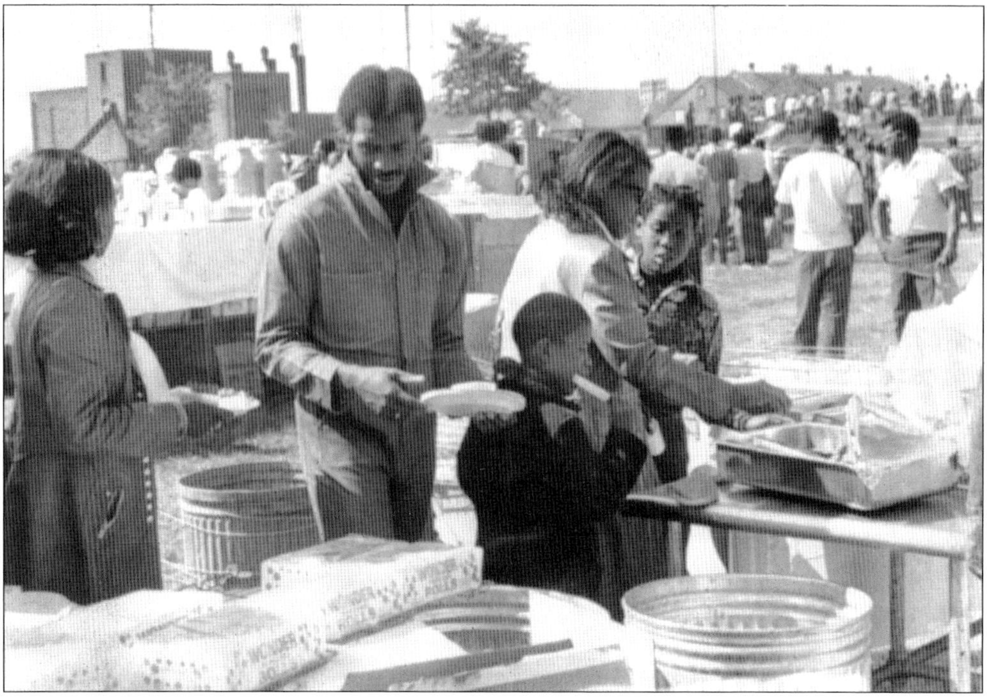

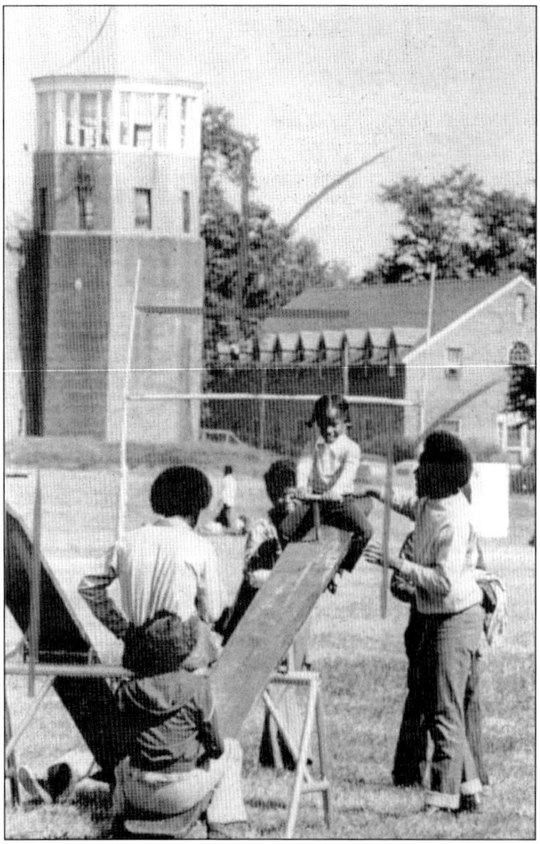

Family Days became eagerly awaited events in the late summer. With the support of the director, they were organized by a committee of inmates and were set up on the prison ball field. Each prisoner was allowed to invite three of his relatives or friends. (Courtesy of DC Archives.)

Games and activities were prepared for all ages to enjoy, and the culinary unit provided picnic-style food. There were ponies to ride, fried chicken to eat, and music from the bands to enjoy. Prison culture required that if an inmate had guests, they were not approached unless invited. (Courtesy of DC Archives.)

Competitive sports were another way to channel physical energy in positive directions. There were two baseball fields at the prison—one at the Workhouse with wooden bleachers, and a regulation-sized field at the Reformatory with brick stands. Lorton teams competed against each other and teams from local businesses, police departments, and even the Federal Bureau of Investigation. Blacks and whites played and rooted together, something notable in the final years of segregation. (Courtesy of DC Archives.)

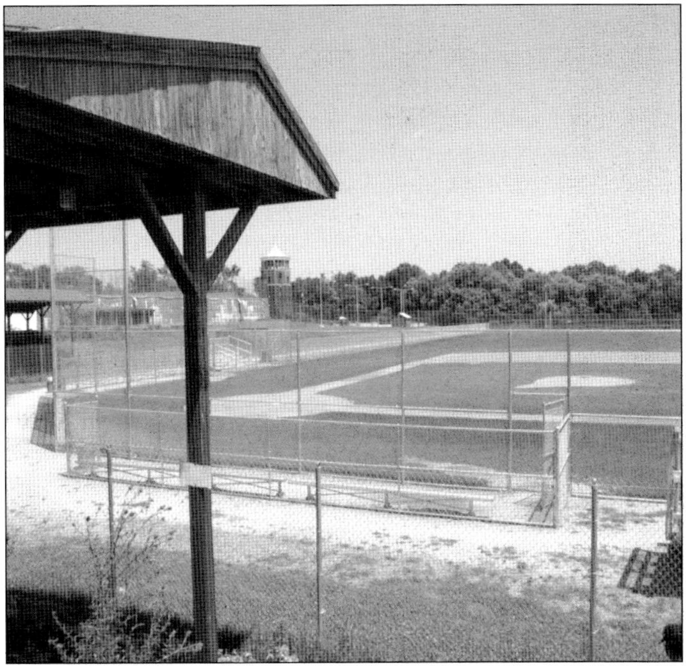

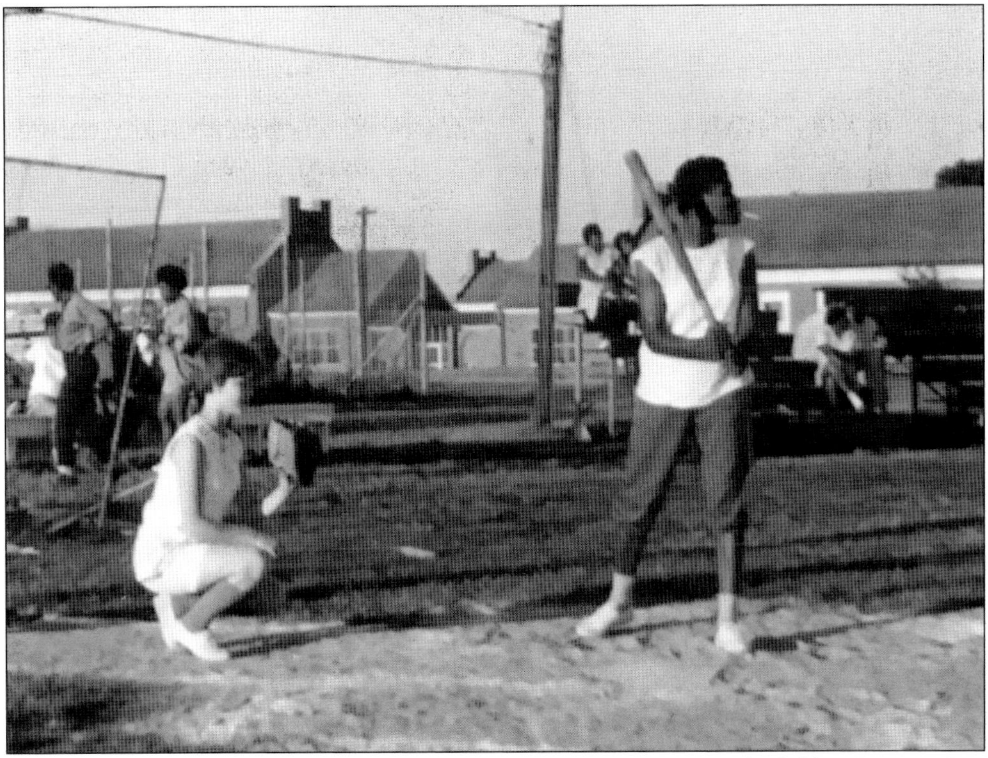

Women prisoners also had the opportunity to play competitive sports on the fields at Lorton. One of the chaplains or correctional officers was often recruited to umpire a softball game between inmate teams and those from the local area that came through to play ball. (Courtesy of the Library of Congress.)

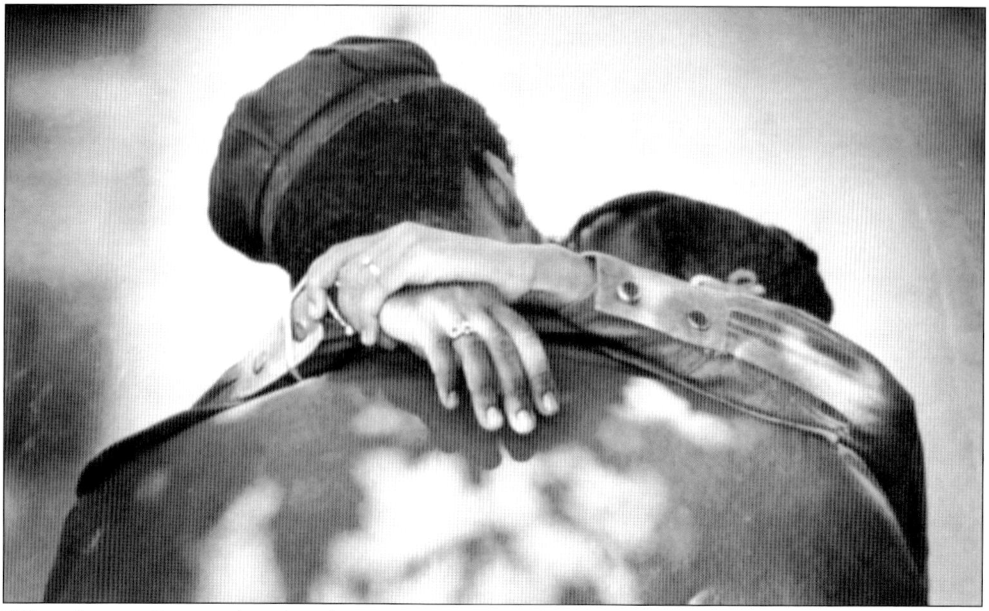

When Lorton Prison closed and inmates transferred to federal prisons throughout the country, one of the downsides was the loss of easy opportunity and transportation to maintain family and community ties. Regular visitation boosted the morale of inmates and gave them incentive and hope. Often, a prison escape was prompted by a problem at home and the need to be there. Being together, even for a short, supervised time, helped. (Courtesy of DC Archives.)

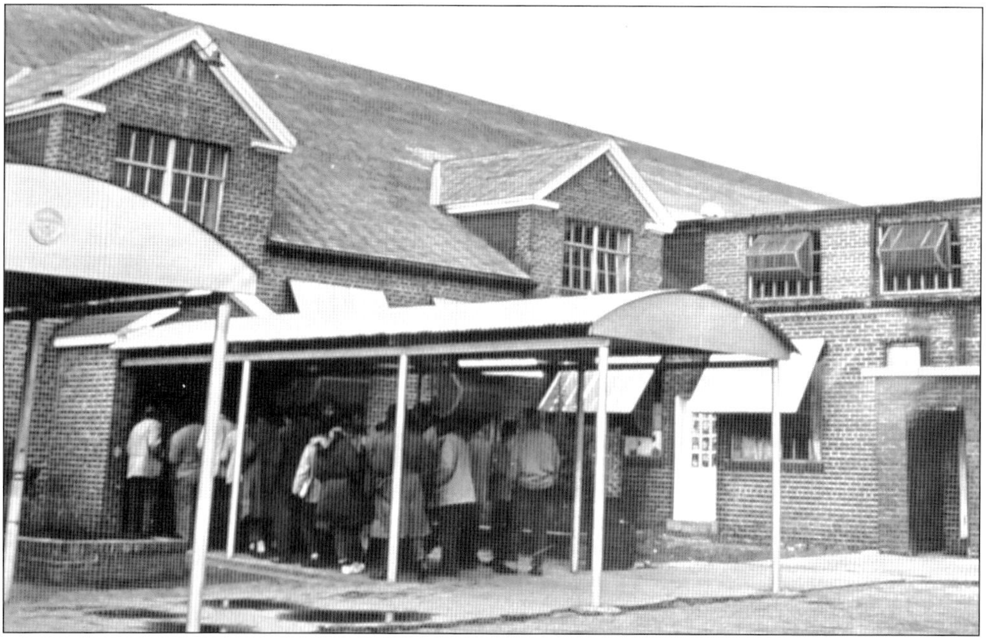

Inmates gathered at the mess-hall doorway while awaiting the time to enter and eat. It was a common area for all inmates and staff and thus became a focal point for protests. In March 1985, 170 inmate mess-hall workers staged a work stoppage by refusing to leave their cells. They presented a list of 14 grievances; including increasing shakedowns for contraband knives and forks as prisoners exited. The protest was peaceful causing "minor disruptions." (Courtesy of DC Archives.)

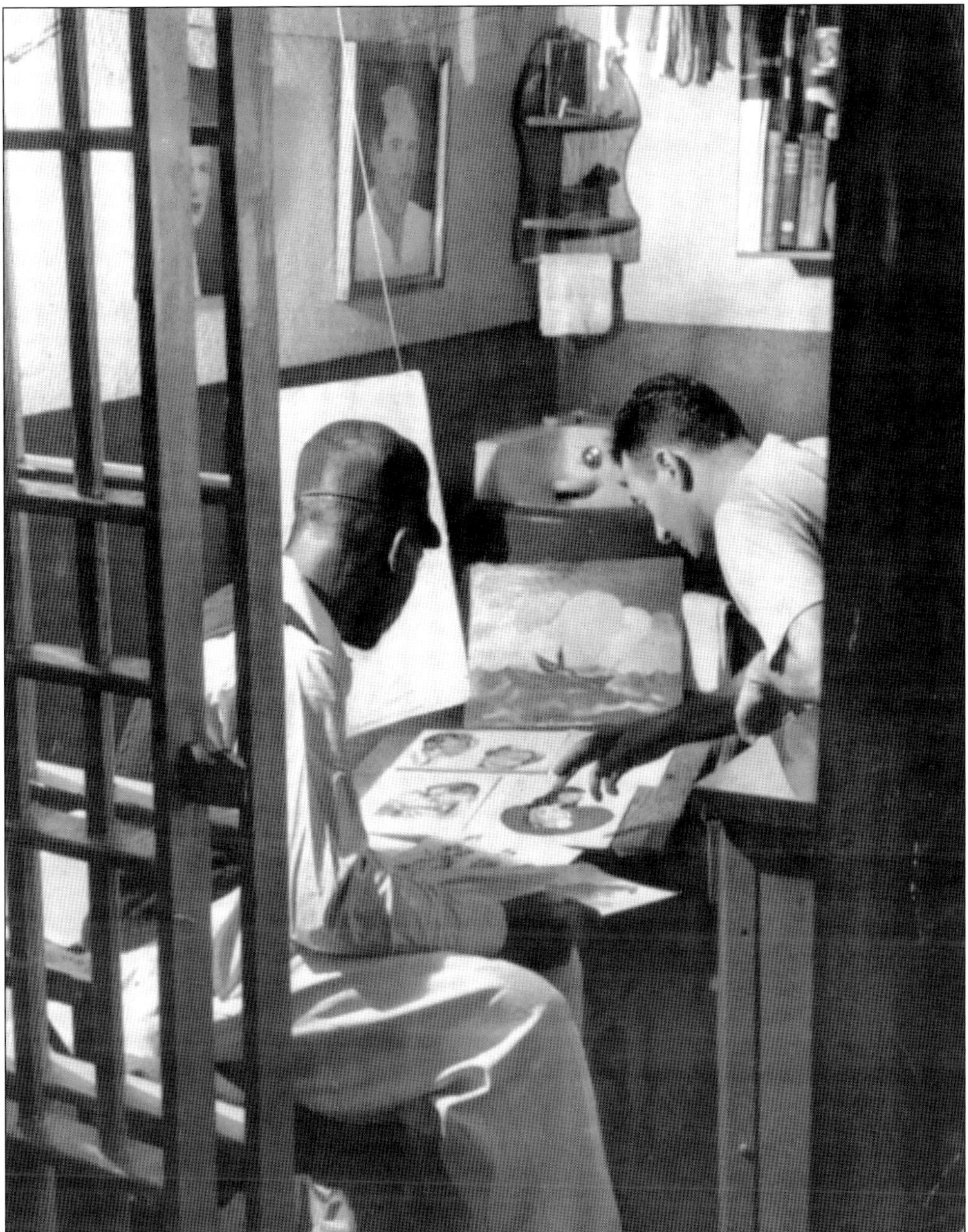

Formal art classes were offered by the education department for inmates wanting to develop their skills. They also shared and critiqued one another. They painted on the walls of their cells and created murals in the dining halls and recreation area or on the brick walls of the buildings outside. Often, the art became a gift to a member of the prison staff. (Courtesy of DC Archives.)

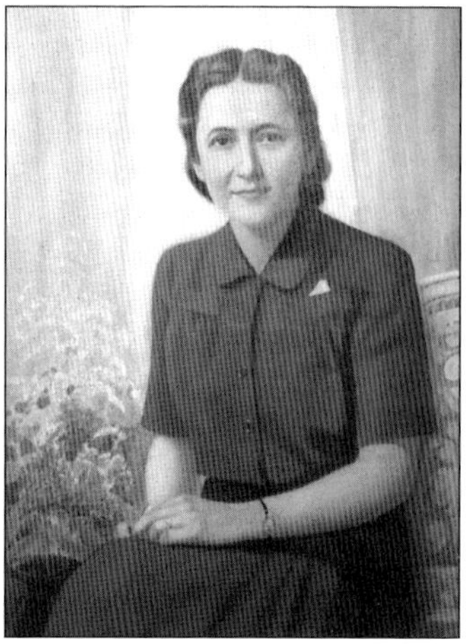

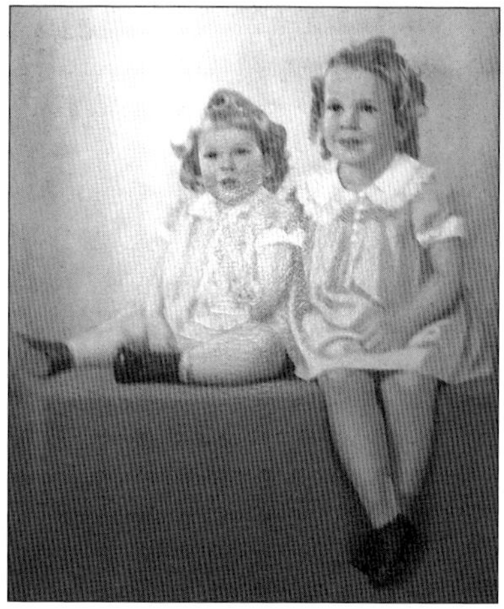

There was always art at the Workhouse. Superintendent Huff commissioned an inmate artist to paint oil portraits of his wife and two daughters in the 1930s. Huff was an early advocate for parole believing it was too hard for some to immediately integrate back into society on the outside. He allowed parolees to live temporarily at the prison, including some in his own residence. The Huff daughters donated the pictures to the museum. (Courtesy of the Huff family.)

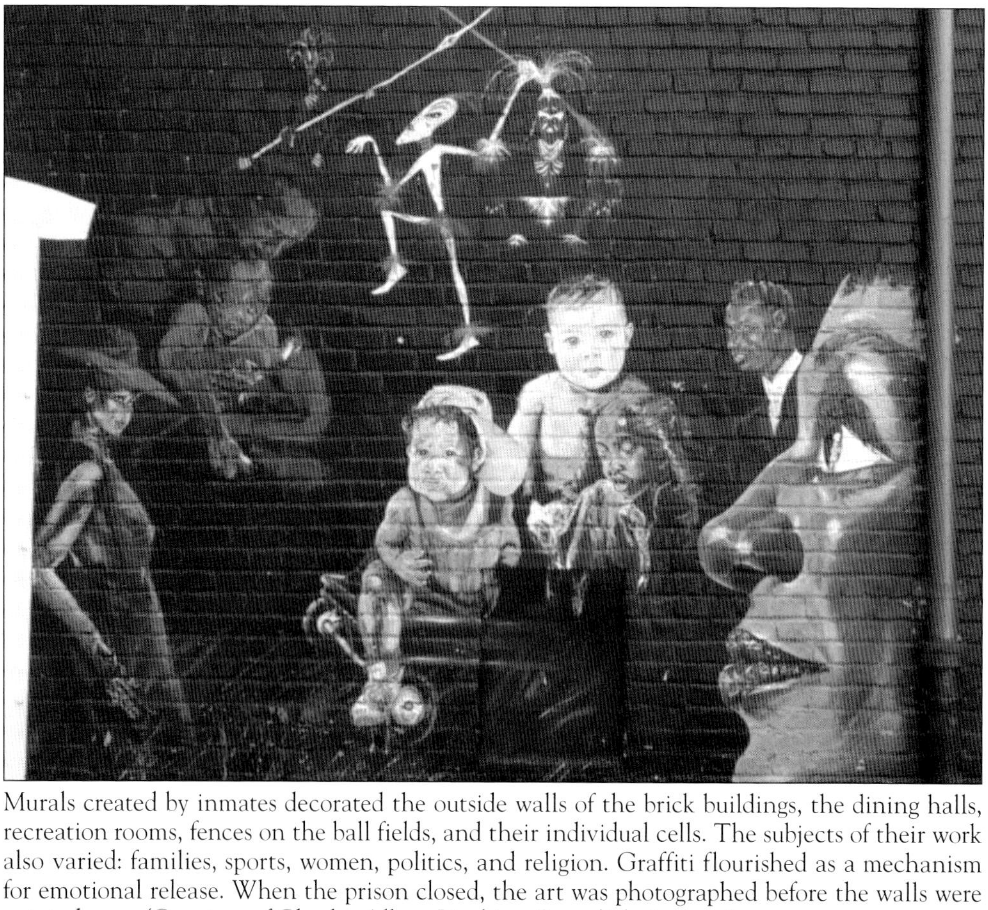

Murals created by inmates decorated the outside walls of the brick buildings, the dining halls, recreation rooms, fences on the ball fields, and their individual cells. The subjects of their work also varied: families, sports, women, politics, and religion. Graffiti flourished as a mechanism for emotional release. When the prison closed, the art was photographed before the walls were painted over. (Courtesy of Charles Albert Huckins, Stonelight Images.)

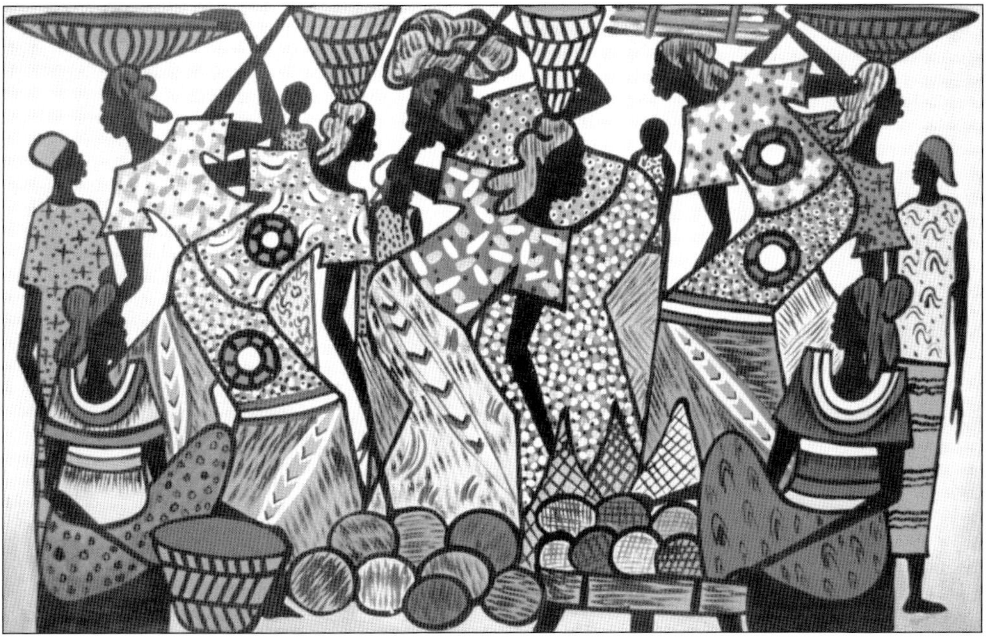

Prison art was as varied as the prisoners themselves. They chose a variety of mediums and a wide range of subjects depending on their own experiences, interests, and dreams. Some pictures show prison-artists enjoyment in experimenting with techniques and colors. (Courtesy of Charles Albert Huckins, Stonelight Images.)

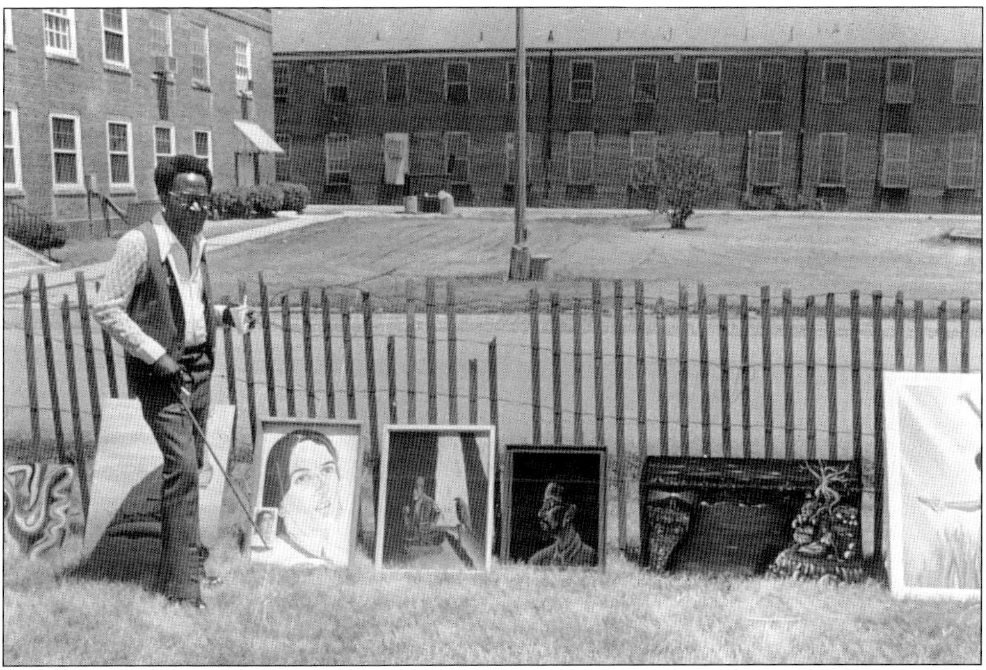

Prisoners had an opportunity to display and sell their art at exhibits on the quad. A rectangular snow-fenced area was set up and artists stood by as their pictures leaned against the fence. Art was a positive way for inmates to deal with the anger, frustrations, and other aspects of prison life. (Courtesy of DC Archives.)

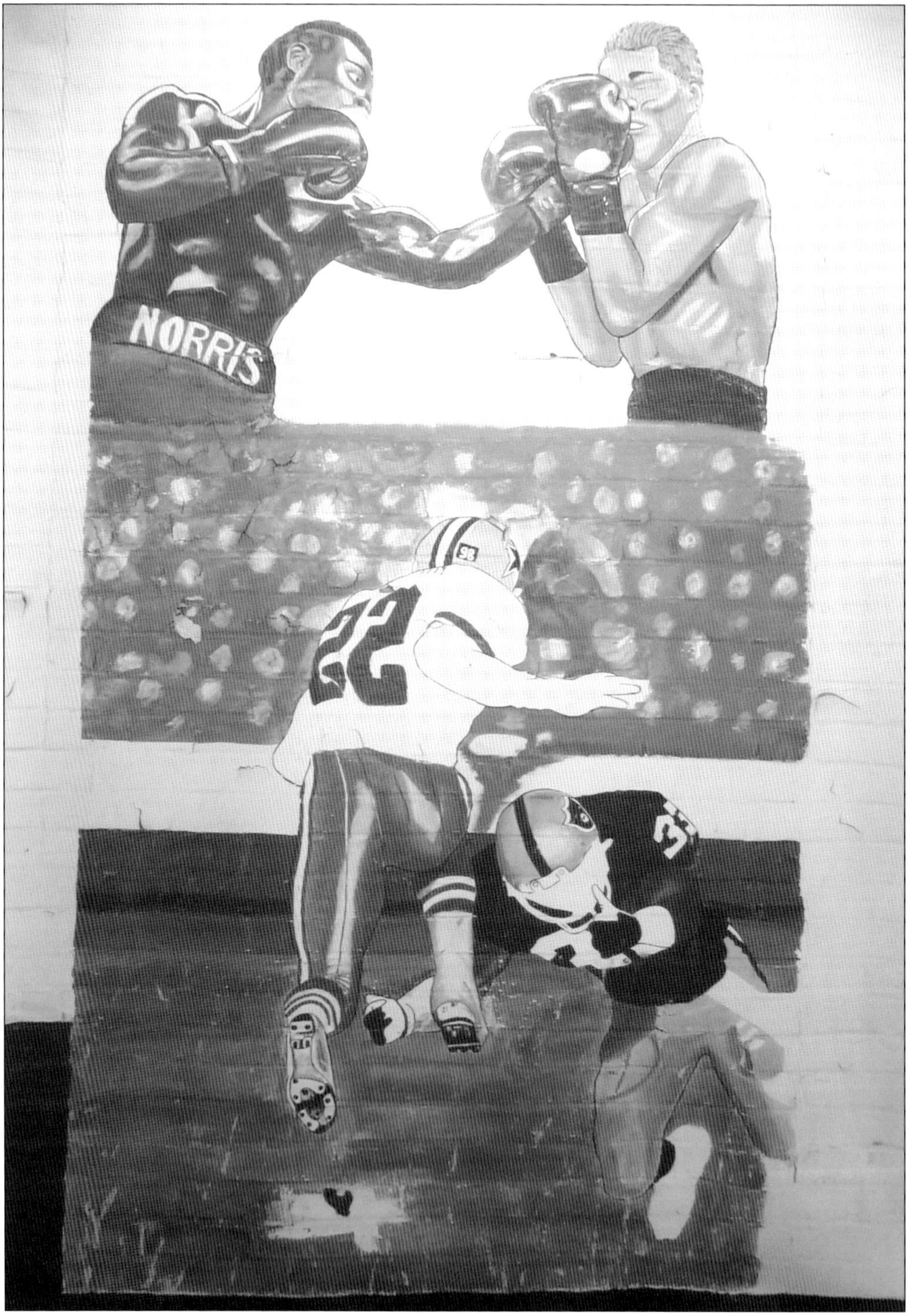

Sports was another favorite topic of prison artists. Various sports, teams, players, and their colors or numbers were showcased. When the prison closed, the county contracted for all the pictures, inside and outside, to be photographed. Because of the previous lead paint, the inside walls were then treated and repainted. (Courtesy of Patrick O'Neill.)

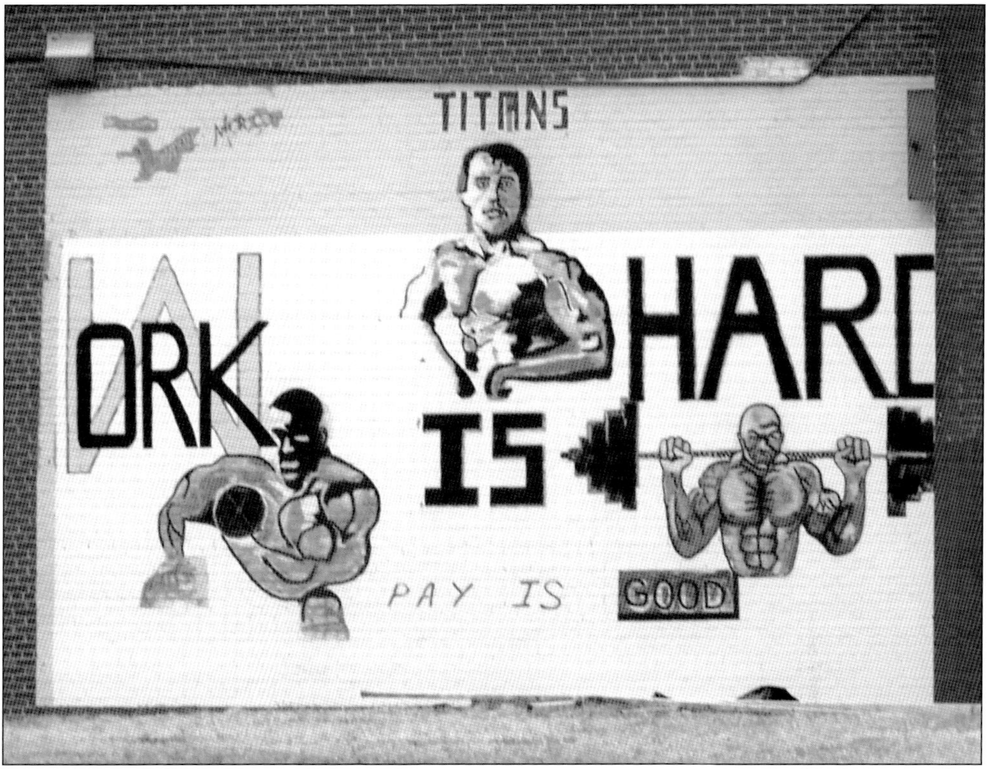

A large outside mural filled a huge billboard at the Youth Center playing field. It subtly integrated a bit of philosophy for coping with prison and later life. Because the Lorton Youth Center was the first to be built solely for young offenders, it became a laboratory to find the best methods for interceding and redirecting young lives in a more positive way. (Courtesy of Don Sweeney, Fairfax County Park Authority.)

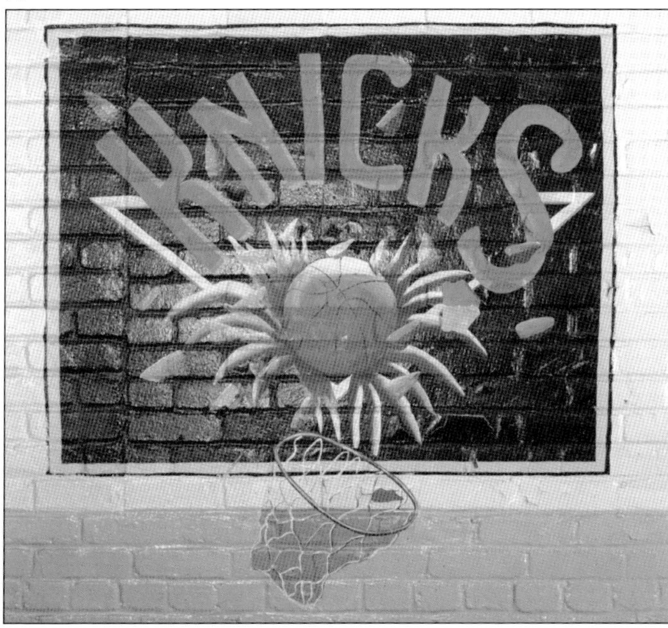

Art was part of the new academic and vocational curriculum at the Youth Center when it opened. Along with physical and recreational activities, the programs aimed at the "resocialization" of the young men sent there. When the center opened in September 1960, it was the first institution that opened in response to the Youth Corrections Act of 1950. (Courtesy of Don Sweeney, Fairfax County Park Authority.)

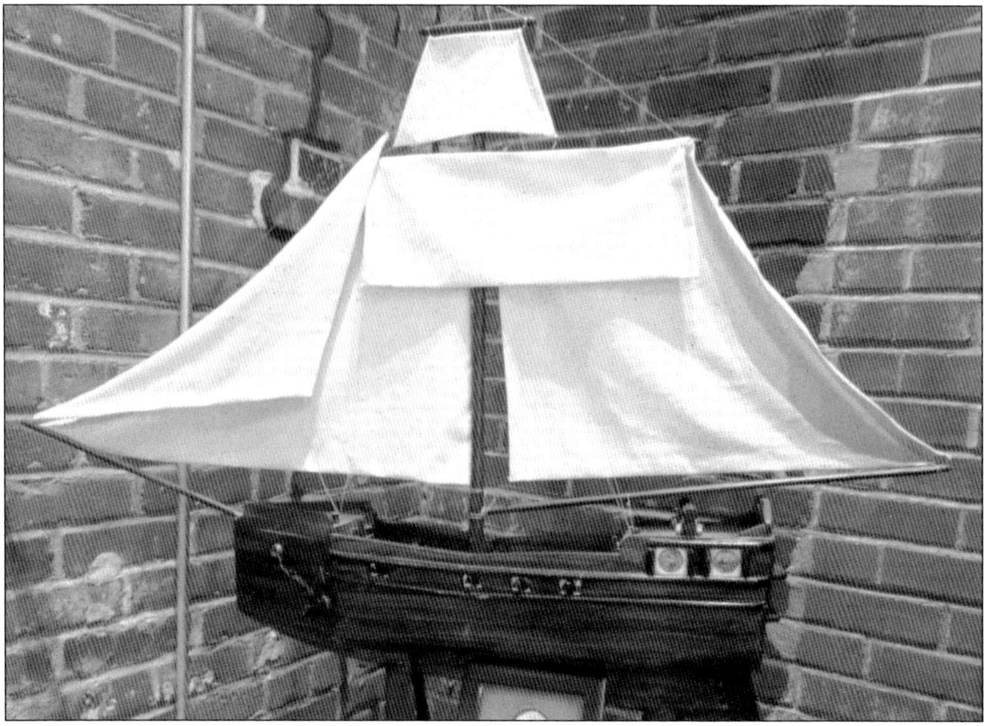

Wood from the furniture factory was used to build this model of an old sailing ship that the inmate gave to a female correctional officer who had been in the navy in World War II. It was in poor shape when it was donated to the museum, but the DC Sailing Club agreed to refurbish it. Puzzled by the flat sails, they guessed that the builder may have never seen a sailing ship and was using a two-dimensional picture. (Courtesy of Patrick O'Neill.)

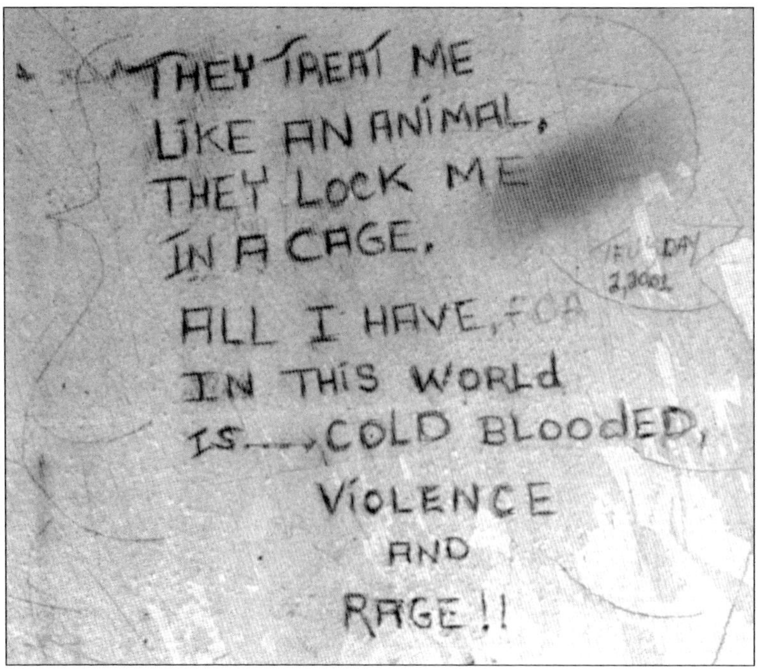

Frustrations and anger could also be expressed and released through art and—when written large on a prison cell wall—could speak for the artist; in this case, he combined two art forms. After the prison closed, this was photographed in one of the cells at Maximum Security. (Courtesy of Charles Albert Huckins, Stonelight Images.)

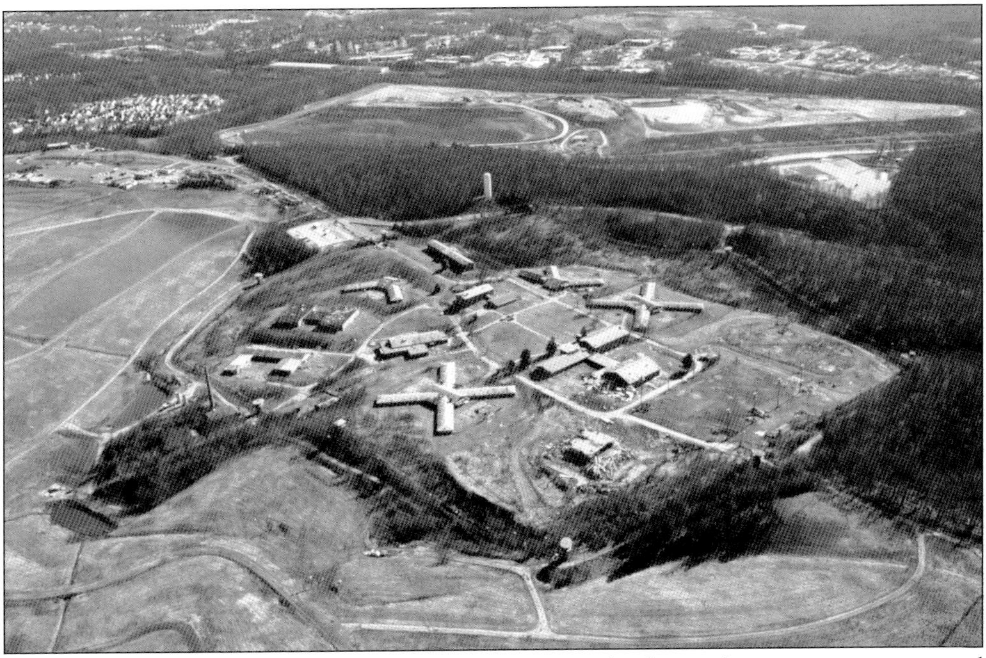

The Youth Center at Lorton was opened in 1960. It was the first such institution constructed specifically to accommodate those sentenced under the Federal Youth Corrections Act that targeted young offenders between the ages of 18 and 22 and urged their segregation from the more hardened adults. It was thought they would be rehabilitated by intensive programs and a mandatory period of parole supervision. (Courtesy of the Library of Congress.)

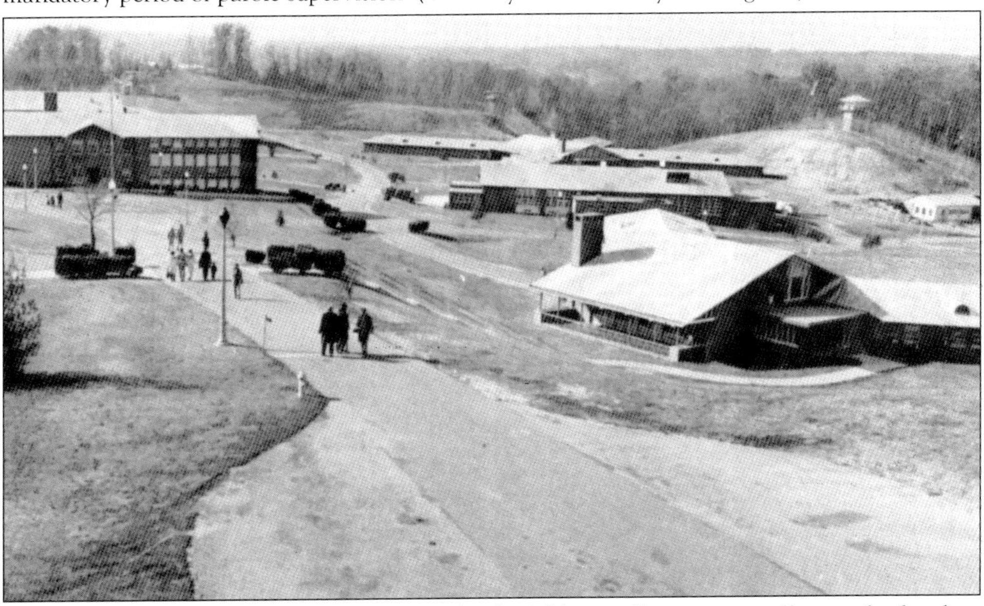

The layout of the Youth Center was designed to look like a college campus allowing for freedom of movement within the 12-foot fence enclosing the compound. Each inmate had his own room. A team approach was used in deciding and providing treatment for each individual inmate. The three key personnel assigned to each case were the classification and parole officer, the psychologist, and the correctional officer. (Courtesy of DC Archives.)

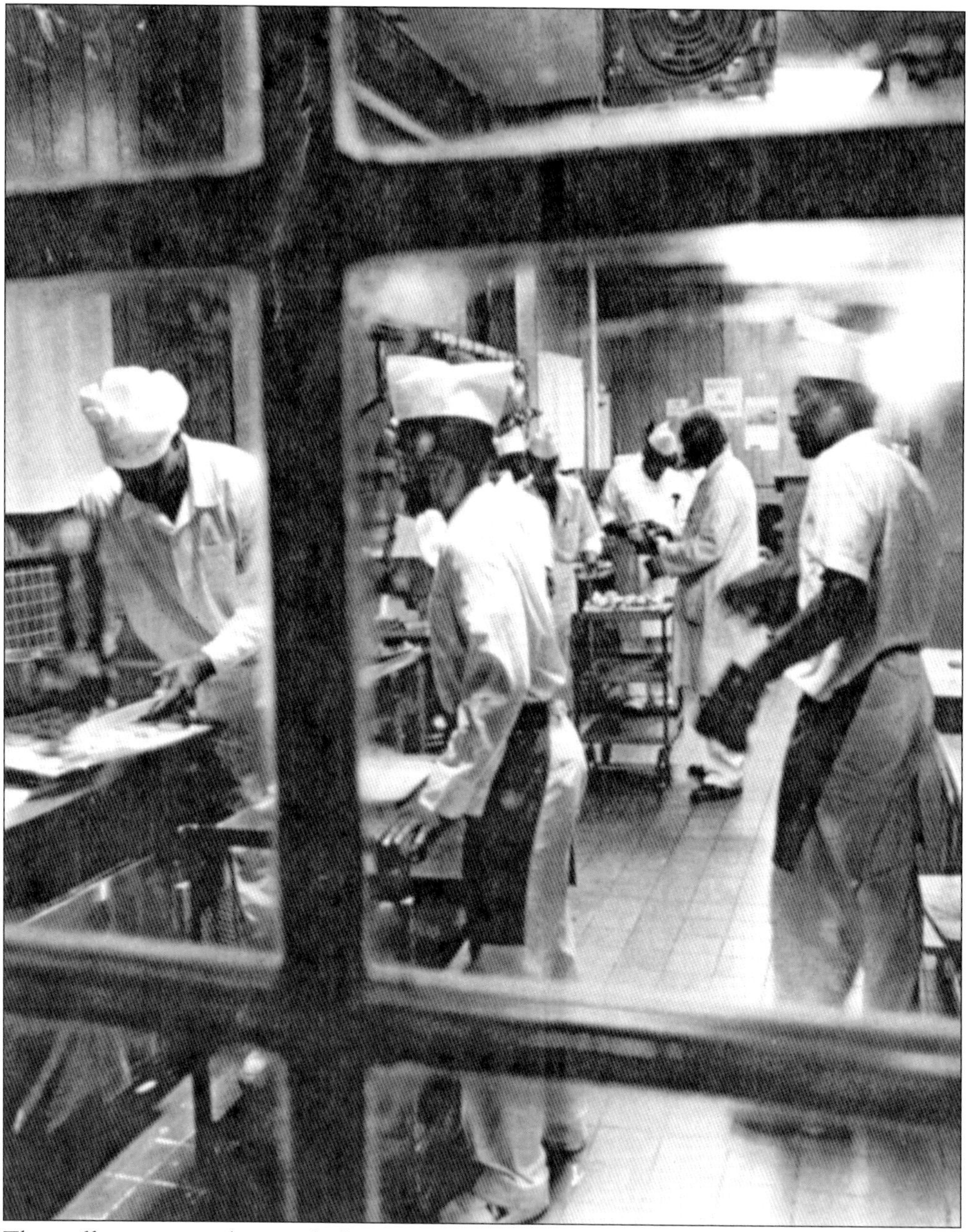

The staff supervising the mess halls were called stewards. Their work uniform was white. While working in the kitchen and preparing food, prisoners doffed their prison dungarees and blue shirts and put on the familiar distinctive attire of cooks in many restaurants. The hat distinguishes the student from the teacher. (Courtesy of DC Archives.)

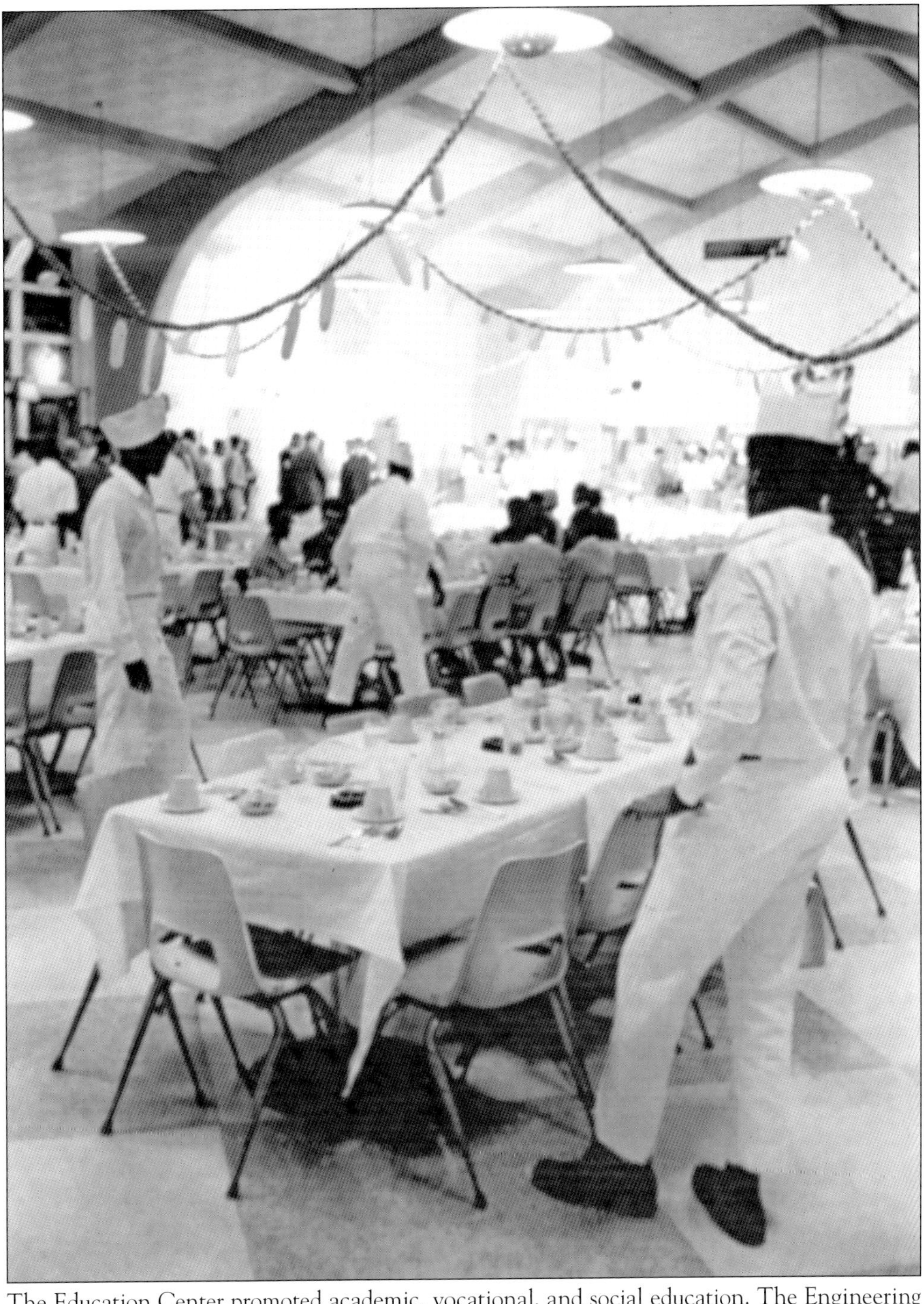

The Education Center promoted academic, vocational, and social education. The Engineering Unit provided on-the-job training for maintenance projects on the buildings, guard towers, security fences, and equipment in the campus area. A variety of arts and crafts and athletic activities encouraged a constructive use of leisure time. The culinary unit provided vocational training in cooking, baking, butchering, waiter service, and sanitation. It also furnished food for award banquets, incentive programs, and athletic and graduation ceremonies. (Courtesy of DC Archives.)

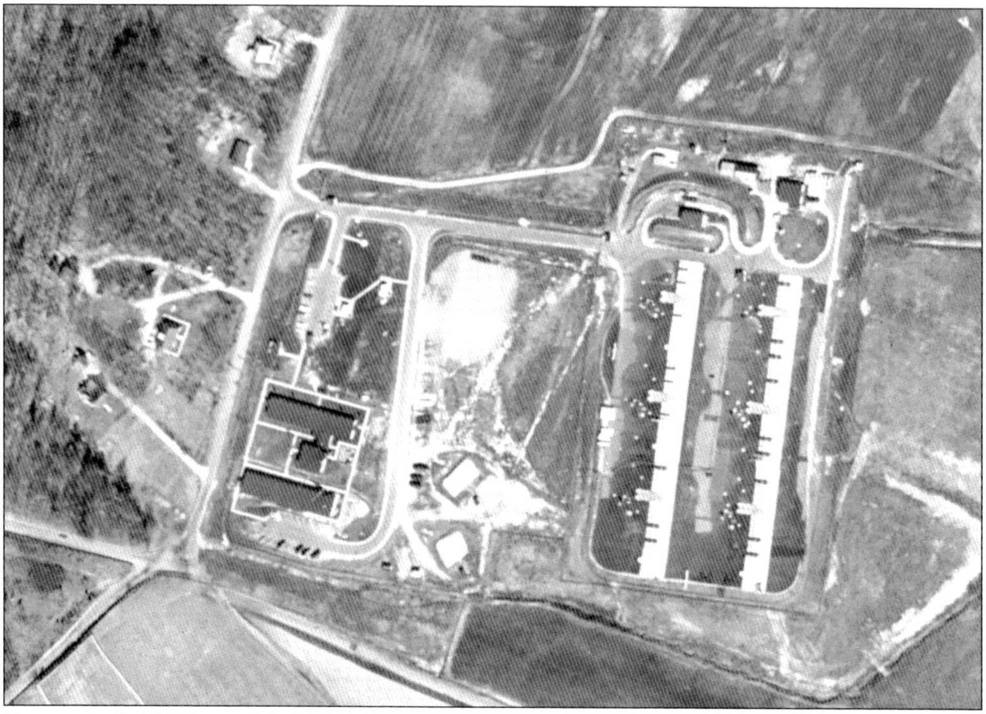

America's Cold War with Russia intensified in the 1950s. As a defense against the Russian Bear Bomber, a series of anti-aircraft missile bases were built. The first and largest of these was located on the prison grounds and named the "National NIKE Site" by the Secretary of the Army. The site was one of several forming a ring around Washington. (Courtesy of the US Army Center of Military History.)

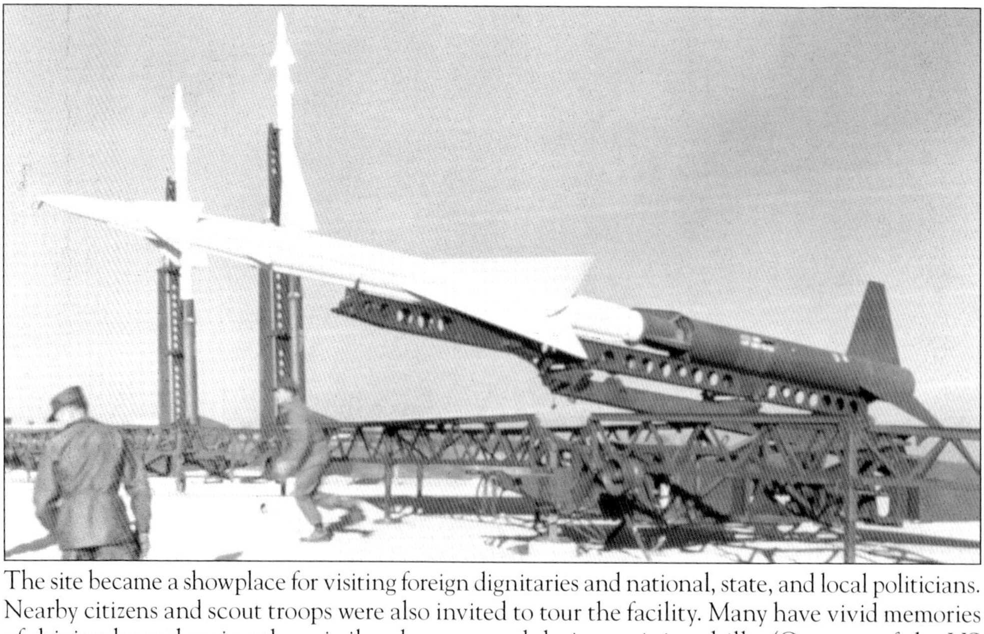

The site became a showplace for visiting foreign dignitaries and national, state, and local politicians. Nearby citizens and scout troops were also invited to tour the facility. Many have vivid memories of driving by and seeing the missiles above ground during training drills. (Courtesy of the US Army Center of Military History.)

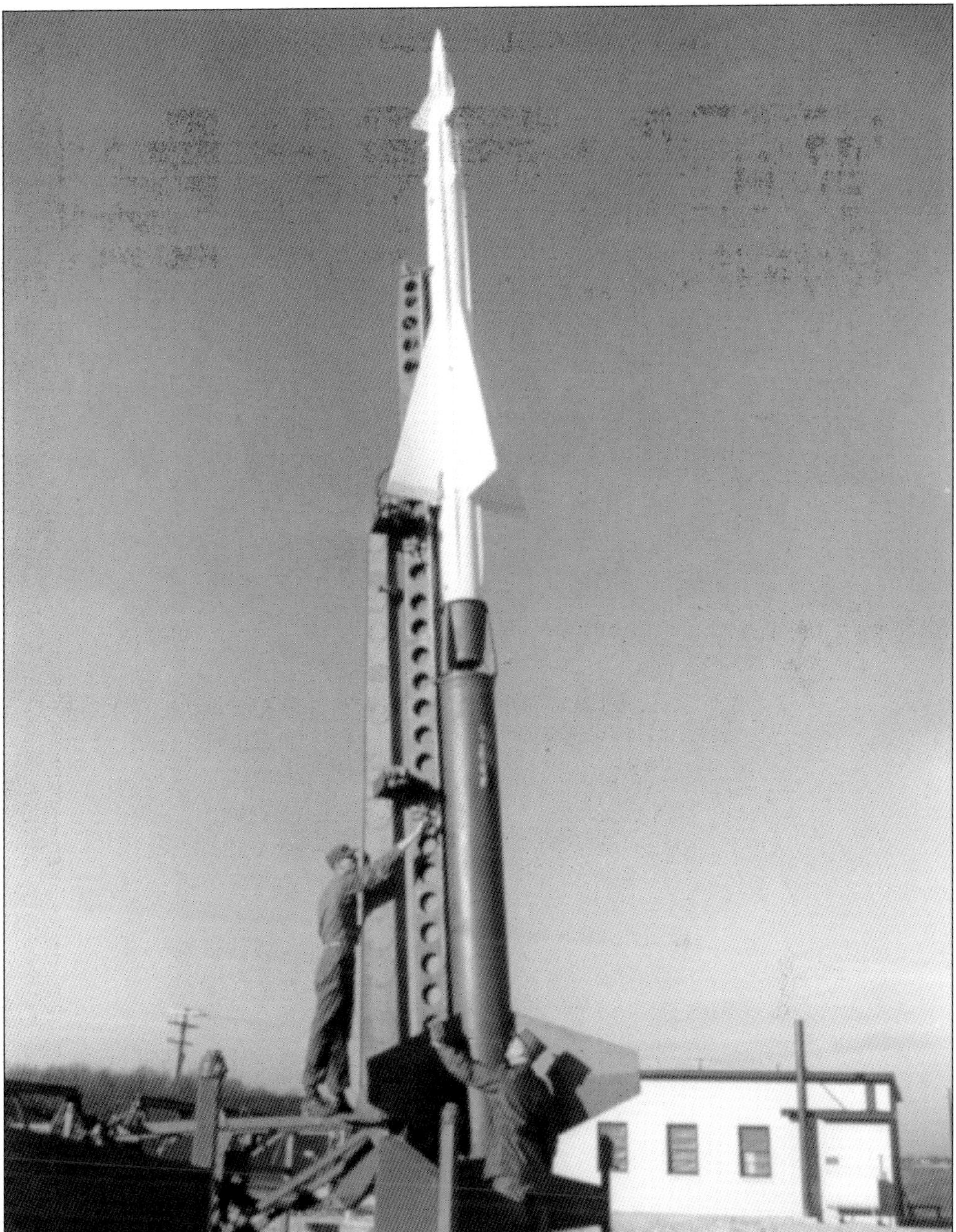

Lt. Col. Marvin Crow oversaw the delivery of the Ajax missiles from White Sands, New Mexico, to Lorton in 1954 and stayed to train the young men manning the site. Crow came to have an encyclopedic knowledge of the entire site and remained involved with the project and local history for many years. (Courtesy of the US Army Center of Military History.)

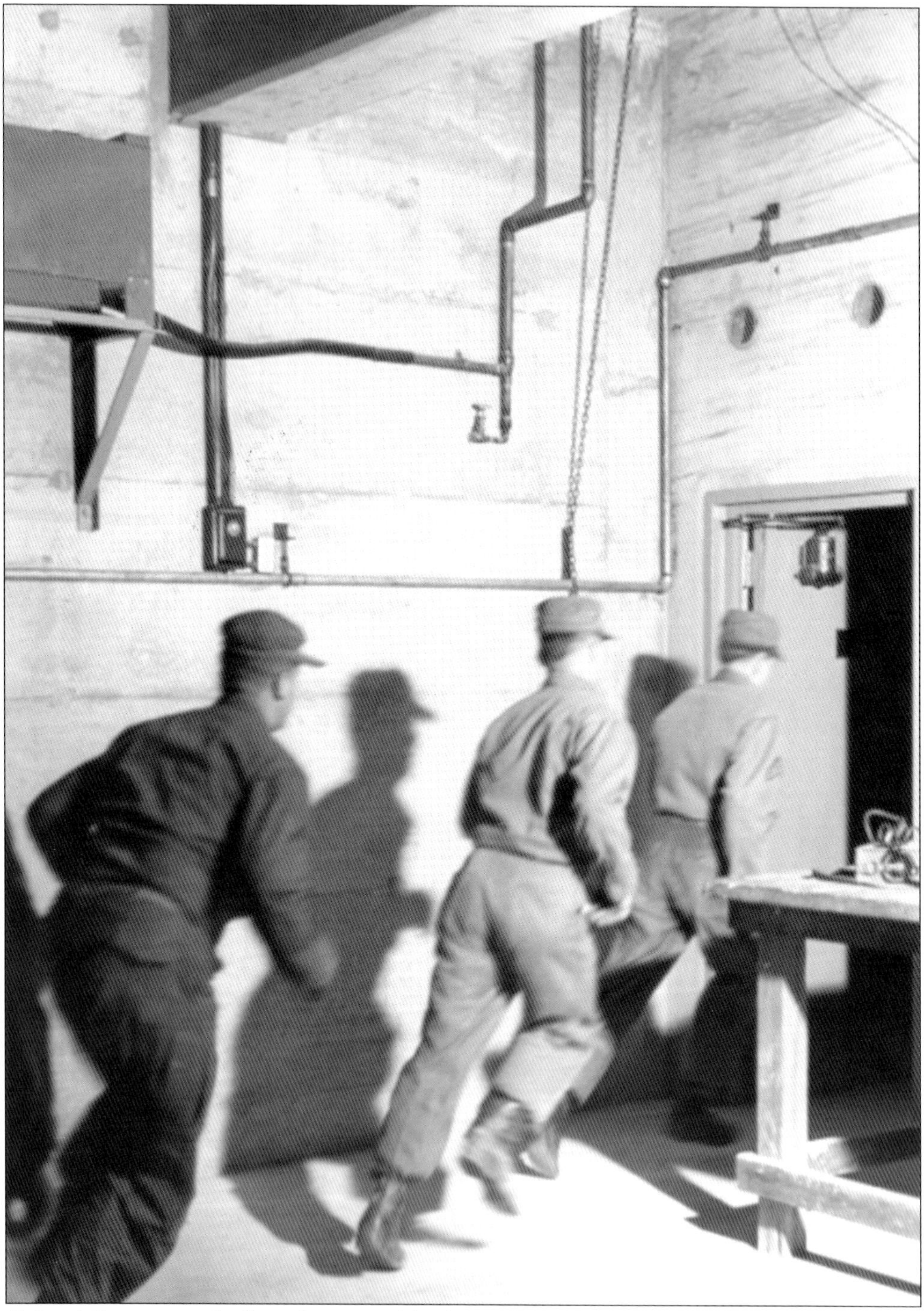

Colonel Crow enjoyed telling the story of the first time a practice drill for launching the missiles was held after the rigorous training of the troops. No one had alerted the prison administration, so when the siren sounded, they thought an escape was in progress and shut down the prison. Better communication plans were subsequently developed. (Courtesy of the US Army Center of Military History.)

Four

The Turbulent Years

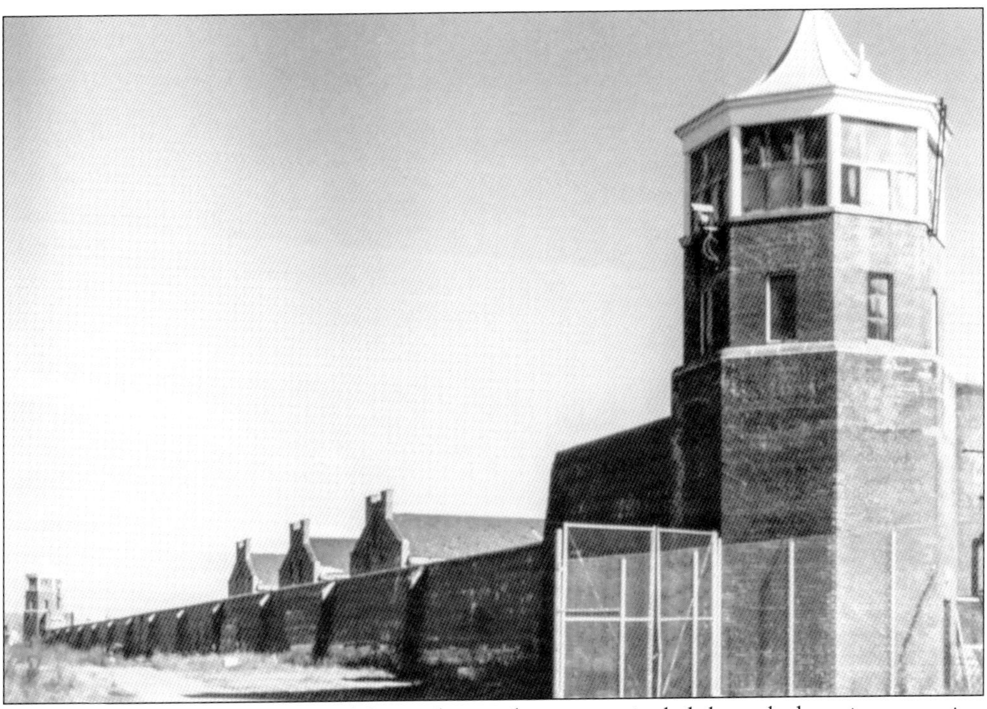

The unrest throughout the United States during these years rippled through the prisons causing physical harm and massive property damage. The old ideals did not seem to work with a new generation of prisoners. The nation was focused on civil rights, and the inmates demanded their rights as prisoners and human beings. A new philosophy for dealing with problems emerged with intended and unintended consequences. (Courtesy of DC Archives.)

DeWitt EASTER, Appellant,

v.

DISTRICT OF COLUMBIA, Appellee

United States Court of Appeals,

District of Columbia Circuit

Date published: Mar 31, 1966

In *Easter v. District of Columbia*, the appeals court ruled in March 1966 that alcoholism was not a crime but a disease; it would be cruel and unusual punishment for a sick person to be sentenced for exhibiting symptoms of an illness. Alcoholics accounted for the majority of men and women sentenced to the workhouses. The effect was an immediate reduction of the workforce for the farm, brickyard, and grounds maintenance. (Courtesy of the US Court of Appeals.)

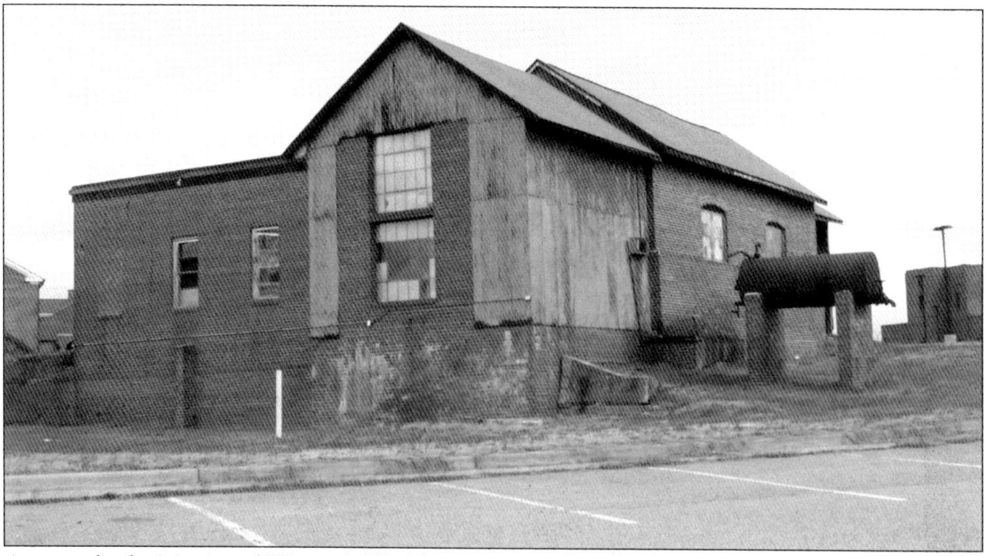

As a result, the Men's and Women's Workhouses were officially closed by 1968, and the remaining inmates were transferred to other prisons. The majority of the buildings and grounds were turned over to the District Department of Health for use as an alcoholic rehabilitation center. After 55 years, the cannery and swine ranch ceased operations and the brickyard shut down permanently. The latter was also caused by a reduced demand for bricks. (Courtesy of Fairfax County Department of Planning and Development.)

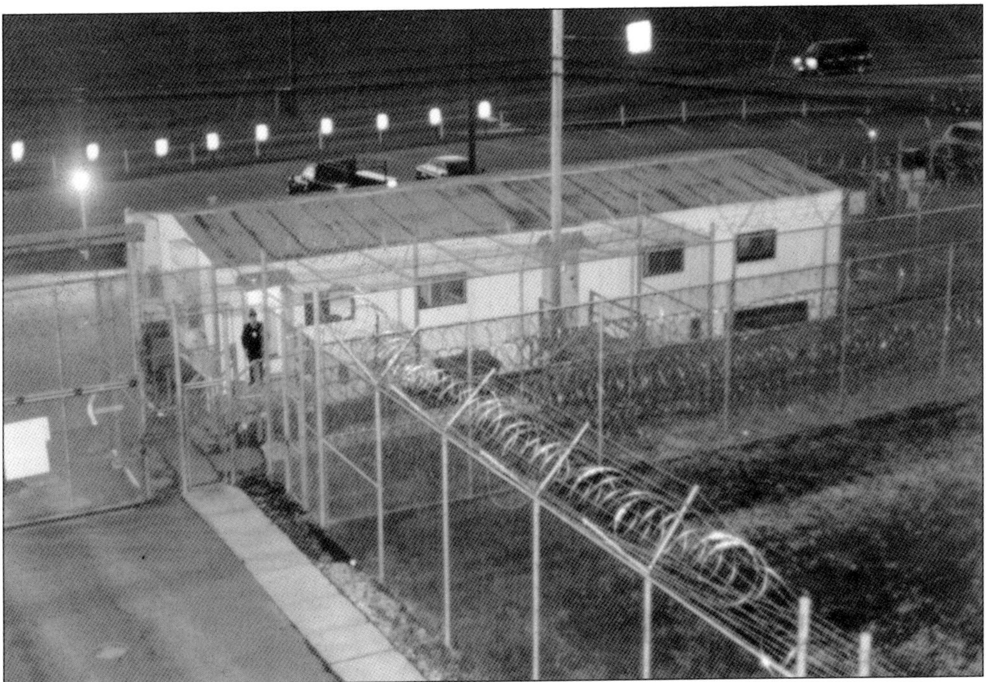

Two dormitories at the Men's Workhouse were retained at the time of the closure. They were used to house the minimum-security prisoners who maintained the agricultural and dairy operations. They also ran the railroad, sewage treatment, and water purification plants. The office staff was housed in trailers on the site. "Minimum Security" replaced "Workhouse" as the new name for this part of the complex. (Courtesy of DC Archives.)

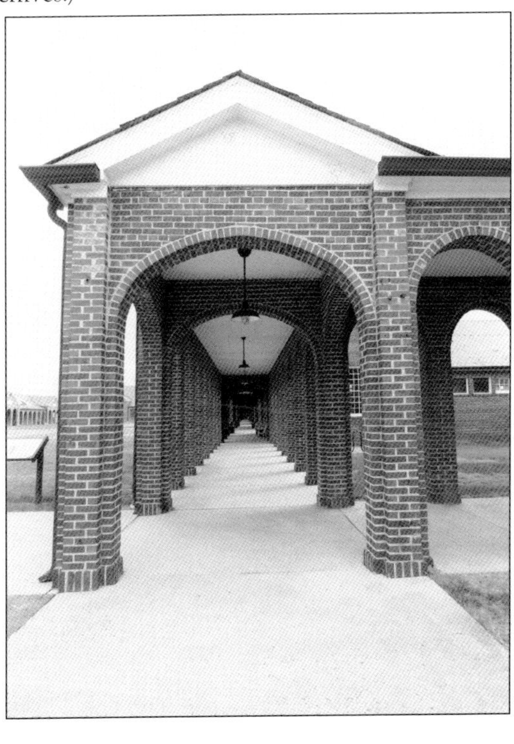

In 1967, Pres. Lyndon Johnson appointed a presidential commission on crime in the District of Columbia. It was directed to explore the causes of crime and delinquency; the adequacy of the existing systems of law enforcement, criminal justice, and corrections; and to recommend improvements for crime prevention and improvement of law enforcement and administration of justice. He also appointed a commissioner and a nine-member council to replace the former three DC commissioners. (Courtesy of the Library of Congress.)

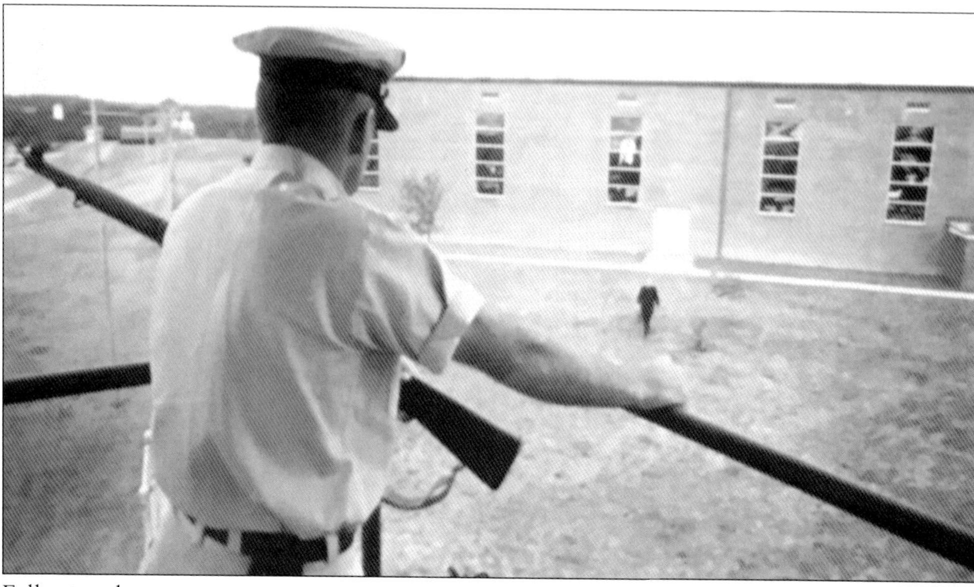

Following the crime commission's recommendations, the correctional complex was reorganized in 1968. The Reformatory and Penitentiary were deactivated and renamed. The reformatory became Central Facility. It was often referred to as "Central" or "the Hill" by staff and inmates. Its stated capacity was 935 and housed felons and misdemeanants. Its population included many sentenced on drug-related charges, reflecting the new, stricter laws. (Courtesy of the Library of Congress.)

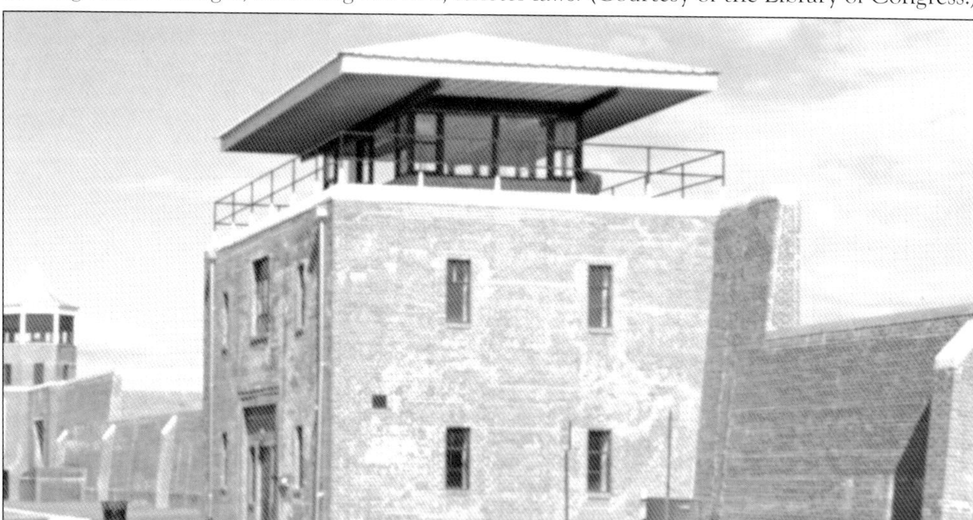

The Penitentiary became Maximum-Security. It housed the worst offenders: the incorrigible, career criminals, those thought dangerous to the safety of the staff and other inmates, and severe disciplinary transfers from other institutions. Many were serving long sentences for drug-related charges with no hope of parole. Thus, though there were shops within the walls, there was little incentive to cooperate or work. (Courtesy of Patrick O'Neill.)

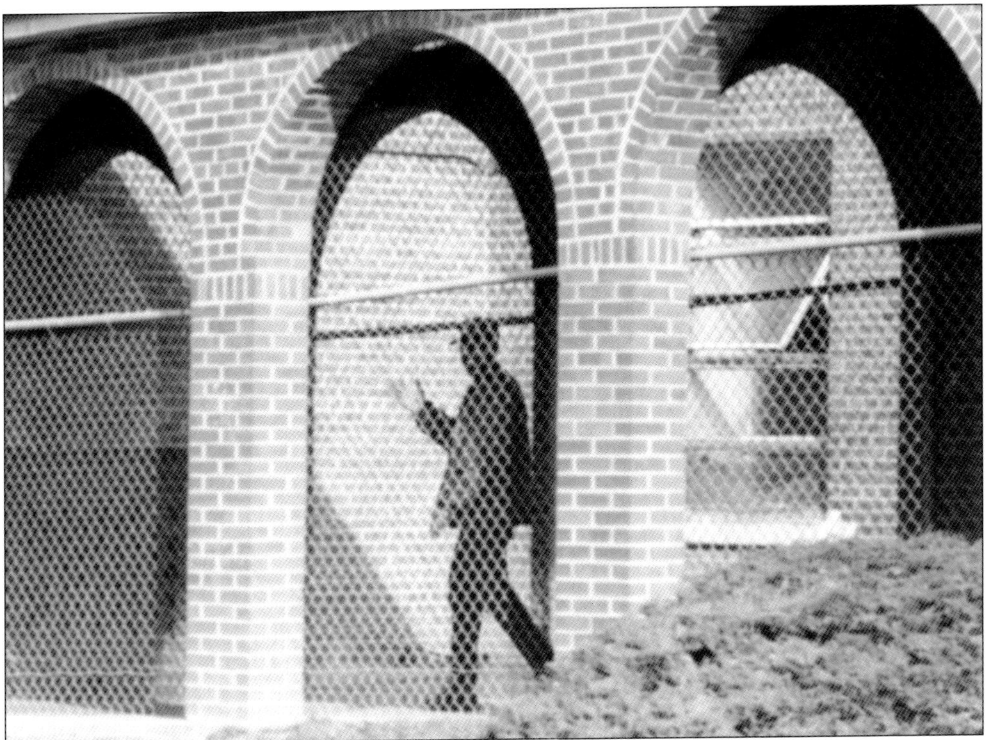

Alarmed by the number of escapes and reports of violence within the prison, politicians in Virginia demanded an audit by the General Accounting Office (GAO), particularly with security management at the Lorton Complex. Included in their report were GAO recommendations that the perimeter security should be tightened, as well as security inside the prison. (Courtesy of DC Archives.)

In response, all areas of the prison without walls were fenced off with razor wire and guard towers were erected at intervals and perimeter lighting improved at the fence line. The number of correctional officers increased, and routine patrol of the perimeter roads was established. In 1976, electronic surveillance equipment was installed on the fence line permitting tower officers to observe it on closed-circuit television. (Courtesy of Fairfax County Department of Planning and Development.)

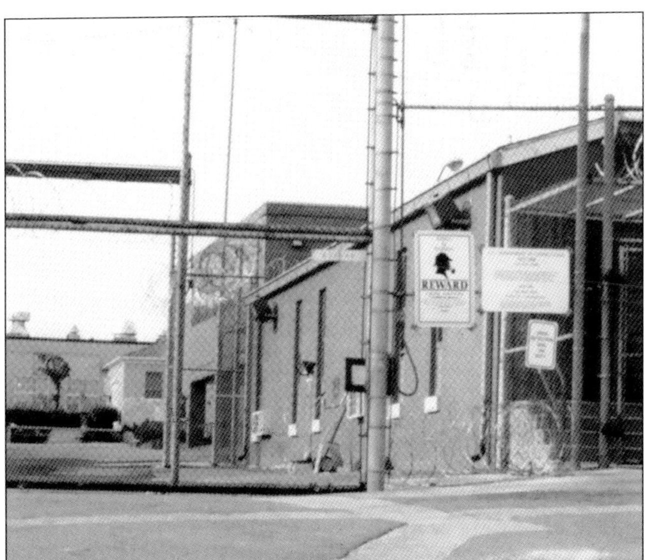

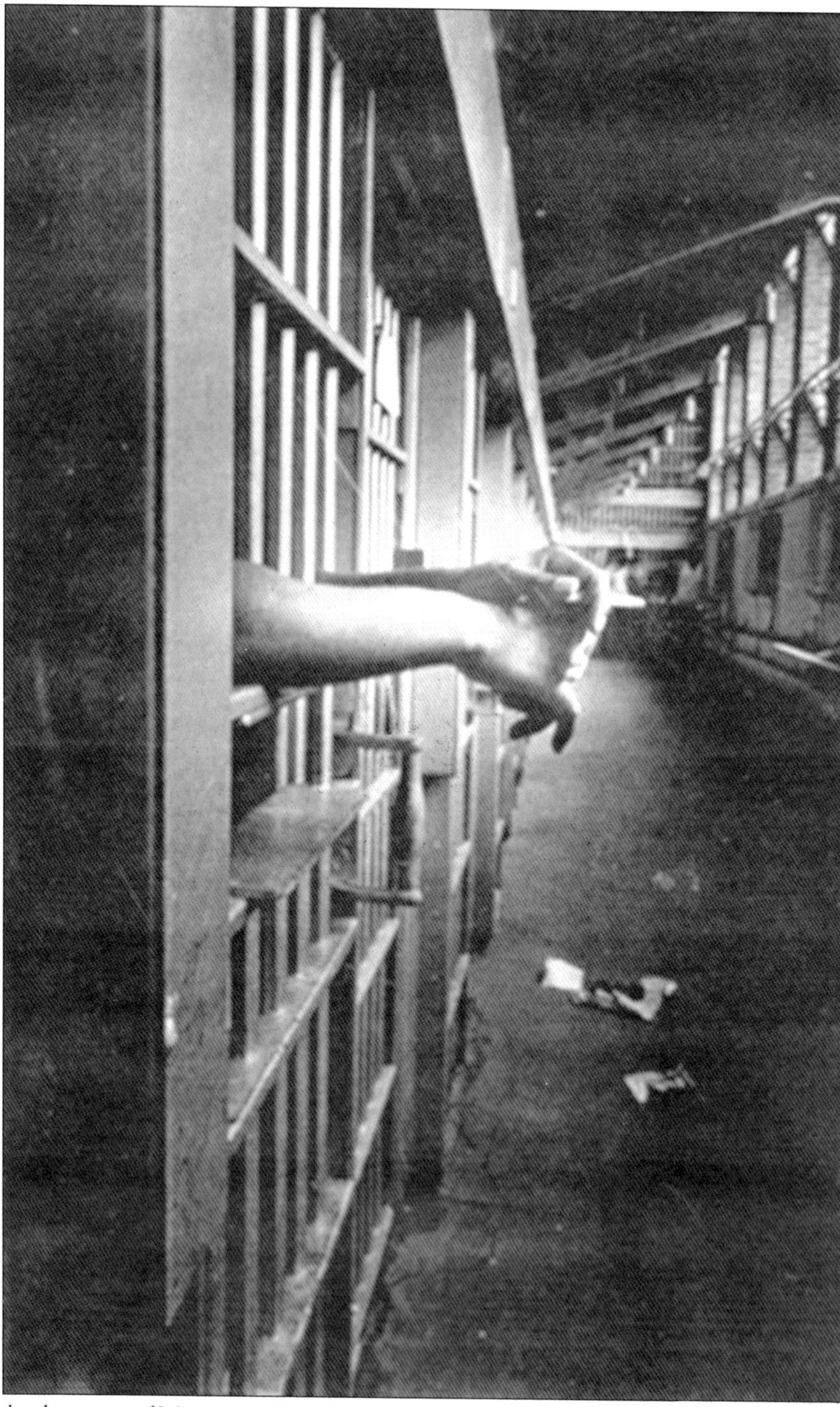

At the back corner of Maximum Security were seven isolation cells referred to as the Hole. They were for those who had killed a fellow prisoner, assaulted a guard, or tried to escape; sometimes, they were sent there for their own protection. Prisoners sent here spent 23 hours a day in a five-by-seven-foot cell with one hour of recess and nothing to do but brood. They were allowed no personal possessions and only religious or legal reading material. (Courtesy of DC Archives.)

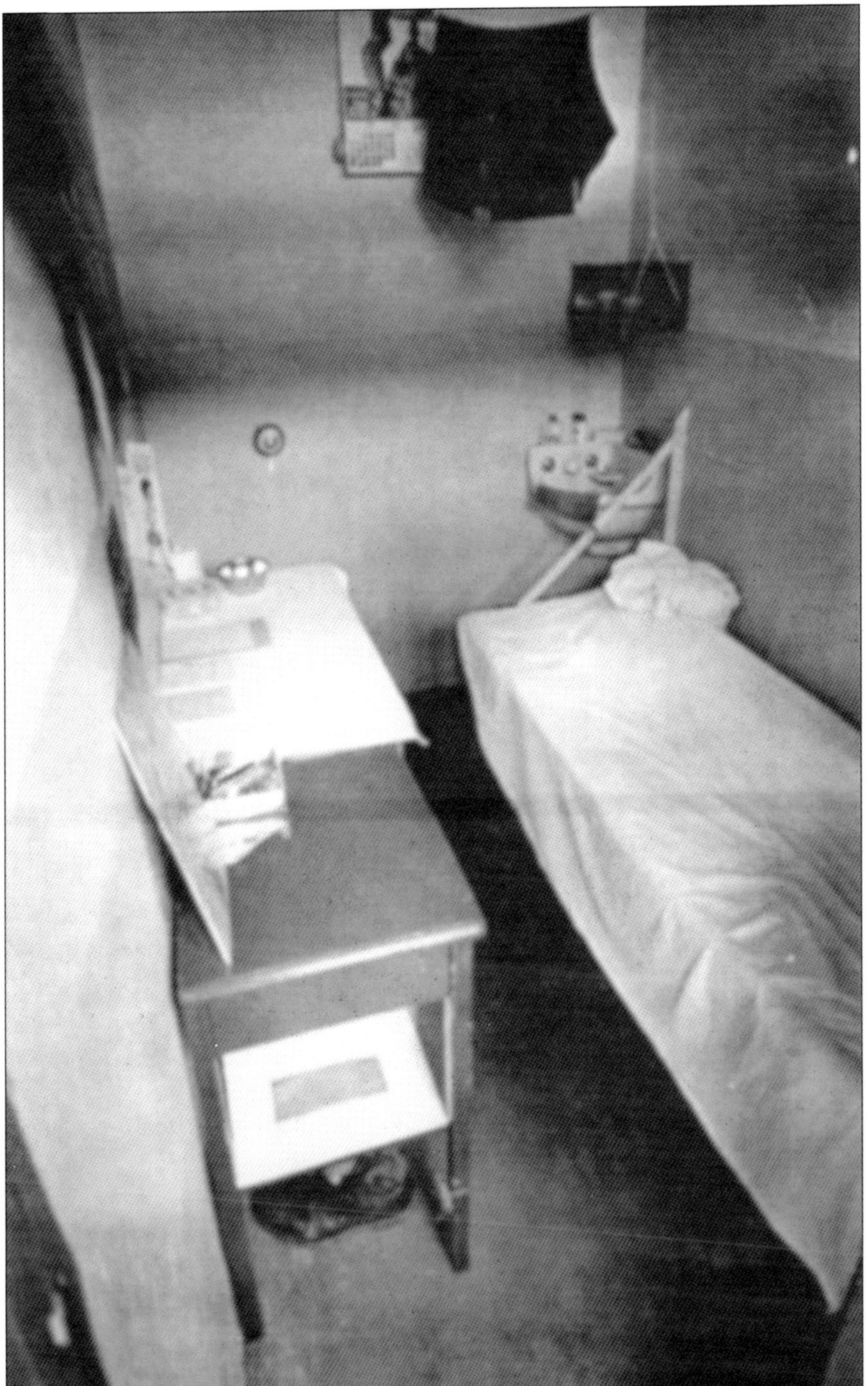

While inmates at the Workhouse and Reformatory still lived dormitory style, much like at military barracks, prisoners at Maximum Security were assigned to single cells. Each one was equipped with a wash basin, toilet, cot, and small desk. There was little room to move around. One building at each of the other facilities had a few "punishment cells" to encourage better behavior from unruly inmates. (Courtesy of DC Archives.)

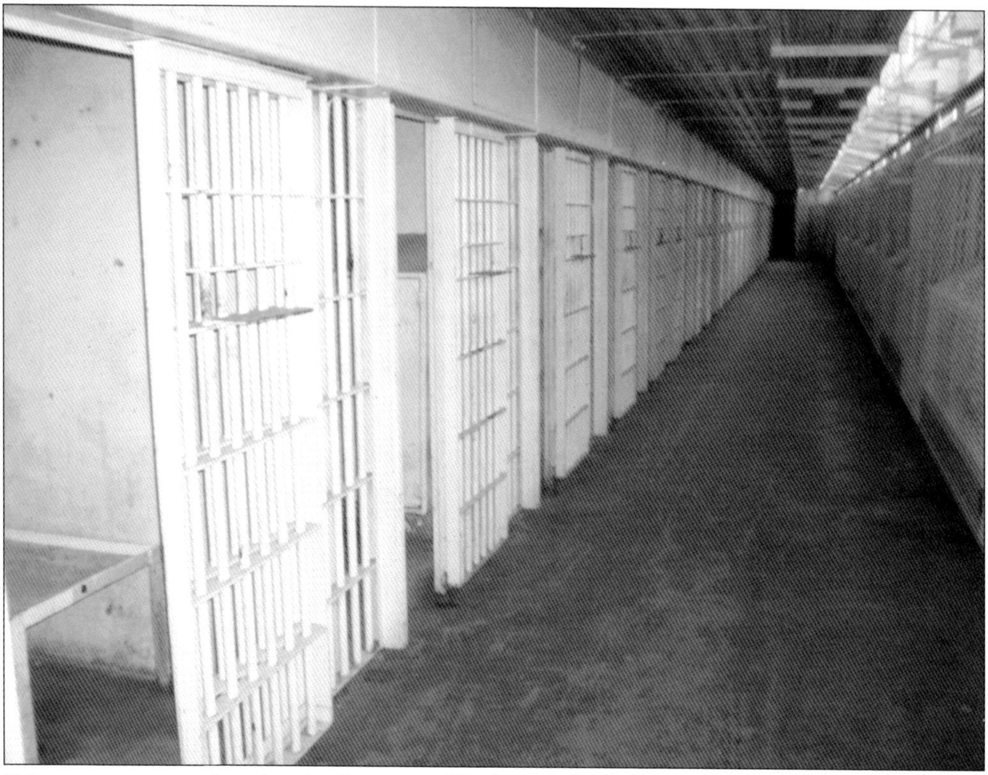

Prisoners were transferred to the Occoquan Facility to relieve the overcrowding at Central. A cell block was added to one of the dormitories. Each cell was designed for one man, but sometimes it became necessary to add a second bunk. Cells were used for unruly prisoners, those suffering withdrawal from substance abuse, and others needing special protection. When the museum moved to its permanent home in Building No. 2, the cell section was kept intact and refurbished. (Courtesy of Patrick O'Neill.)

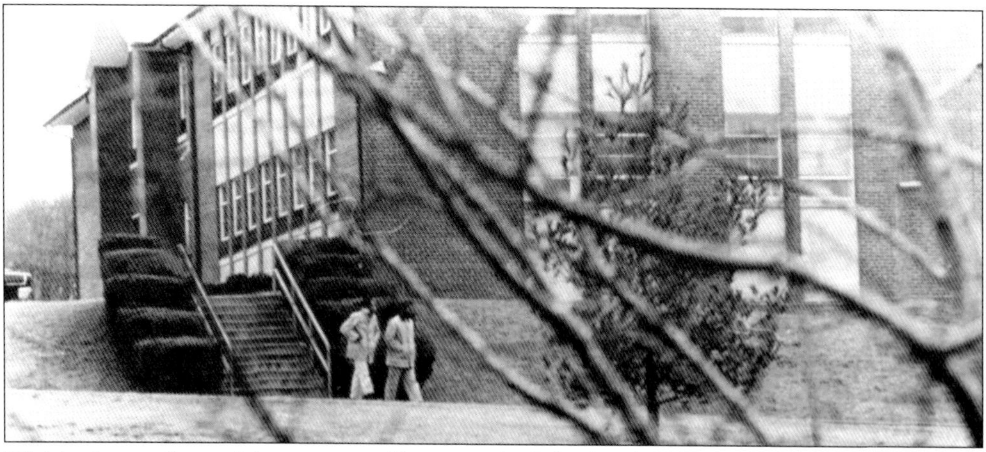

Within the confines of the prison itself, inmates had the freedom to move around at will as they walked among the dorms, shops, mess hall, and other buildings, much as they would on a college campus. Maximum Security with its high brick walls loomed over them, a visible reminder of the consequences of bad behavior. Staff also moved among them, and this allowed for friendly interaction. (Courtesy of Fairfax County Department of Planning and Development.)

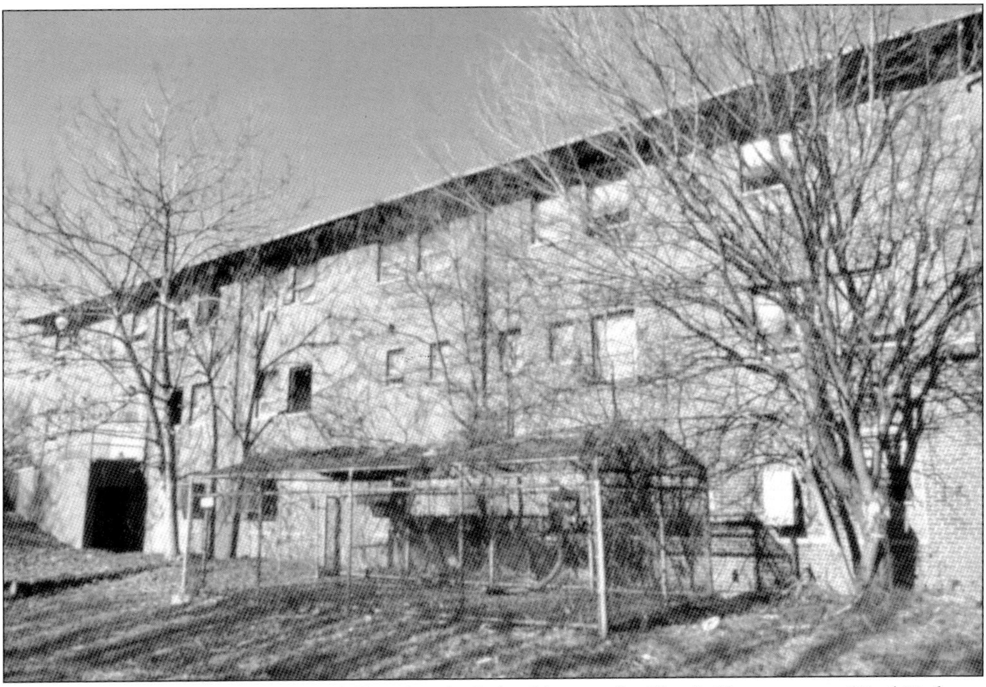

Dug into the hill under the ground-floor level of a building at the Youth Center was a Civil Defense Emergency Operations Center bunker operated by the DC Office of Emergency Management. It was thought any shock from a nuclear attack on Washington would be absorbed by the terrain. Various governmental agencies had cubicles in the bunker to retain the ability to communicate and conduct operations in case of an emergency, it was stocked with food, water, radar detection equipment, and other necessities for a prolonged stay. There was also a contingency plan to bring the president if necessary. When dismantled in 2003, most of the original equipment and artifacts remained. (Above, courtesy of Alan McKie; below, courtesy of William Koch.)

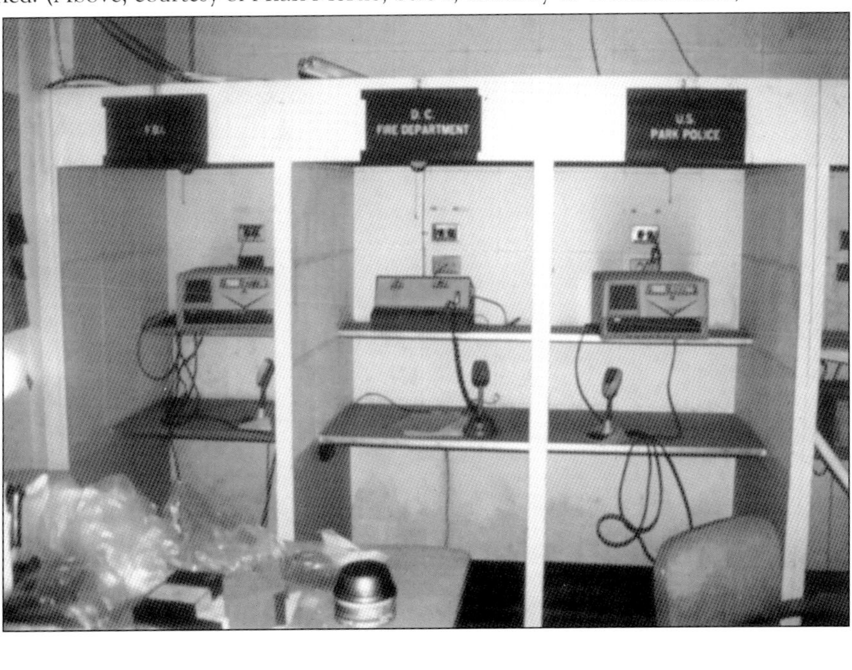

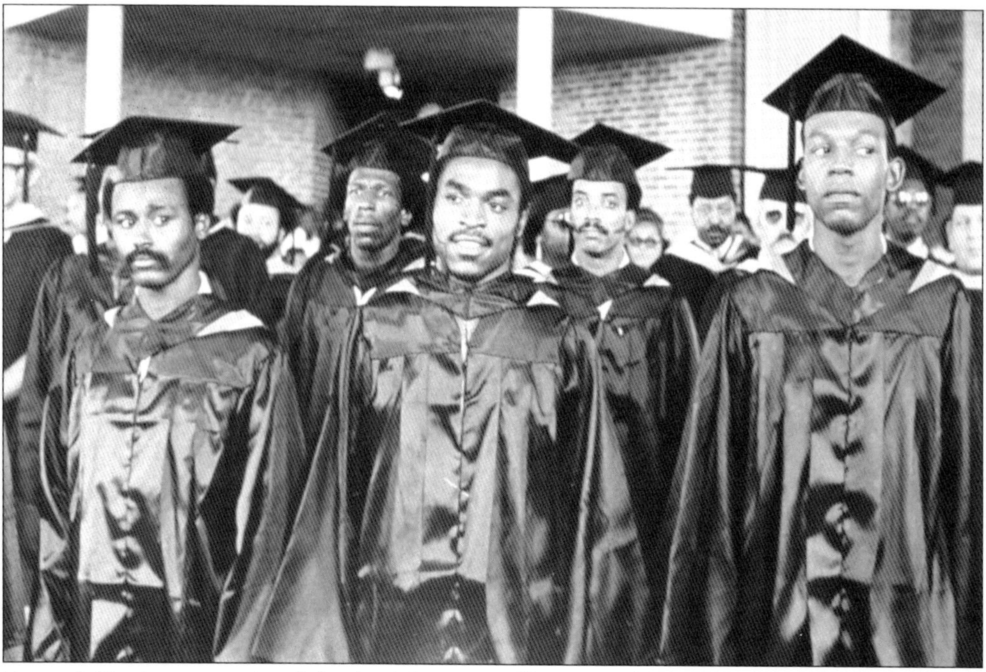

Kenneth Hardy was appointed the third director and began implementing the Crime Commission's monumental recommendations. He instituted a system of furloughs whereby inmates were released on day-long or weekend passes. A prison college program was developed; prisoners took undergraduate courses at Federal City College. More than 600 inmates engaged in self-help programs. Nine work-release and halfway houses were established, and residents received intensive rehabilitative treatment. An employment division helped place ex-inmates in jobs. (Courtesy of the People's Archive, DC Public Library.)

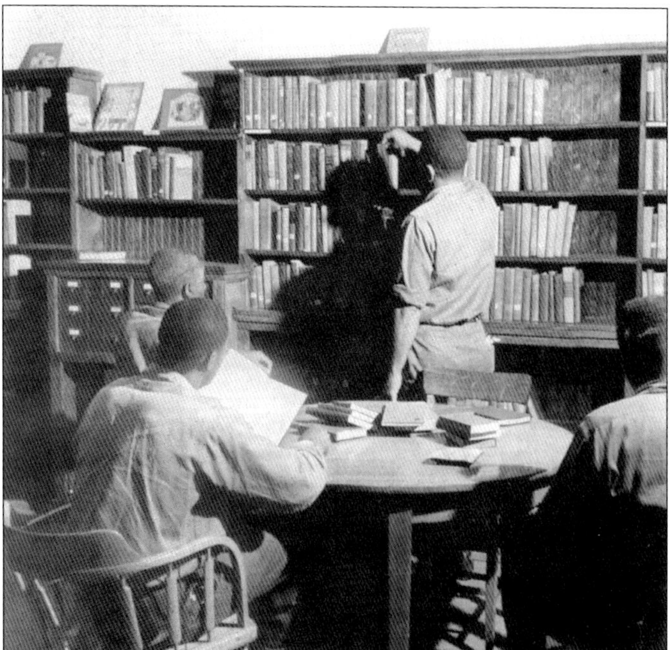

A law library consisting of donated law books and a copy of the DC Penal Code occupied a section of the Reformatory library. As some prisoners studied them carefully, they became "jailhouse lawyers" willing to take on pleas for other prisoners unable to afford an attorney. Petitions filed against the DC Department of Corrections forced officials and correctional officers to spend valuable time replying and testifying in court. (Courtesy of the People's Archive, DC Public Library.)

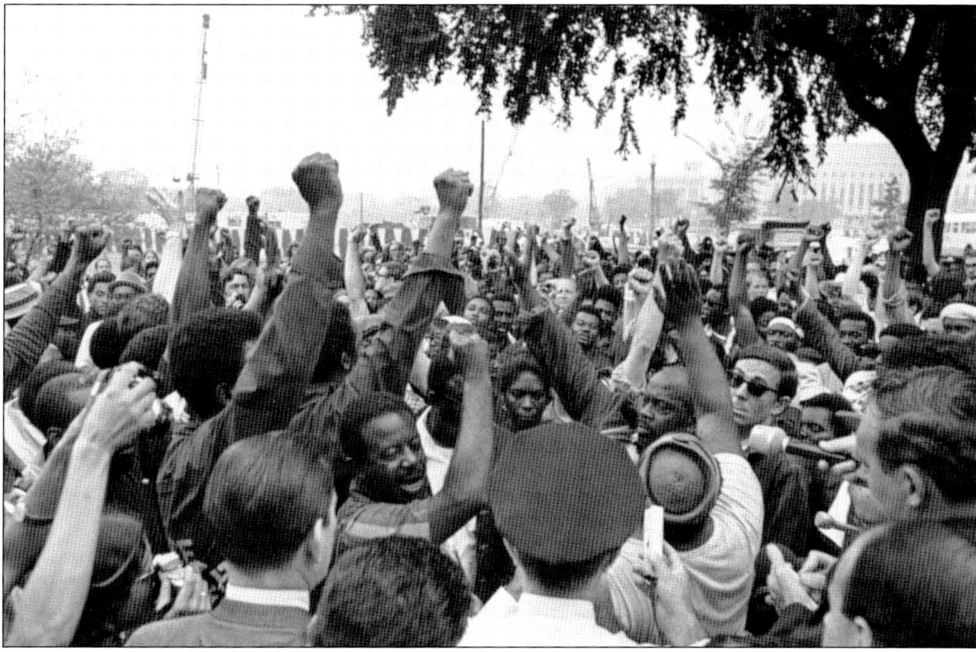

Beginning with the Civil Rights Movement, Washington, DC, became a focal point for marches and demonstrations, including Vietnam War protests, women's rights marches, and the Poor People's Campaign. It culminated in 1968 with the riots after the assassination of Dr. Martin Luther King Jr. Some participants were taken to Lorton on a "catch and release" tactic. Ringleaders, including many prominent people, were tried and when convicted served their sentences at the Minimum-Security Facility. (Courtesy of the Library of Congress.)

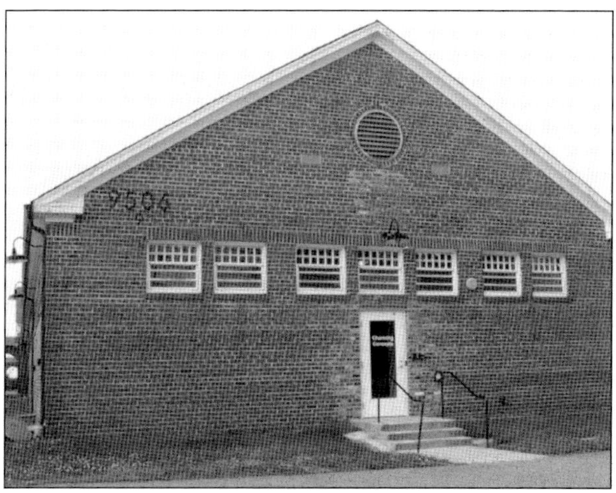

After the protestors left in 1968, the Occoquan site became part of the rehabilitation center for alcoholics to relieve the overcrowding at the former Women's Workhouse. Stays at the center were mostly voluntary, and people began complaining about men wandering the streets of the nearby neighborhood and drinking. In 1971, the Veteran's Administration agreed to cover the cost of treatment for alcoholic veterans. (Courtesy of Fairfax County Department of Planning and Development.)

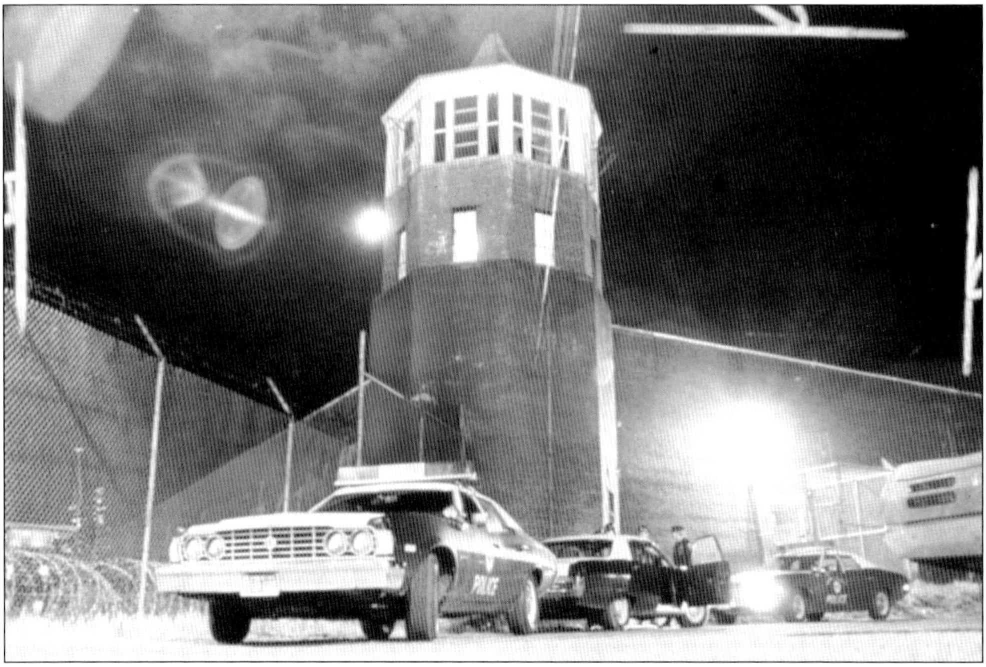

Three prison correctional officers and three inmates were seriously injured in a disorder at Lorton Reformatory in September 1969. Trouble erupted in the Maximum-Security compound when 100 prisoners refused to return to their cells after the dinner hour. Fires were set in the mess hall, the furniture repair shop, a dormitory, and a nearby workshop. County police and state troopers manned the outside fences to prevent breakouts. (Courtesy of the Fairfax County Department of Fire and Rescue.)

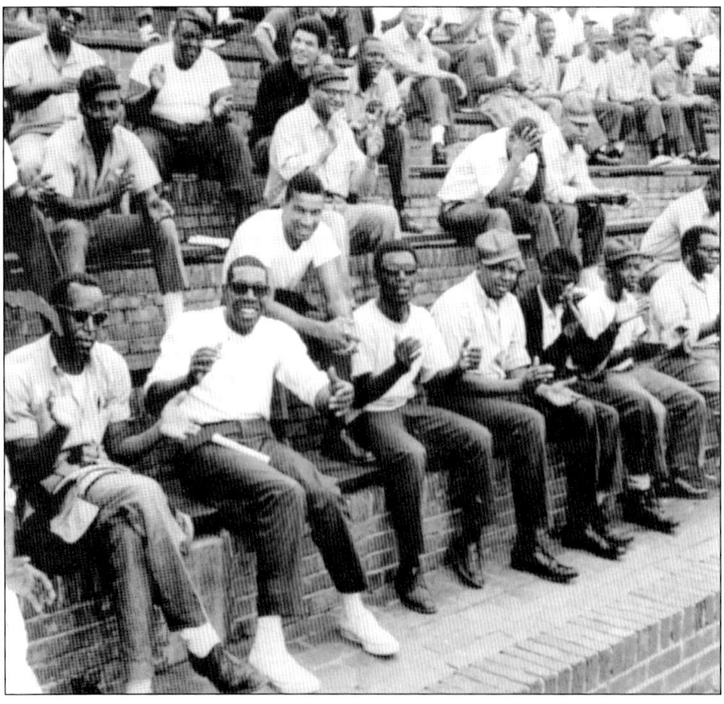

The racial makeup of the inmate population also changed in the 1970s, as a result of demographics and the growth of the suburbs. By the end of the decade, it was estimated that 98 percent of the inmate population was black. There was a similar increase in the number of black staff officers which grew to 55 percent. (Courtesy of Stefan Hembre.)

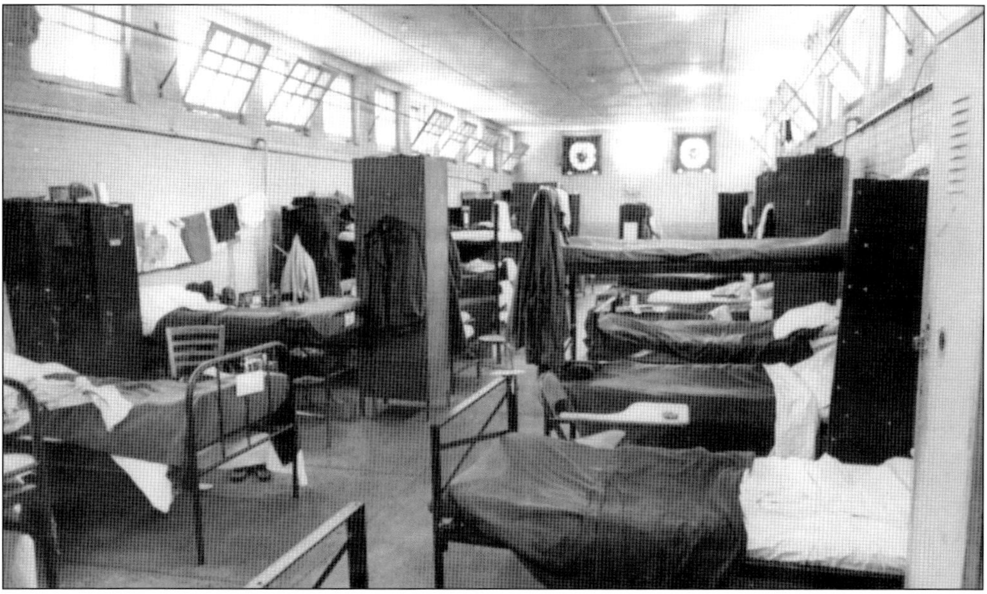

The Court Reform and Criminal Procedure Act of 1970 was passed. It sought to increase the efficiency of the District courts and police department by adding and training more personnel. One unintended consequence was an increase in the inmate population causing more severe overcrowding, peaking in the summer of 1972 at 56 percent. (Courtesy of Fairfax County Department of Planning and Development.)

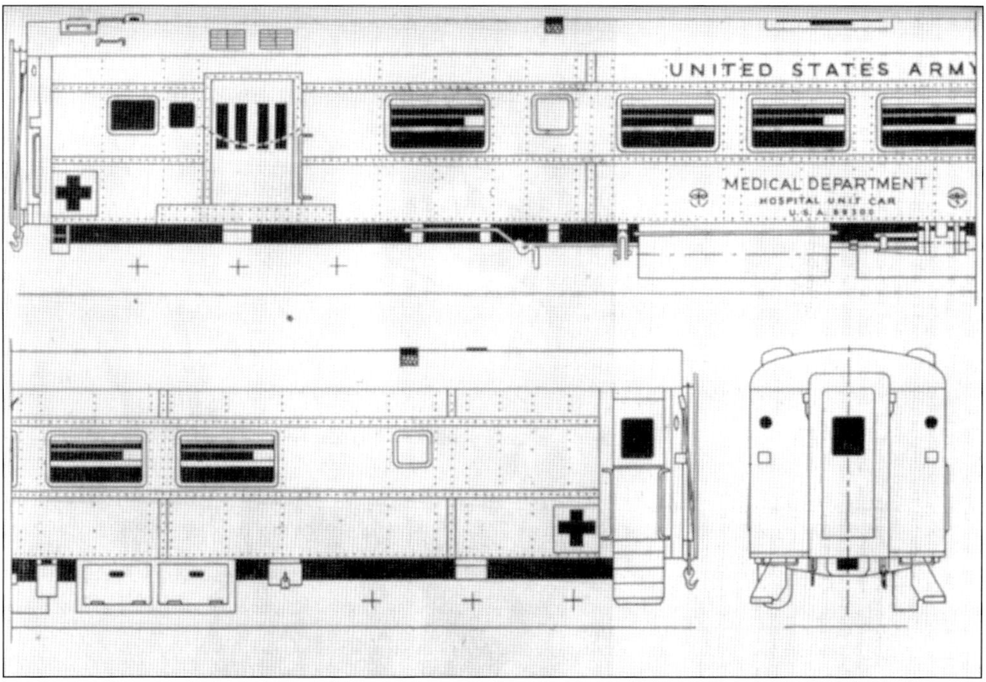

Due to the overcrowded conditions at the prison in the 1970s, prisoners were briefly housed in 10 army surplus hospital cars parked on one of the spurs of the L&O Railroad. Vandalism and security problems caused the project to be abandoned a few months after it began. (Courtesy of Patrick O'Neill.)

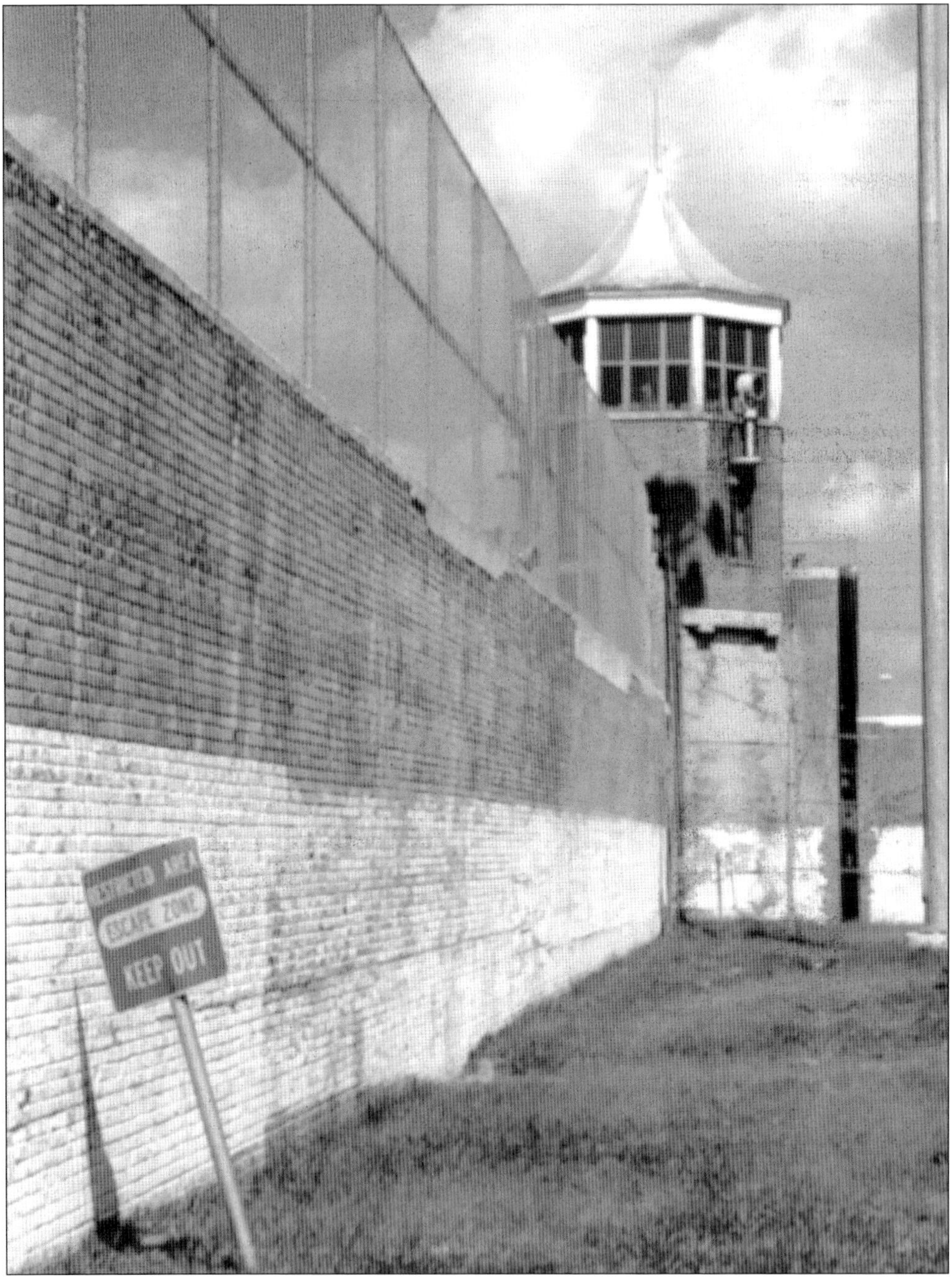

As a direct result of the overcrowding, escapes were more frequent and inmate unrest caused several disturbances. The new more liberal methods of handling prisoners introduced during the 1960 reforms caused tensions and the lowering of morale among correctional officers used to the older traditional ways and who had no voice in making the decisions. (Courtesy of Charles Albert Huckins, Stonelight Images.)

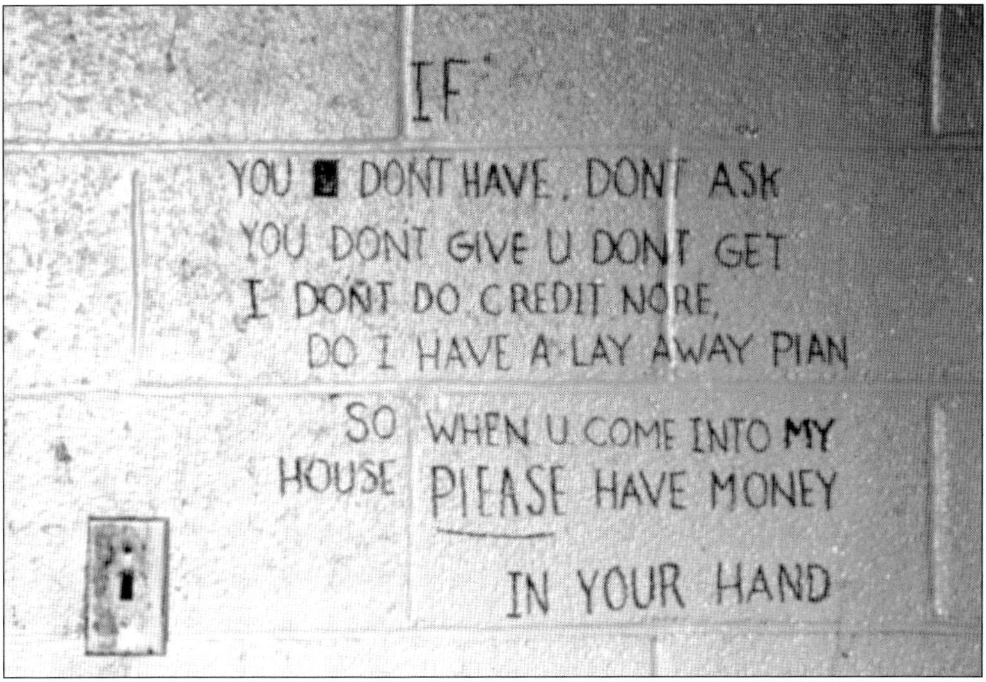

The epidemic explosion of drug usage in the District and nation was reflected at Lorton. More stringent drug laws requiring mandatory sentences added to its already crowded population. It created the need to combat the introduction of contraband drugs to the campus, provide treatment programs for the users, and combat the drug rings operating openly within the prison population. (Courtesy of Charles Albert Huckins, Stonelight Images.)

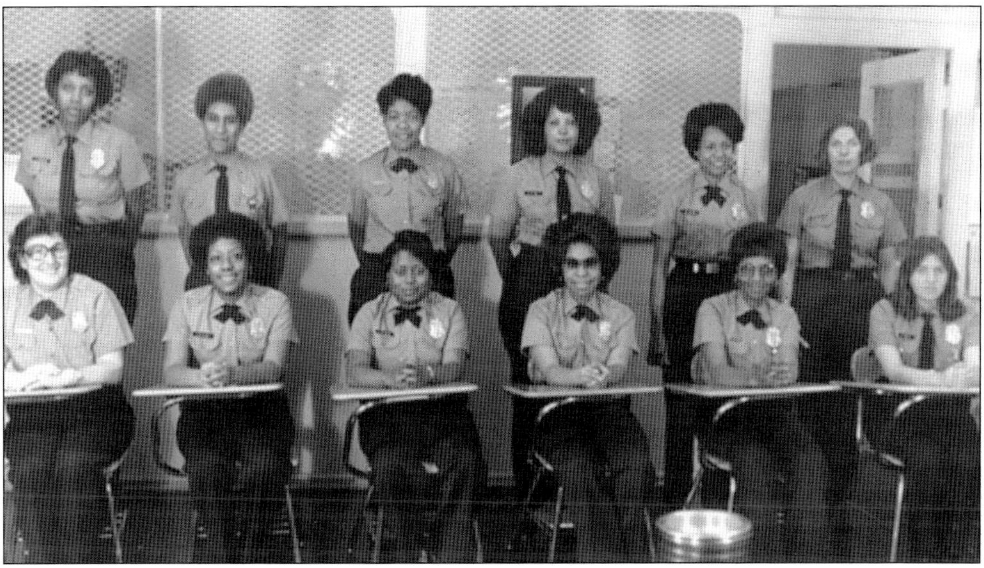

The passage of Title IX in 1972 opened doors for women at the prison complex. Previously, women worked there as nurses, office secretaries, or guards in the women's prisons. Charging that this discriminated against them in terms of promotion, the women sued and eventually won full access to the men's dormitories as well. For a time, this increased tensions with the male inmates and with their fellow correctional officers. (Courtesy of Irma Clifton.)

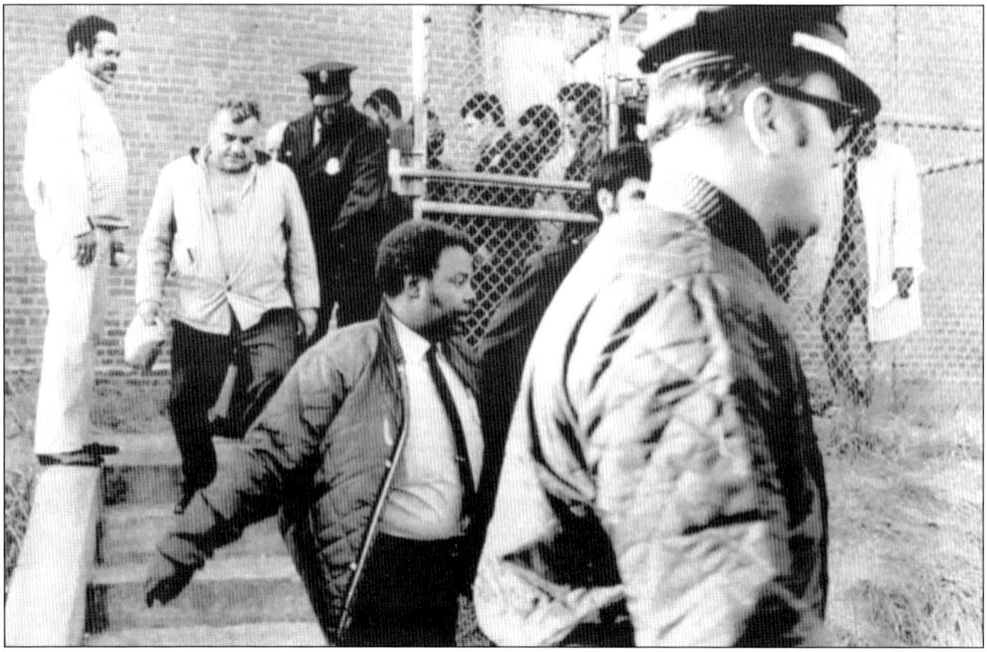

DC Department of Corrections superintendent Kenneth L. Hardy and 11 others were held in Cell Block 1 at the DC Jail in October 1972. The hostage-takers demanded to be freed or threatened violence against their hostages. A negotiated settlement was finally reached after 22 hours. In exchange for the opportunity for hostage-takers to air their grievances before a federal judge and the promise of no reprisals for their actions, Hardy and the others were released. (Courtesy of DC Archives.)

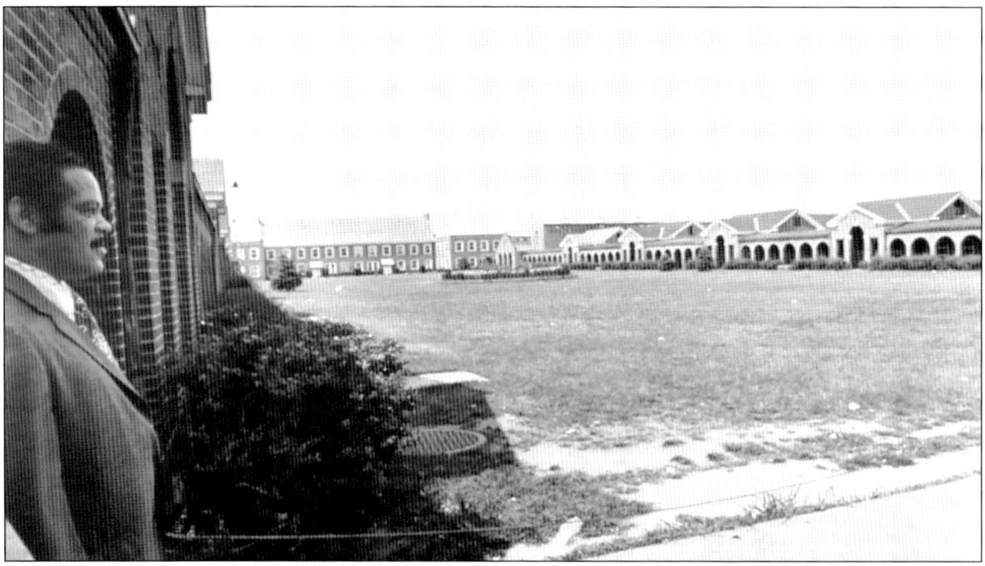

In 1973, Delbert Jackson became the fourth director of corrections and the second black man to hold the position. He described his new penal philosophy and goals: "The winds of change which swept the country after World War II have blown away long-standing preconceptions. There has been a real effort to deal with causative factors and not merely the symptoms." (Courtesy of DC Archives.)

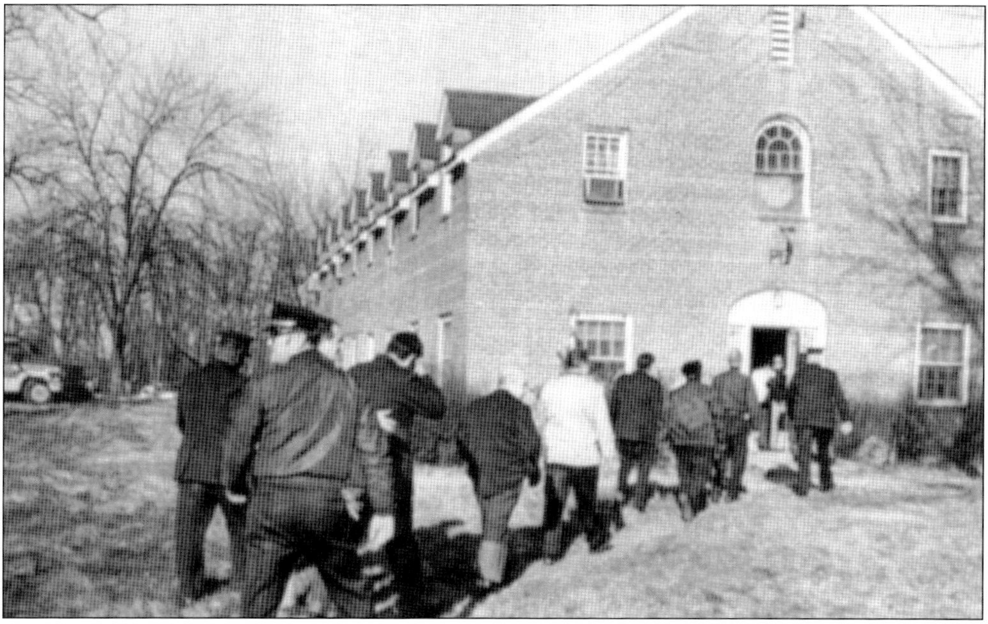

On Christmas Night 1974, about 100 armed inmates staged a takeover of the Maximum-Security section at Lorton, seizing 10 hostages. Four men escaped, but one died in the attempt. Negotiations were held with Director Jackson, and the prisoners' demands and grievances were presented. They included serving their time at Lorton and not being sent to federal prisons. An agreement was reached after 20 tense hours, and the hostages were released. (Courtesy of DC Archives.)

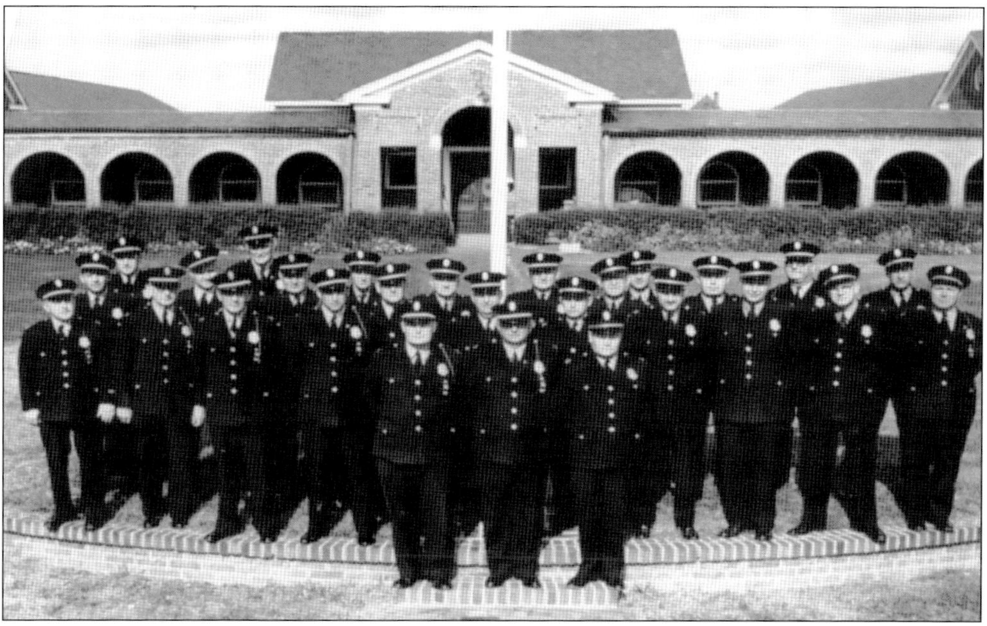

The unrest continued, and after a further series of incidents at Lorton, the president appointed another special committee. It found "torn inadequate facilities and the requirements of physical and mental health; between the militant attitudes of young black men from the troubled ghetto and the conservative philosophies of the white staff members from the rural and suburban communities." (Courtesy of DC Archives.)

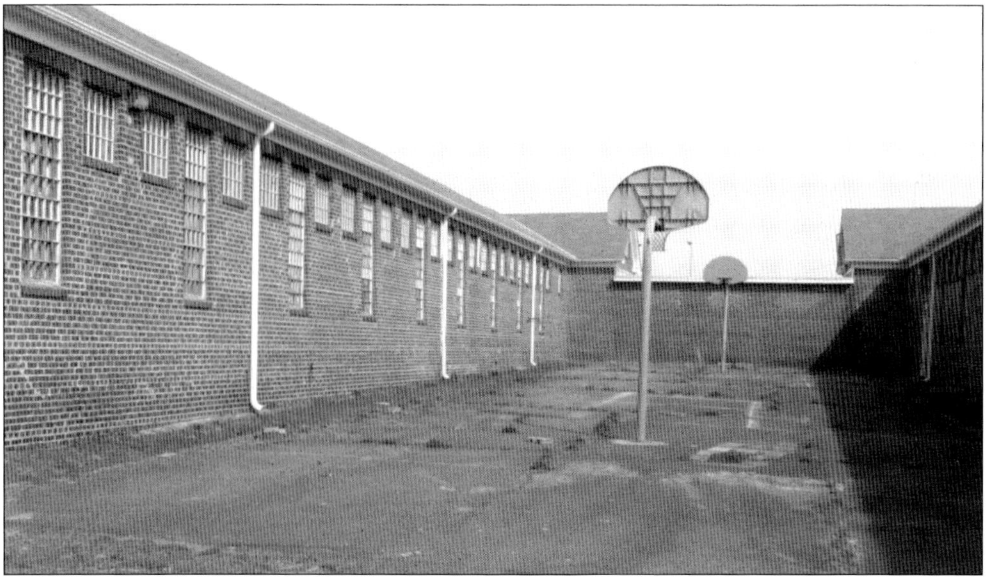

Baseball was still played on the two prison ball fields. Beginning in the 1970s and until the prison closed, basketball was another popular sport There were indoor courts at the gyms, and hoops were set up in the exercise yards between the buildings for play and practice. Among the prisoners, "Lorton Ball" was a way for inmates to exhibit dominance and perhaps alter the power structure inside. (Courtesy of Capt. William Jernigan.)

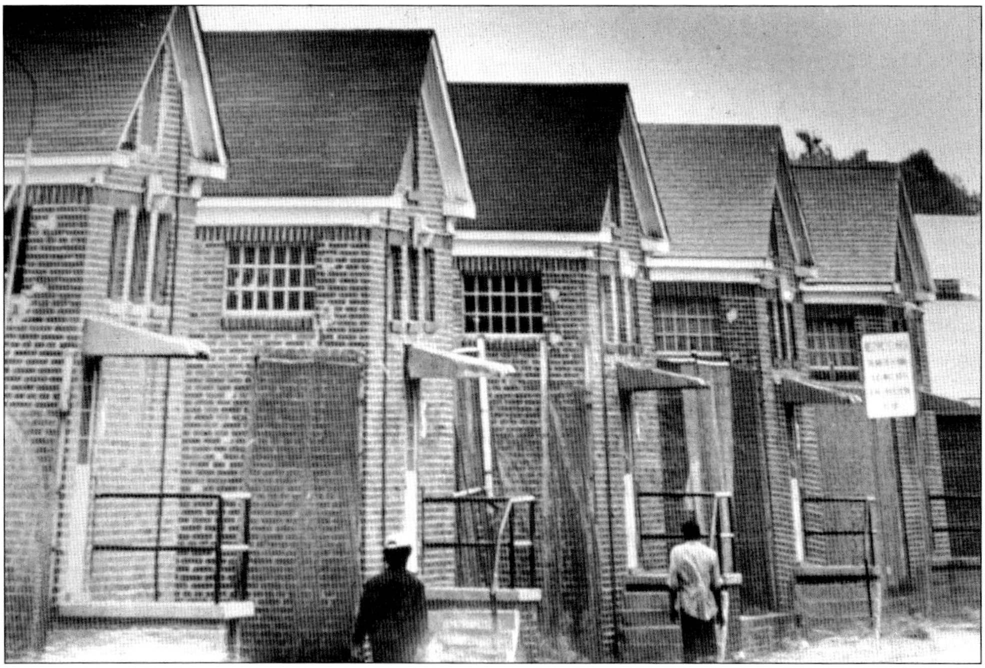

In the 1980s, DC became a major market in the distribution of crack cocaine. It moved from the upscale neighborhoods into suburban areas, and then into the poor black communities. Open-air markets flourished, and in 1985, they became a battleground as dealers fought for a piece of the lucrative trade. By the end of 1985, DC passed all other US cities in per capita drug arrests. The population at Lorton overflowed. (Courtesy of DC Archives.)

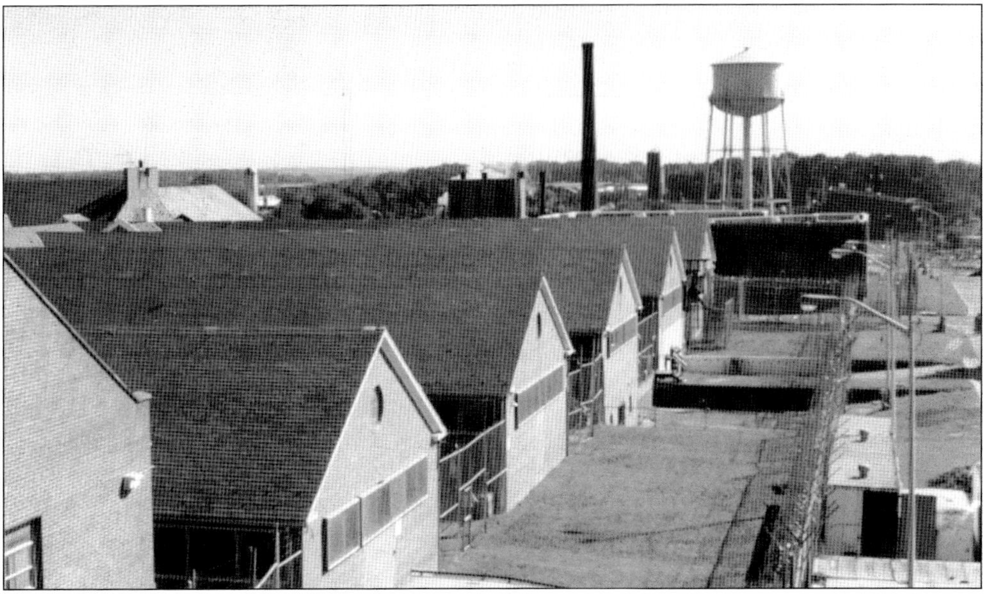

In April 1980, five armed men staged a daring raid into the Minimum-Security Occoquan Facility and gunned down a prisoner before the other frightened inmates. Law enforcement personnel termed it a drug-related assassination as the victim was a convicted heroin dealer from a rival gang, who thought the prison would be safer than the streets. Headline writers had a field day referring to Lorton as "the only prison in the country people were breaking into!" (Courtesy of Fairfax County Department of Planning and Development.)

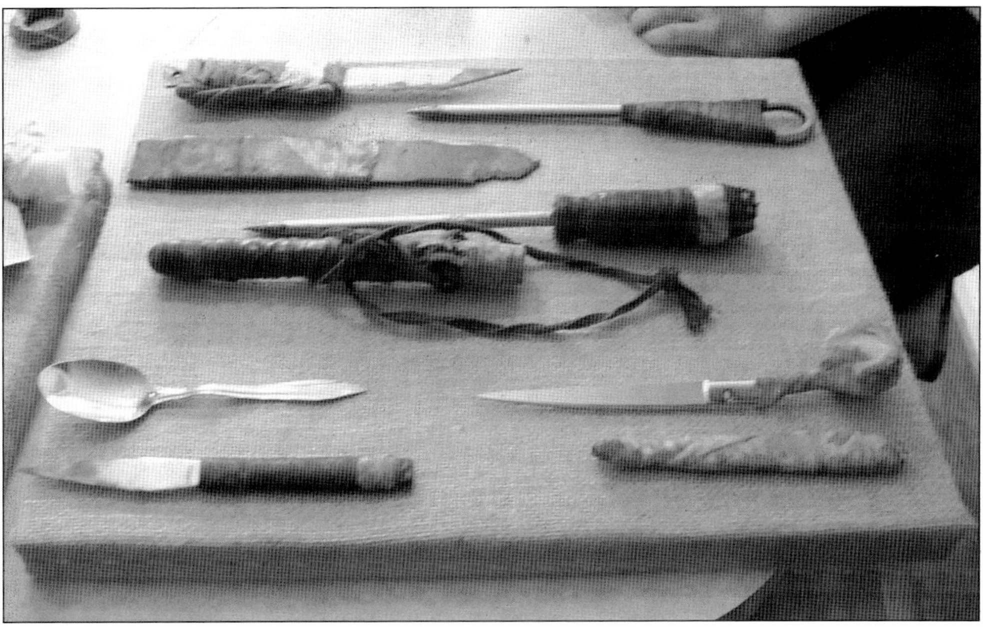

There were at least 17 major disturbances on the Lorton reservation in just over a decade. They occurred in Central, the Occoquan facility, and the Youth Centers. They incurred millions of dollars in damages to buildings already in need of repair. This did not include the stabbings and fighting among groups and individuals living in facilities that seemed to add more each week to an already overcrowded and explosive area. (Courtesy of William Koch.)

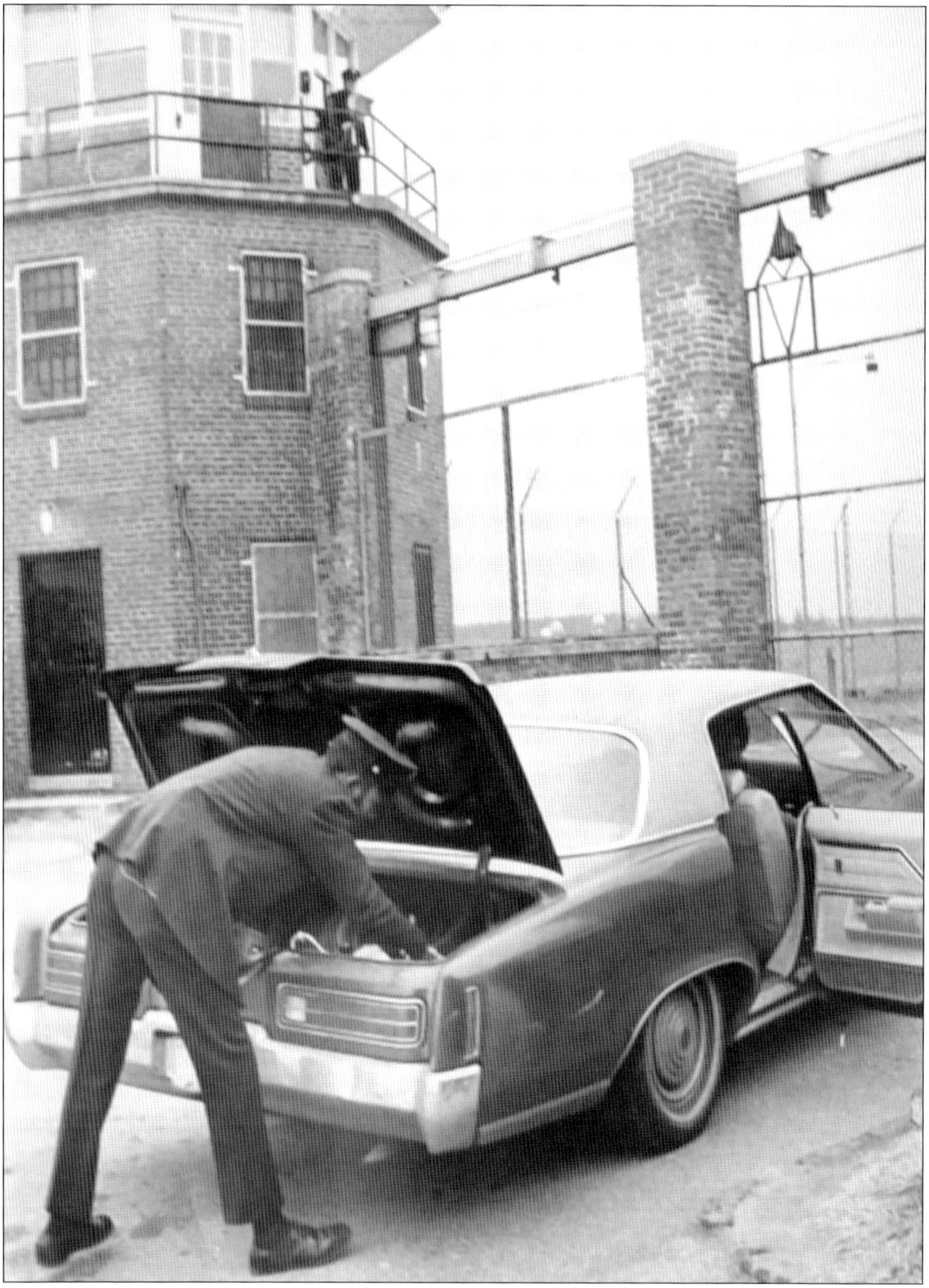

Due to the number of attacks on and by inmates at the Lorton Complex, car checks increased, and random shakedowns were conducted in at least one facility every 60 days. That was in addition to less thorough searches done twice each day by each facility's regular officers. All cars were thoroughly searched for contraband before entering the prison and visitors were routinely searched inside before being allowed to contact an inmate. (Courtesy of DC Archives.)

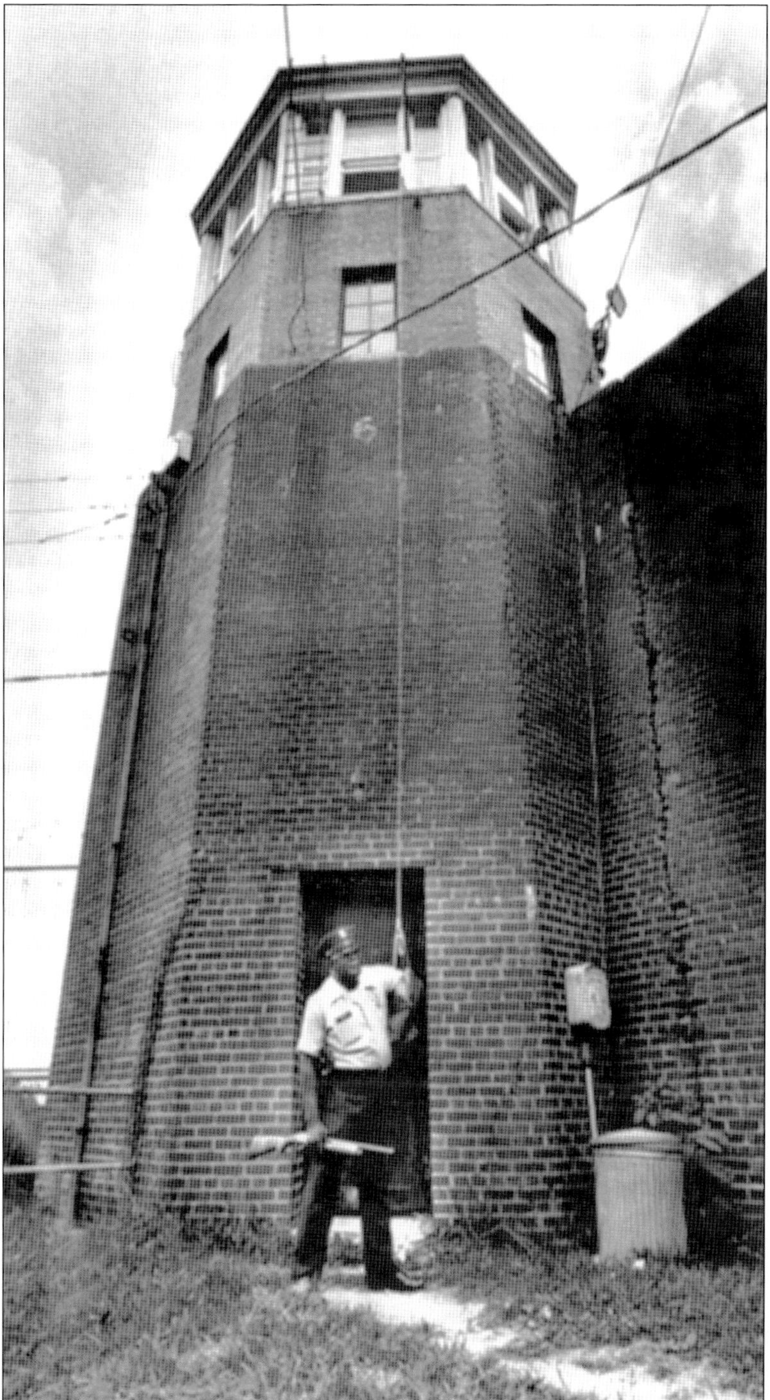

There were at least four towers at each facility, numbered from one through four and up. The room at the top of each tower provided a bird's-eye view of the area beneath. Tower guards watched for early signs of trouble to prevent it from spreading. The guard at the top had the key and lowered it to allow his replacement to unlock the door at the bottom. (Courtesy of DC Archives.)

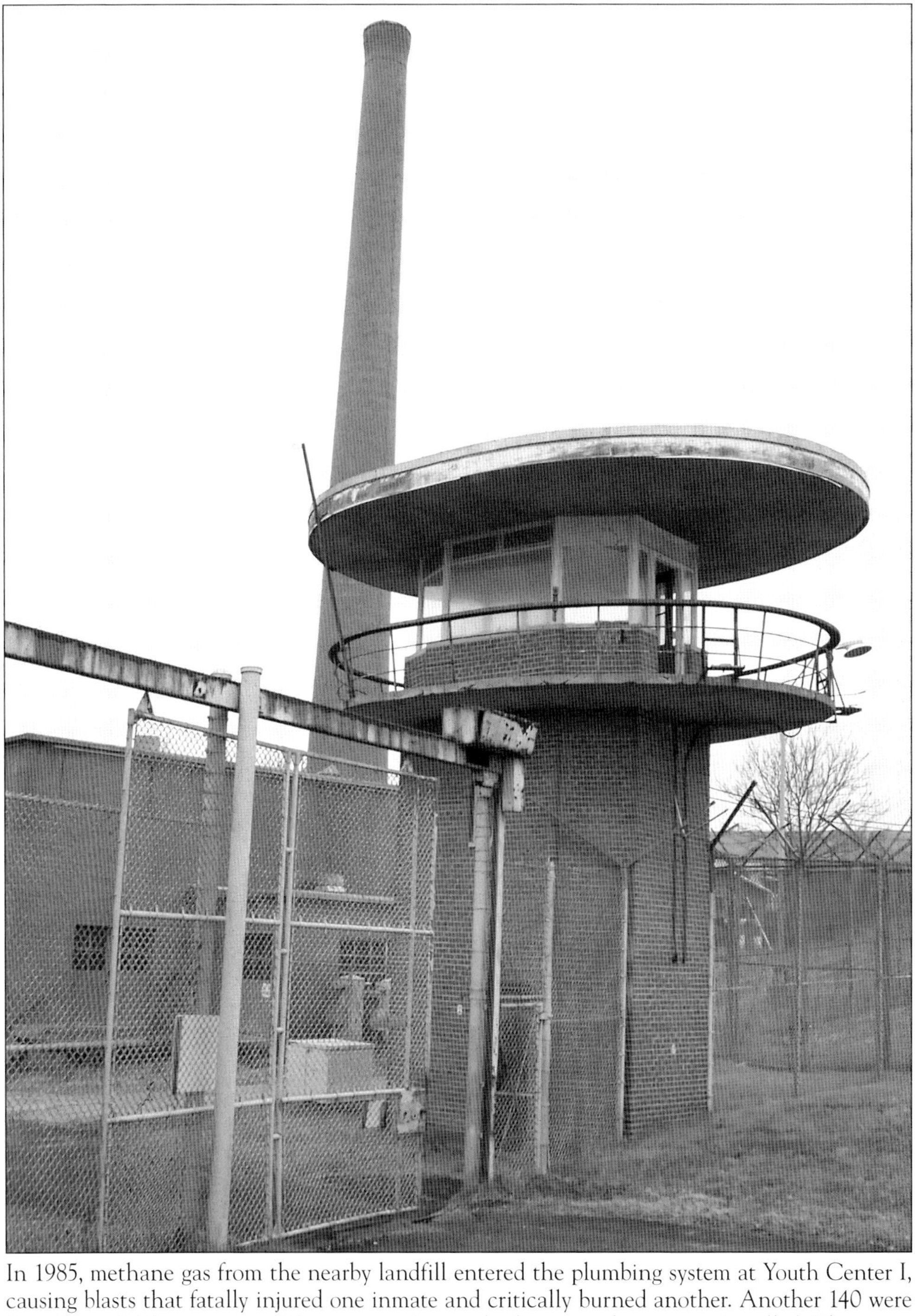

In 1985, methane gas from the nearby landfill entered the plumbing system at Youth Center I, causing blasts that fatally injured one inmate and critically burned another. Another 140 were forced to quickly evacuate while an extensive method to vent the gas was installed. They were temporarily housed in the gym facility at Youth Center II. (Courtesy of Don Sweeney, Fairfax County Park Authority.)

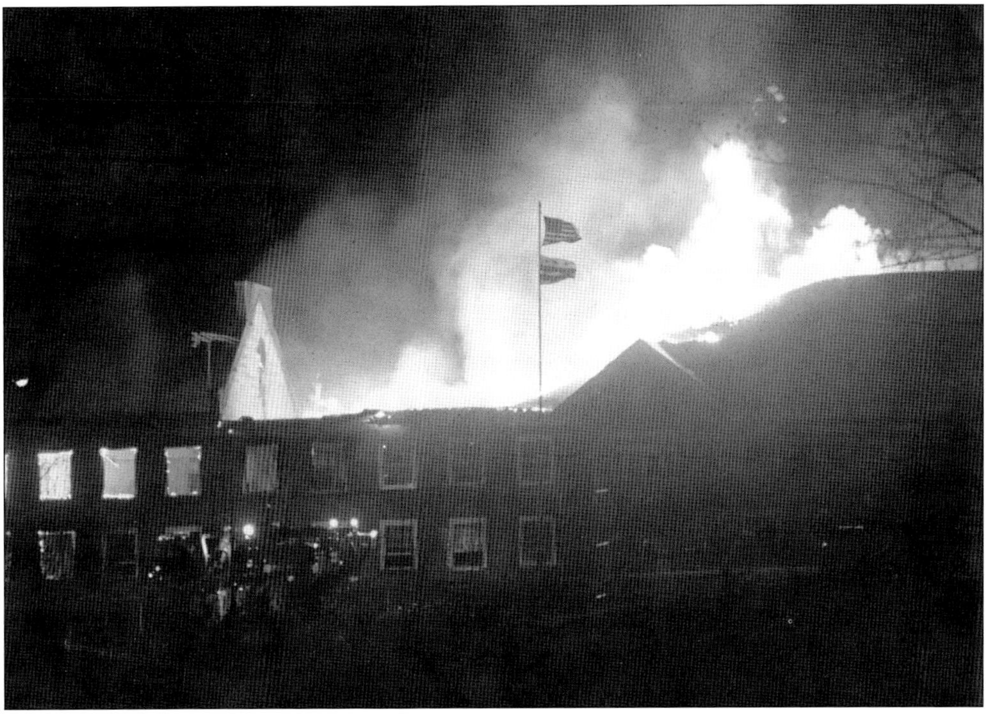

In July 1986, rioting inmates set fire to 14 buildings at Occoquan. Inmates attacked armed correctional officers that were trying to transfer 64 ringleaders of the uprising to the DC Jail. Five buildings were destroyed and two roofs collapsed. Later, helmeted officers fired tear gas and shot guns as a second round of violence occurred at the baseball diamond where the prisoners had been herded away from the smoke and flames. (Courtesy of the Fairfax County Department of Fire and Rescue.)

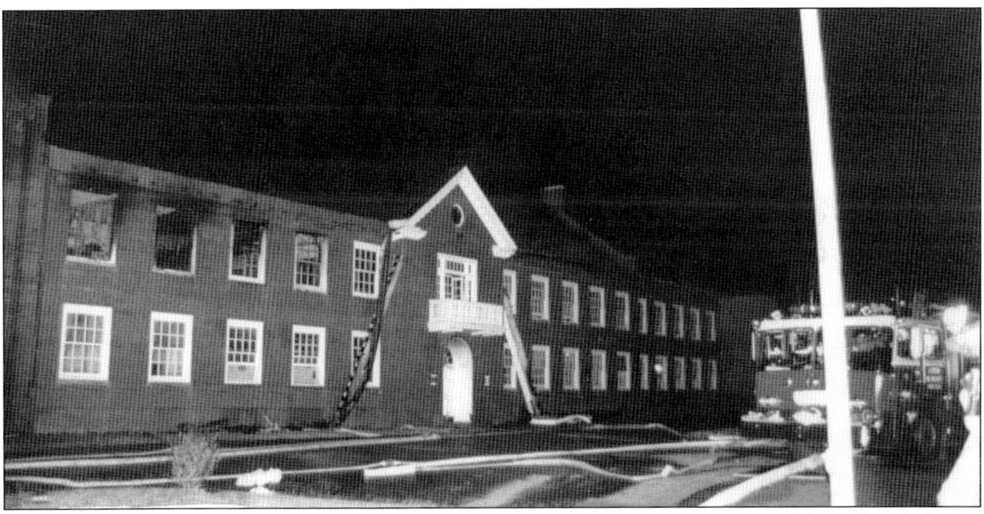

Inmates took advantage of a power failure in January 1989 to set a series of fires that left one inmate dead, two stabbed, and a gutted administration building. Firefighters from Fairfax County refused to enter the grounds until prison guards contained the inmates freely roaming the grounds. A damaged heating system forced the removal of 60 prisoners from one dorm to the DC Jail. (Courtesy of the Fairfax County Department of Fire and Rescue.)

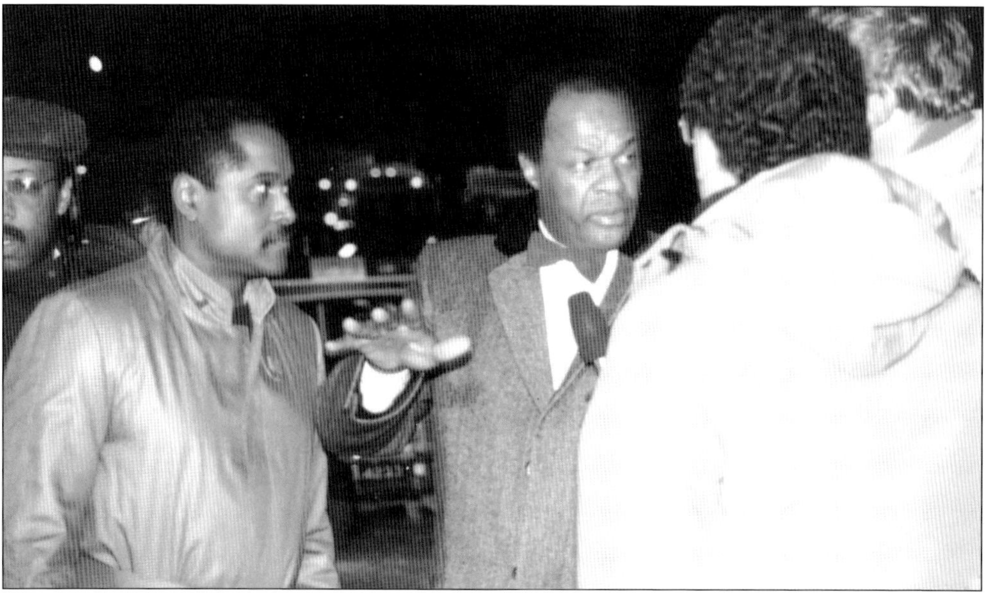

Washington, DC, mayor Marion Barry publicly downplayed the incident incurring the wrath of Fairfax County officials. Relations further deteriorated in 1988 and 1989, with the mayor's proposal to relocate Lorton inmates to a private prison in West Virginia and lease the Lorton prison property to a developer for a large office park and 10,300 homes. Area politicians killed the plan, while local demands to permanently close the prison continued to grow. (Courtesy of the Fairfax County Department of Fire and Rescue.)

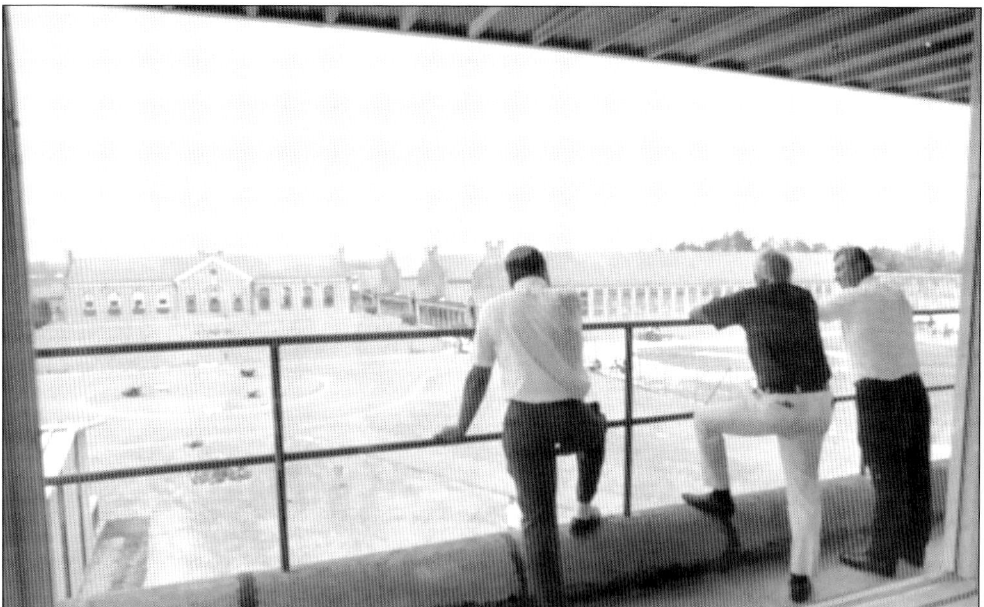

Arguments over whether the prison should go or stay grew fiercer. Each side dug in and waged battle through news outlets and community meetings. Meanwhile, those most affected by the final decision grew fearful. The administration and staff worried about their jobs. The prisoners worried about where they would be sent. Their families worried it would be to a federal prison far from home, with the loss of support and comfort of frequent visitation. (Courtesy of DC Archives.)

Five

The Final Years, Closure, and Rebirth

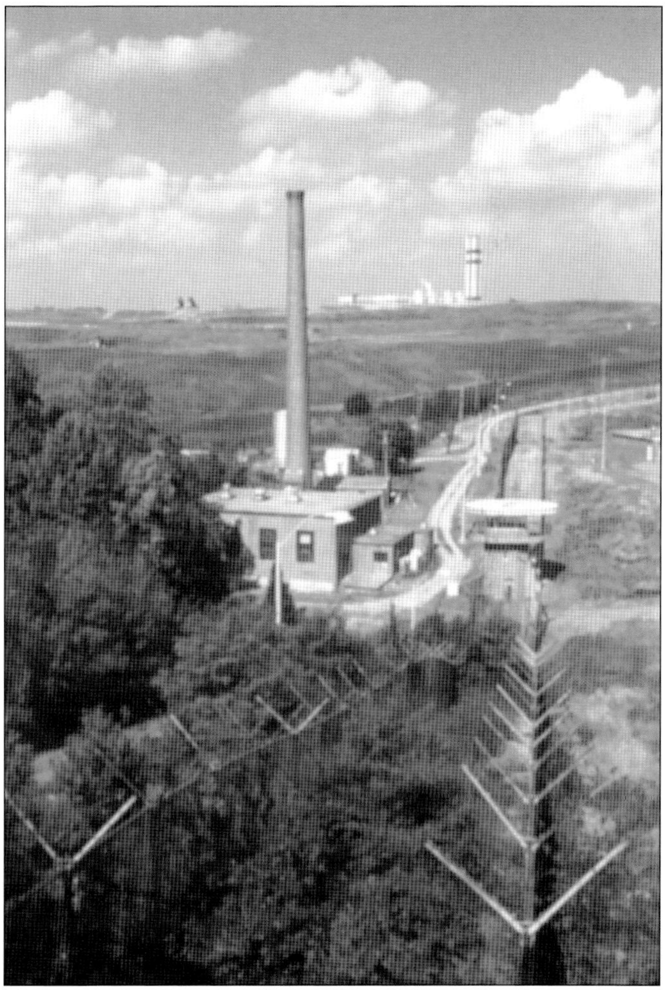

The area surrounding the prisons became less rural. Housing developments swallowed up acres of farmland and moved ever closer to the complex. Newspaper headlines and negative stories continued to affect the attitudes of the local communities toward having a prison in their midst. The overcrowded structures needed costly major repairs beyond the already overstrapped municipal DC budget. It culminated with the closing of the prison and repurposing of the land. (Courtesy of Charles Albert Huckins, Stonelight Images.)

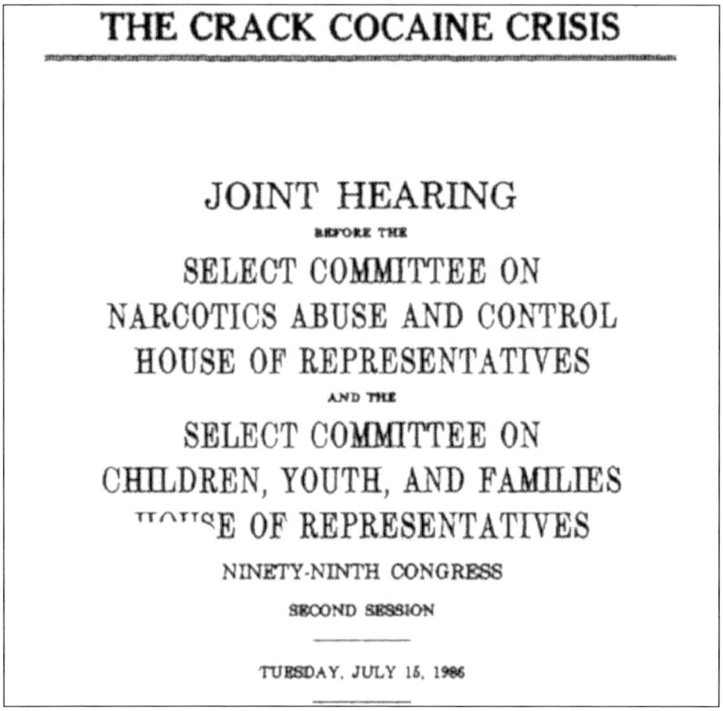

THE CRACK COCAINE CRISIS

JOINT HEARING

BEFORE THE

SELECT COMMITTEE ON

NARCOTICS ABUSE AND CONTROL

HOUSE OF REPRESENTATIVES

AND THE

SELECT COMMITTEE ON

CHILDREN, YOUTH, AND FAMILIES

HOUSE OF REPRESENTATIVES

NINETY-NINTH CONGRESS

SECOND SESSION

TUESDAY, JULY 15, 1986

In the 1980s, DC became a major market in the distribution of crack cocaine. It moved from the upscale neighborhoods into suburban areas, and then into the poor black communities. Open-air markets flourished, and in 1985, they became a battleground as dealers fought for a piece of the lucrative trade. By the end of 1985, DC passed all other US cities in per capita drug arrests. The population at Lorton overflowed. (Courtesy of the Library of Congress.)

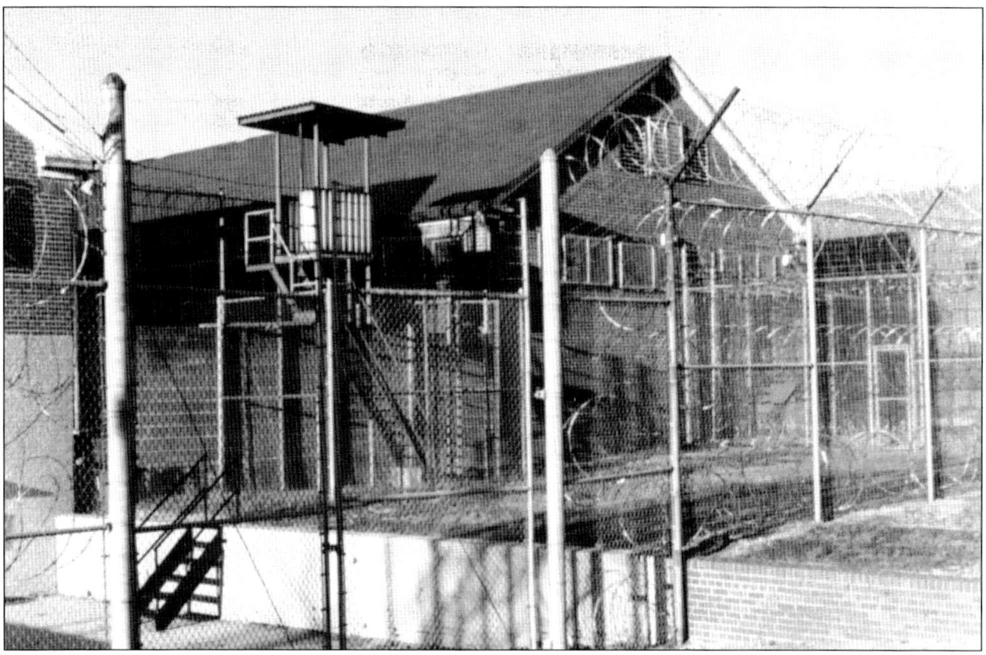

Sanford Ashford's design for a college campus–like look for the prison was shattered with the erection of metal fencing topped by razor wire at the Workhouse. No unique brick towers, but utilitarian ones were attached at corners of Workhouse dormitories. The Workhouse now resembled a fortress. Even the walkways on the quad side of the building were fenced in, creating access only at certain points and making it easier for crowd control at signs of trouble. (Courtesy of DC Archives.)

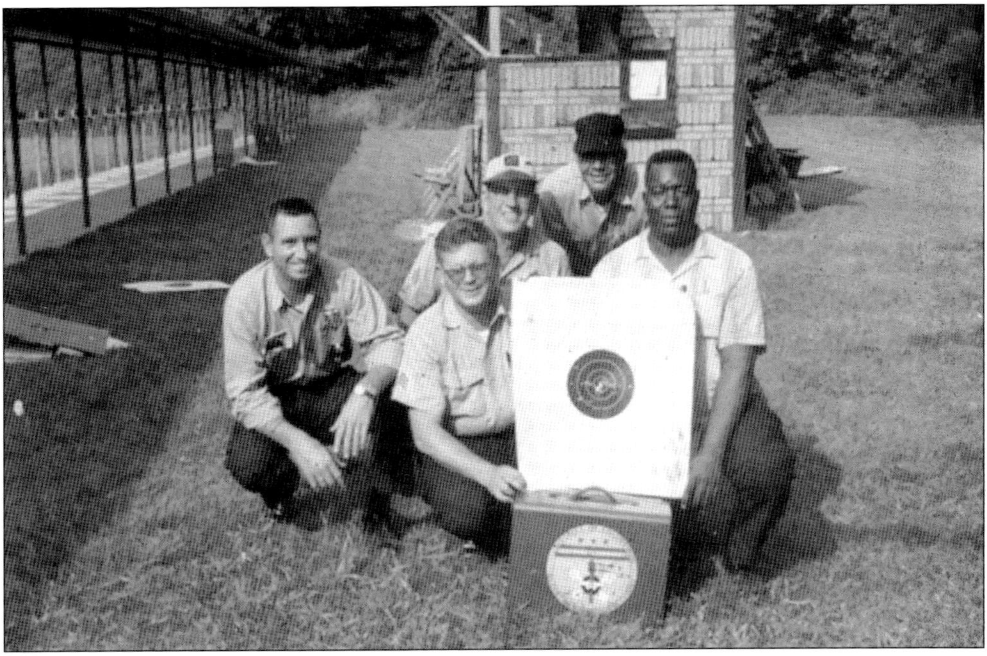

As the population of the prison continued to overflow its designed capacity, incarceration replaced rehabilitation as the dominant philosophy. The rifle team continued to compete, but now an Emergency Response Team (SWAT) was formed at Lorton in response to the growing tension between staff and prisoners and among the inmates themselves. They received training and were drilled in methods of handling challenging situations. (Courtesy of DC Archives.)

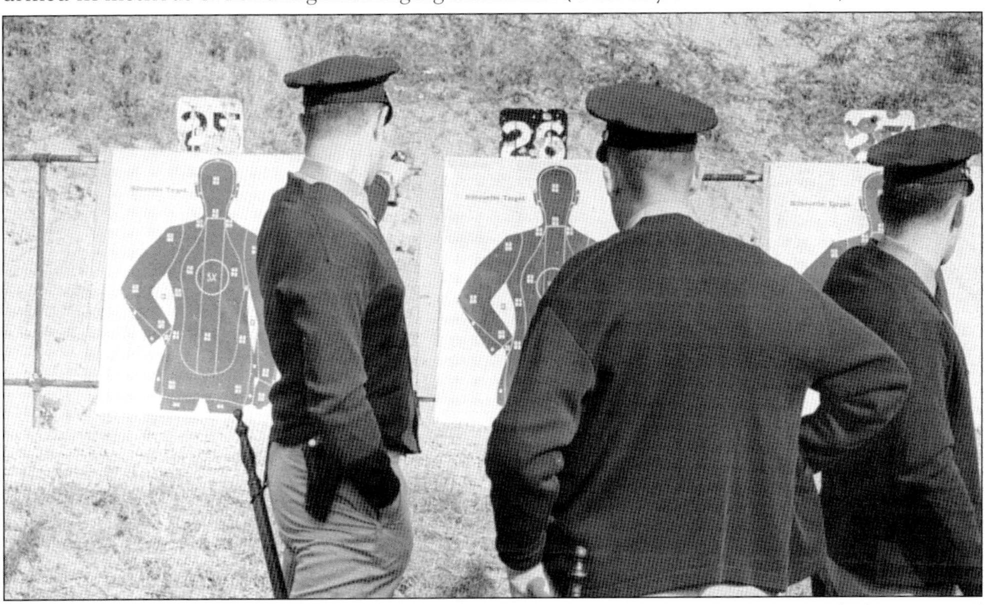

The adverse attention by the news media to escapes and incidents at Lorton led to several investigations into the operations at the prison complex. The furlough program was put on hold; a casualty of the negative publicity. The previous friendly, cooperative relationships developed over the years with the surrounding communities further ruptured when bullets fired from a prison practice range landed in a nearby housing development. (Courtesy of DC Archives.)

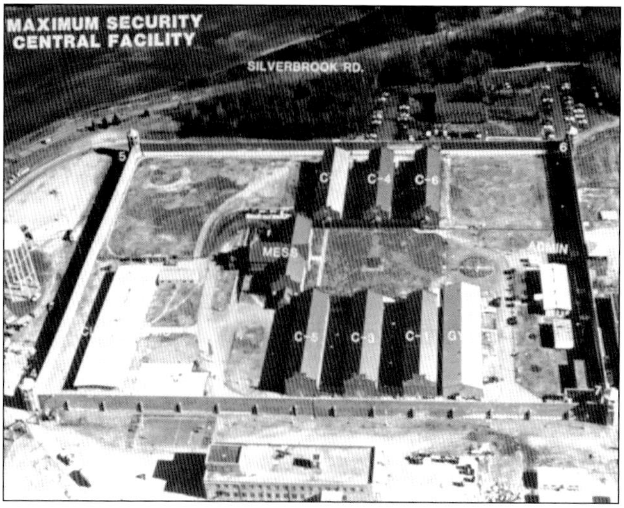

Maximum Security occupied ten acres within the Reformatory site and was surrounded by a high, thick, brick wall that extended deep into the ground to prevent tunneling. Brick towers guarded the four corners. Yet, Snowden Ashford's ideas were incorporated into the arrangement of brick dormitories with a quad area in the middle. "Max" was self-sustaining, with its own mess hall, library, recreation area, shops, and offices. The sally port is at lower right. (Courtesy of Laura McKie.)

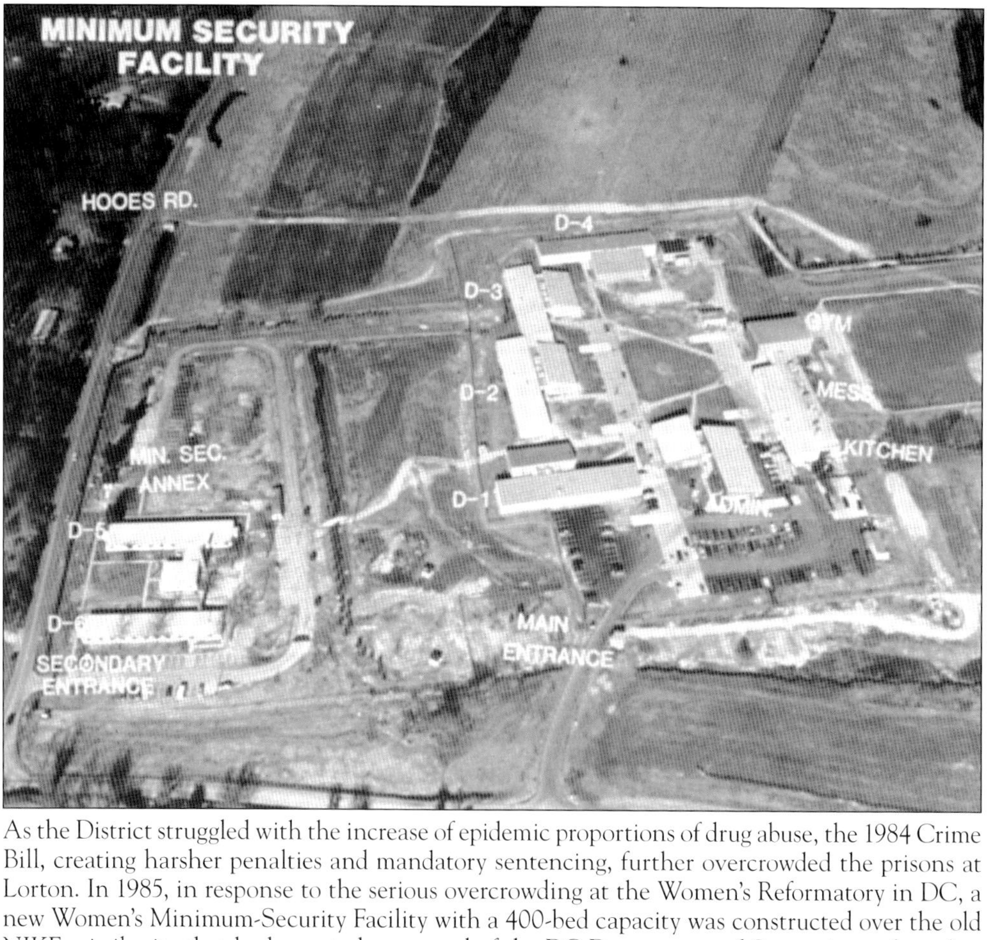

As the District struggled with the increase of epidemic proportions of drug abuse, the 1984 Crime Bill, creating harsher penalties and mandatory sentencing, further overcrowded the prisons at Lorton. In 1985, in response to the serious overcrowding at the Women's Reformatory in DC, a new Women's Minimum-Security Facility with a 400-bed capacity was constructed over the old NIKE missile site that had reverted to control of the DC Department of Corrections when that site was closed in 1974. (Courtesy of Laura McKie.)

In 1993, DC mayor Sharon Pratt Kelly proposed an addition to the maximum-security facility at Lorton. It was part of a package to reduce violent crime in the District by relying more on enforcement and punishment. Tom Davis, chairman of the Fairfax County Board of Supervisors, led the community-wide protest. A hastily constructed modular facility to house 400 inmates was built behind the shops at the Reformatory. (Courtesy of Laura McKie.)

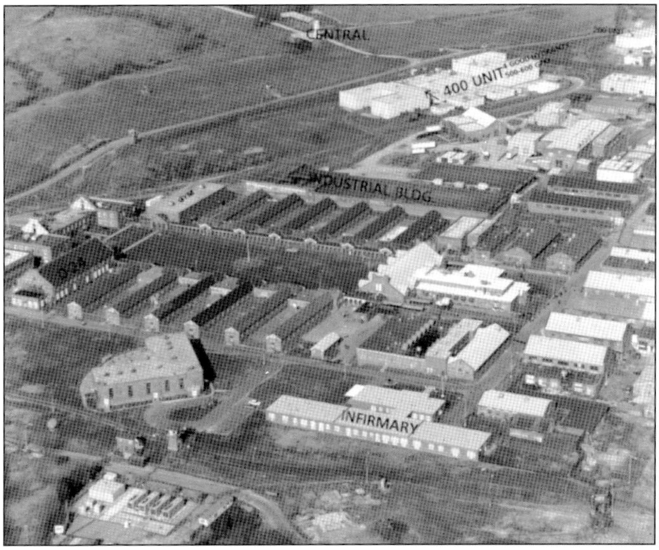

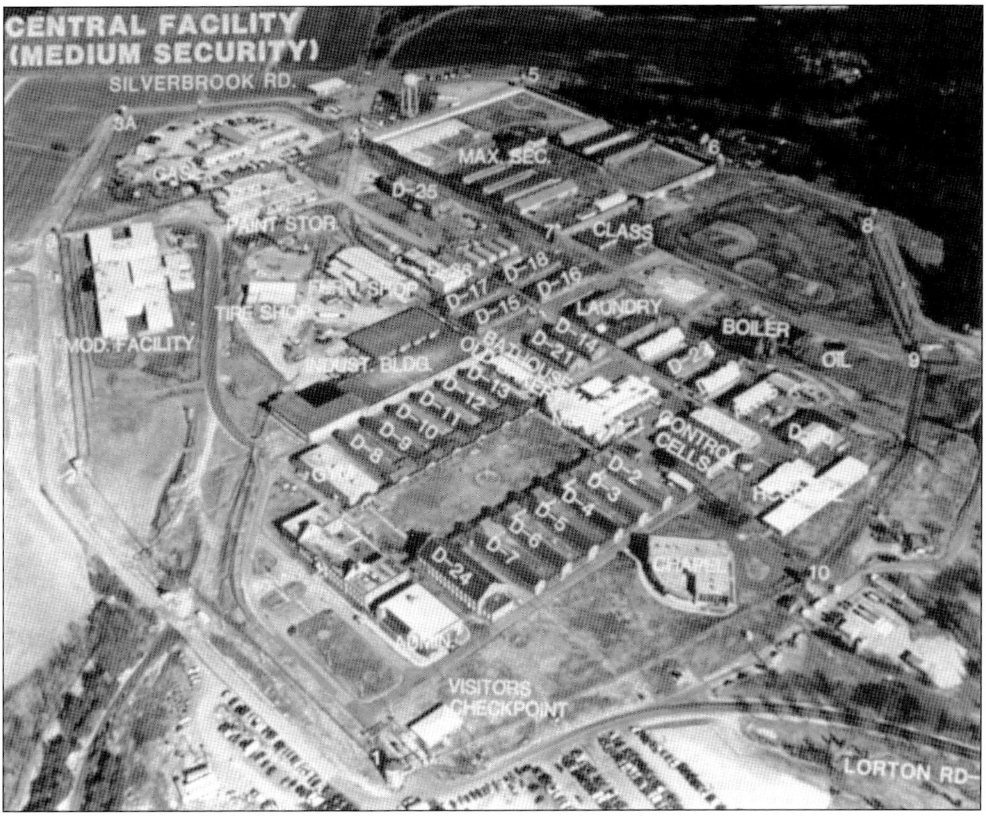

The last attempt to save the prison was made in 1997 by Pres. Bill Clinton. He submitted an $885 million plan to renovate and expand the prison, double its capacity to 10,000 inmates, and put it under the US Bureau of Prisons. Congress objected. The National Capital Revitalization and Self-Government Improvement Act of 1997 was enacted to reform the troubled criminal justice system in DC. It required the closing of Lorton Prison by December 31, 2001. (Courtesy of DC Archives.)

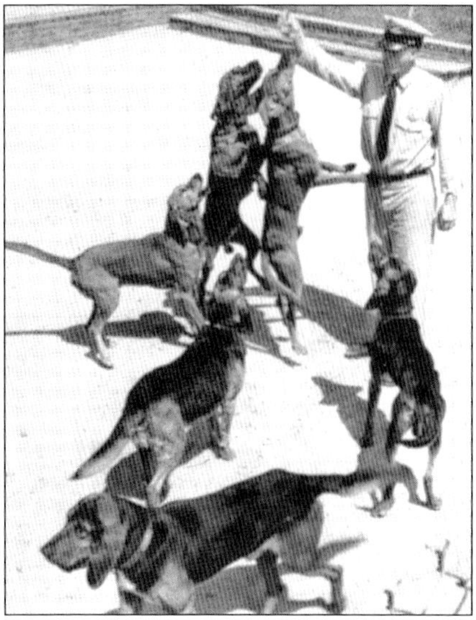

Bloodhounds were sometimes used to track escapees through the densely wooded area surrounding the prison. They also assisted local authorities in locating lost children. Dogs were kept at the residence of the officer training them. The use of bloodhounds was discontinued in the 1960s when the Shirley Highway (now Interstate 95) was built, believing the road would interfere with the scent. They returned in the 1990s when officer Kevin Kocher was hired and brought his own dogs. (Courtesy of Irma Clifton.)

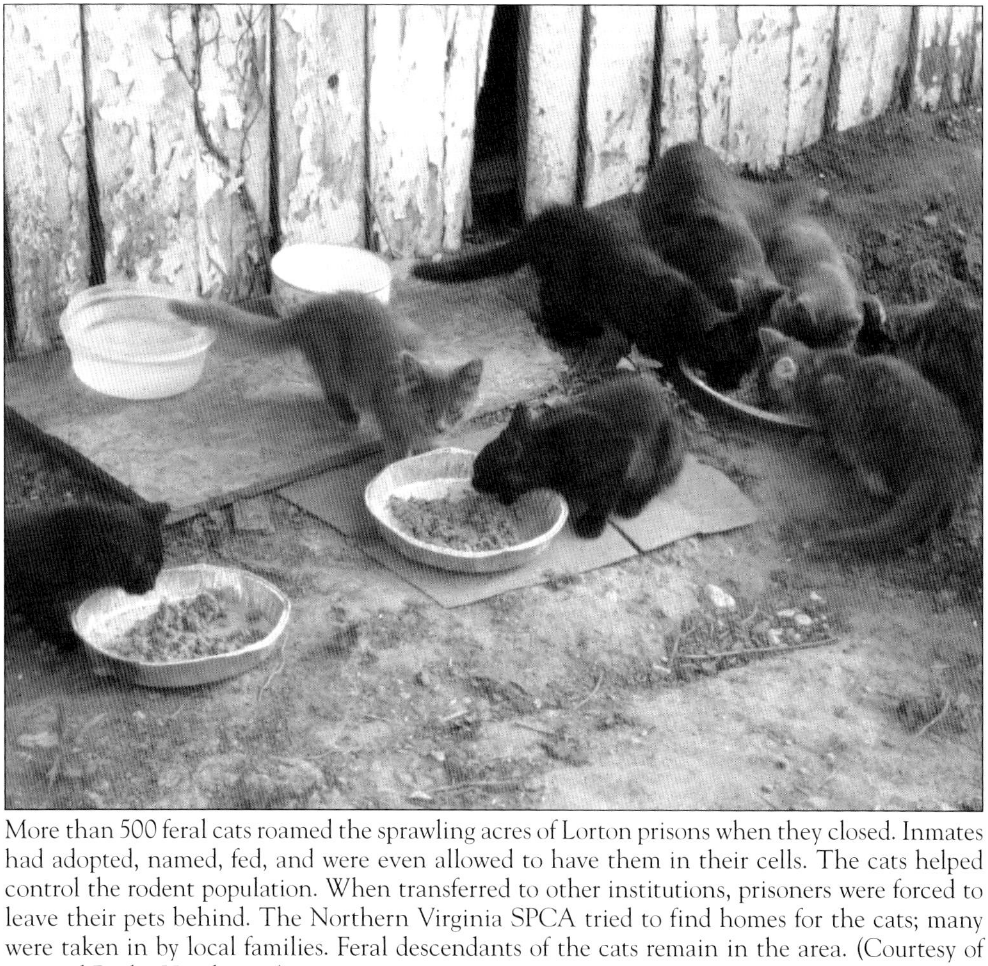

More than 500 feral cats roamed the sprawling acres of Lorton prisons when they closed. Inmates had adopted, named, fed, and were even allowed to have them in their cells. The cats helped control the rodent population. When transferred to other institutions, prisoners were forced to leave their pets behind. The Northern Virginia SPCA tried to find homes for the cats; many were taken in by local families. Feral descendants of the cats remain in the area. (Courtesy of Jim and Becky Henderson.)

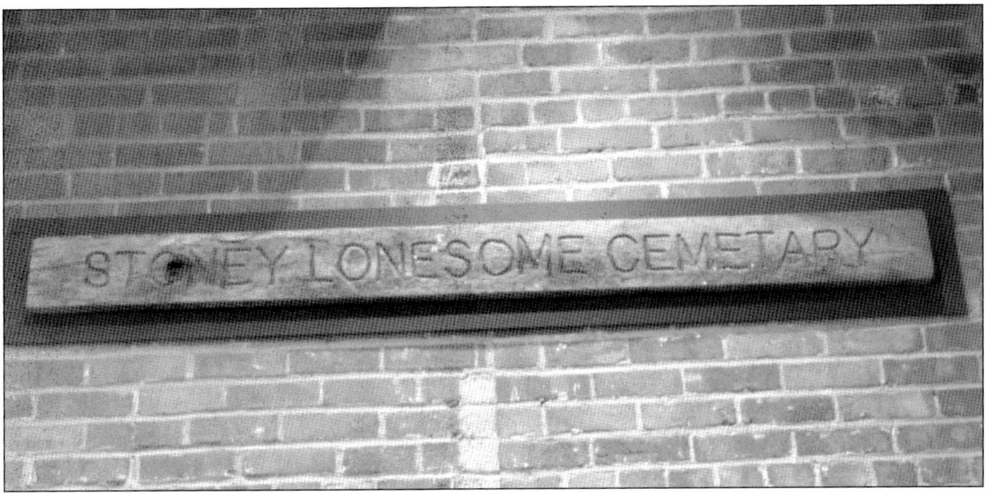

Land was set aside for a prison cemetery built around 1920. No surviving records indicate the number of burials or identities of the dead. Historians estimate the number as between 50 and 100. Inmates carved this sign for the cemetery. The earliest burials were probably men or women who succumbed to disease or fatal work-related injuries. Some may have caught the Spanish flu during the 1918 epidemic. (Courtesy of Patrick O'Neill.)

When no one claimed the body of a prisoner who died while incarcerated, the prisoner was buried in Stoney Lonesome, the prison cemetery. A pine coffin was made in the furniture factory, and the grave was dug by inmates. A graveside service was conducted by the chaplain with friends in attendance. Bricks made by the inmates were sometimes used to mark the graves. (Courtesy of Patrick O'Neill.)

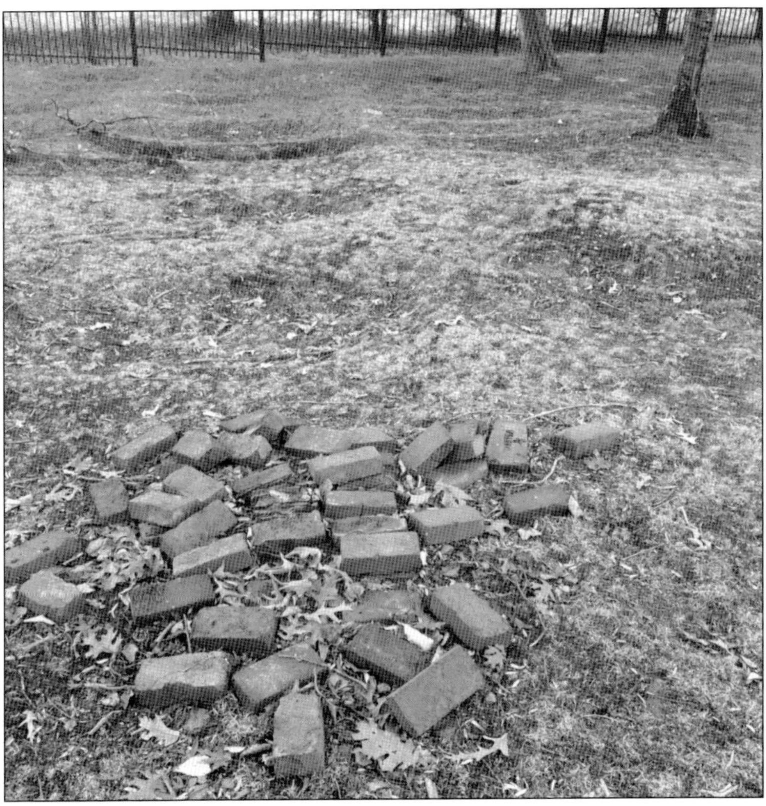

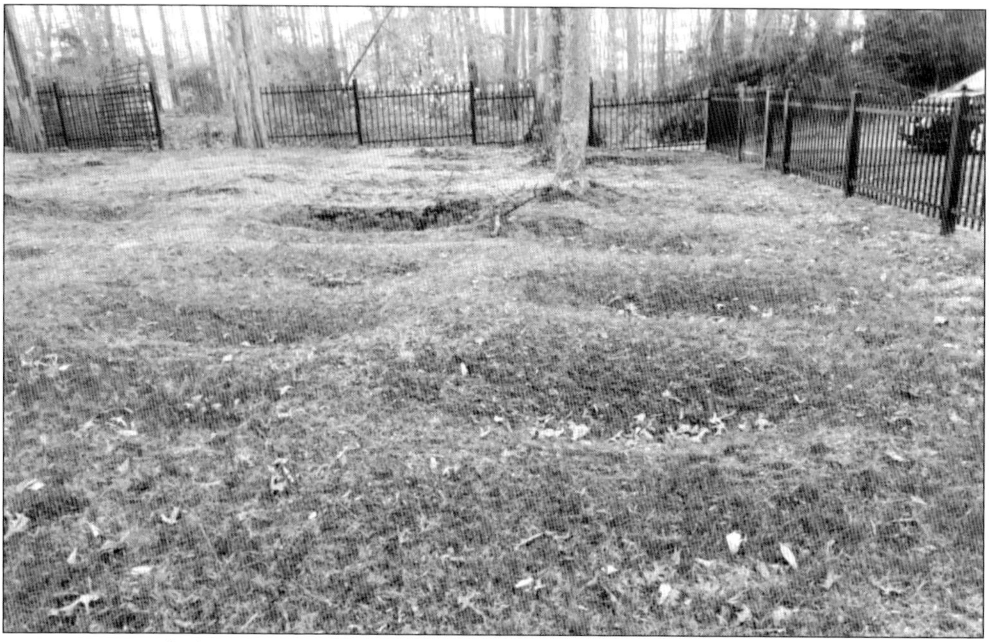

Few stones mark the graves of the deceased prisoners buried at Stoney Lonesome. However, indentations in the soil can be seen indicating a grave site. The cemetery now lies within the boundary of the Fairfax County Water Authority located at the old Women's Workhouse site. They accepted the responsibility to care for the only prisoners remaining at Lorton, and an iron fence now encompasses the cemetery. (Courtesy of Patrick O'Neill.)

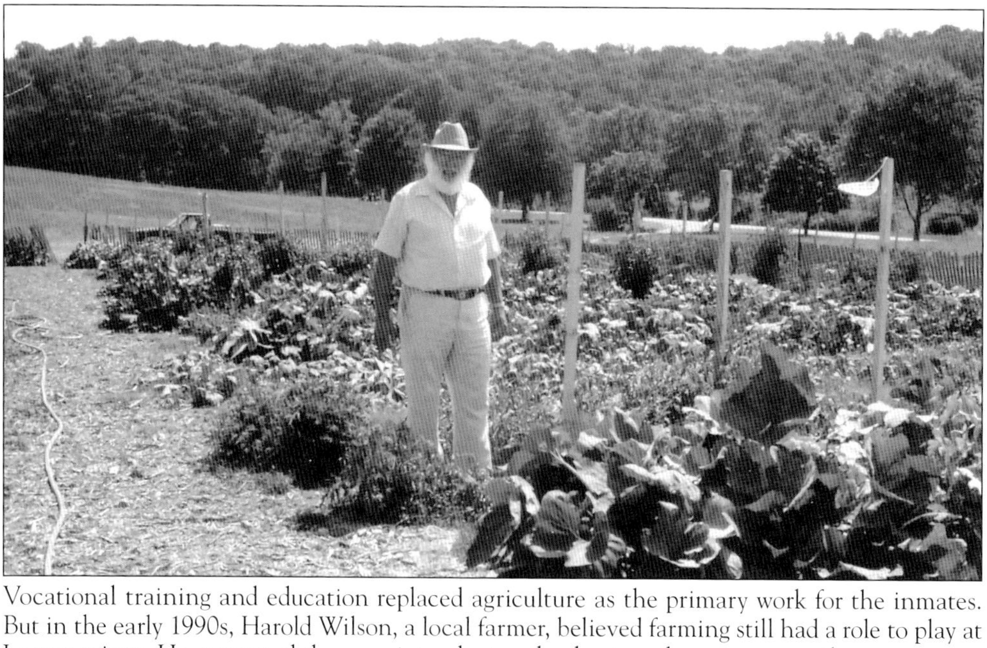

Vocational training and education replaced agriculture as the primary work for the inmates. But in the early 1990s, Harold Wilson, a local farmer, believed farming still had a role to play at Lorton prison. He contacted the superintendent and volunteered to manage a pilot program on the prison grounds. Prisoners volunteered to participate under Wilson's supervision. A variety of crops were grown, and produce was shared with the prison kitchens and charitable organizations in DC. (Courtesy of John Wilson.)

The dairy farm with its supporting hay and corn crops was the last industrial operation to go at Lorton. It was also the last remaining commercial dairy in Fairfax County. In its last year, it had produced 1,600 gallons of milk. Its sales, including other dairy products, topped $1 million. The cows were sold off at the 1998 auction. The buildings would not get the needed repairs. (Courtesy of Fairfax County Department of Planning and Development.)

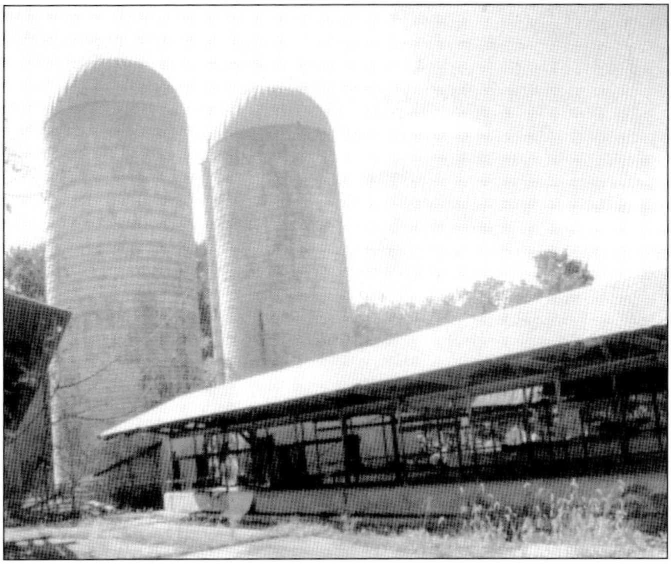

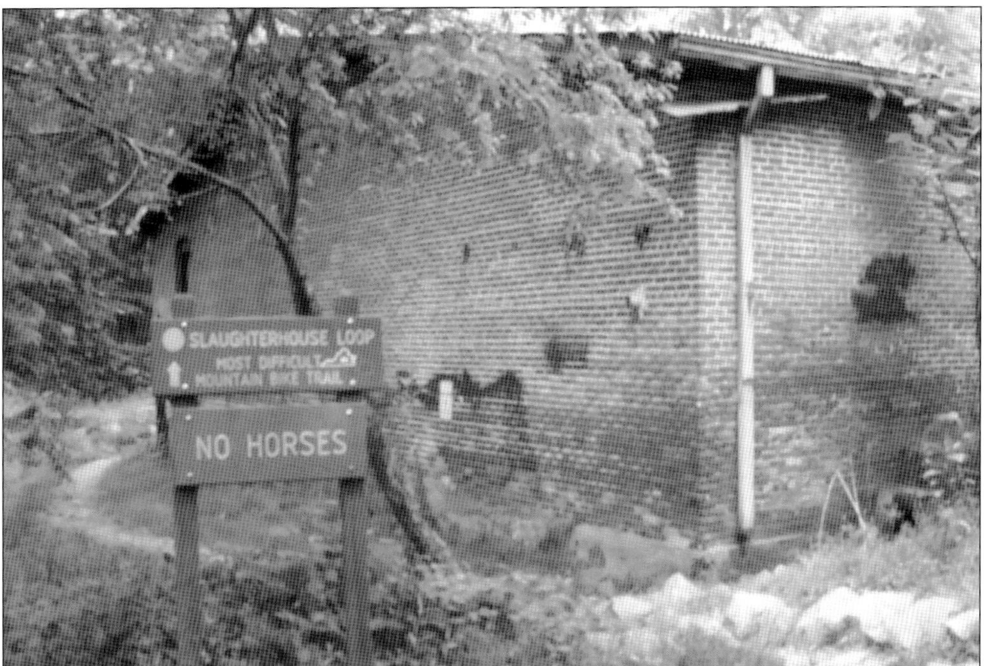

In October 1998, Congress passed the Lorton Technical Corrections Act. It required that before the property was sold and turned over, Fairfax County must develop a reuse plan that would maximize the use of land for open space, parkland, or recreation. The county board of supervisors appointed a citizens task force to work with the county planning staff to develop the plan. Their plan was adopted by the board of supervisors in July 1999. (Courtesy of Fairfax County Department of Planning and Development.)

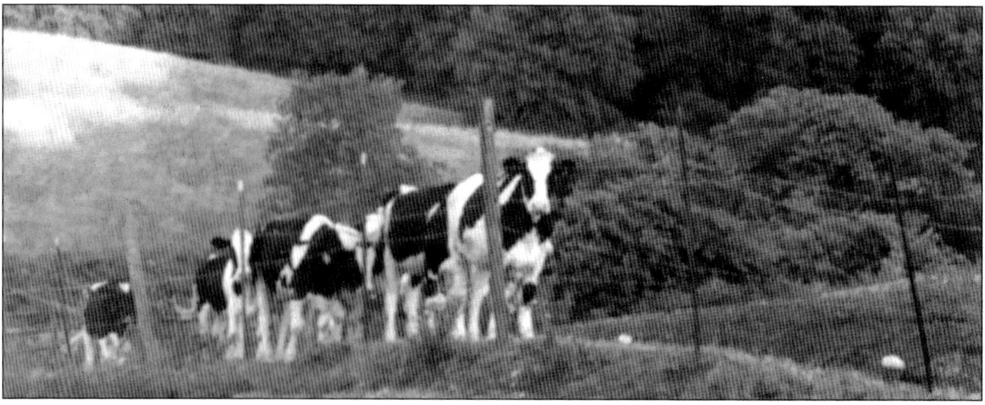

Prisoner exodus from the complex began in 1998 when inmates from the Youth Center, the Modular Facilities at Central, Medium Security, and Occoquan I and II were transferred to federal prisons. That year, the cows returned for their final milking and the dairy operation ceased; the last industrial operation to go. In 1999, Minimum Security on Furnace Road followed. In 2001, Maximum and Central prisoners were transferred. The final prisoners departed on November 30, one month early. (Courtesy of Irma Clifton.)

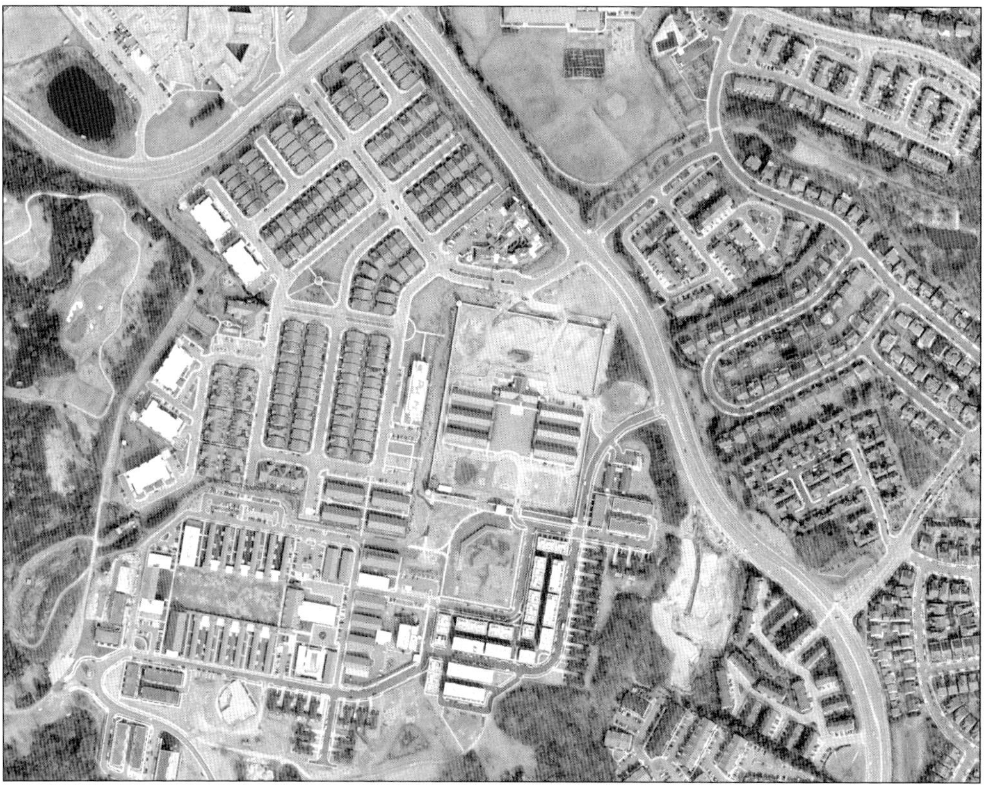

A complicated land swap in 2002 involved the federal government, Pulte Homes and Fairfax County. Pulte homes bought the 810-acre property known as Meadow Wood Farm in Mason Neck; then traded that property for 210 acres of federally owned prison land to build Spring Hill housing development. The remaining pristine reserve property was given or sold to Fairfax County and became part of the Meadowood Recreation Area operated by the Bureau of Land Management. (Courtesy of Larry Clark.)

Behind the walls of the old penitentiary, the Lidl grocery chain constructed a new market. It was the "anchor store for the shopping district going up around it. Behind the tower, the top floors of the townhouses are visible. The occupants and residents of the single-family homes and condos are within convenient walking distance. (Courtesy of Patrick O'Neill.)

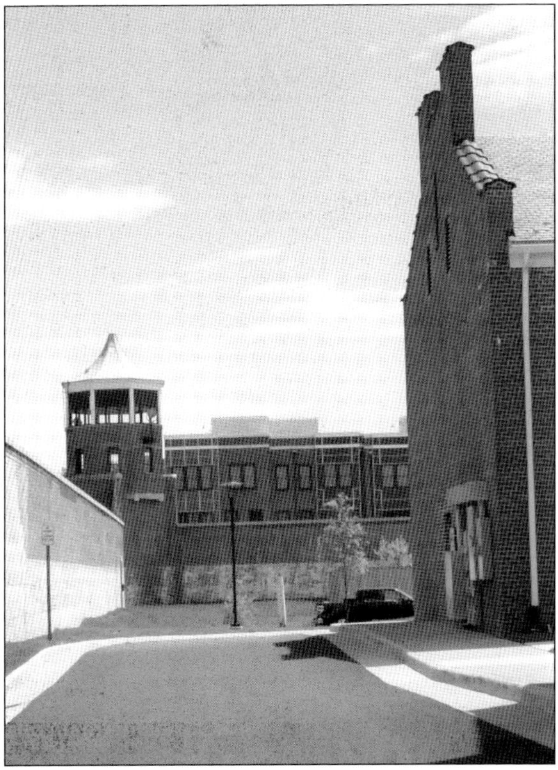

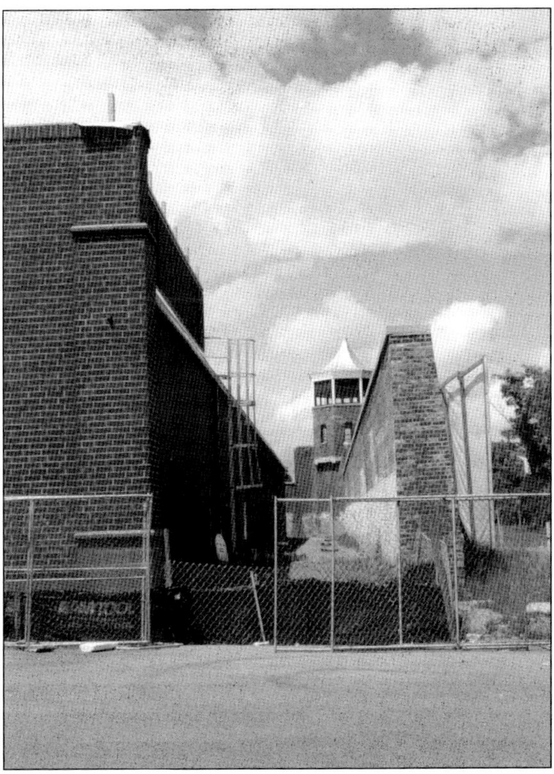

A far cry from the picks and shovels used by the first inmates at Lorton as they built their own prison, today's construction workers have the most modern equipment to help with repurposing the buildings at the old Central Facility. Because the shopping area needed access from the road, a portion of the Penitentiary wall was torn down. It provides the opportunity to realize how thick it was. (Courtesy of Patrick O'Neill.)

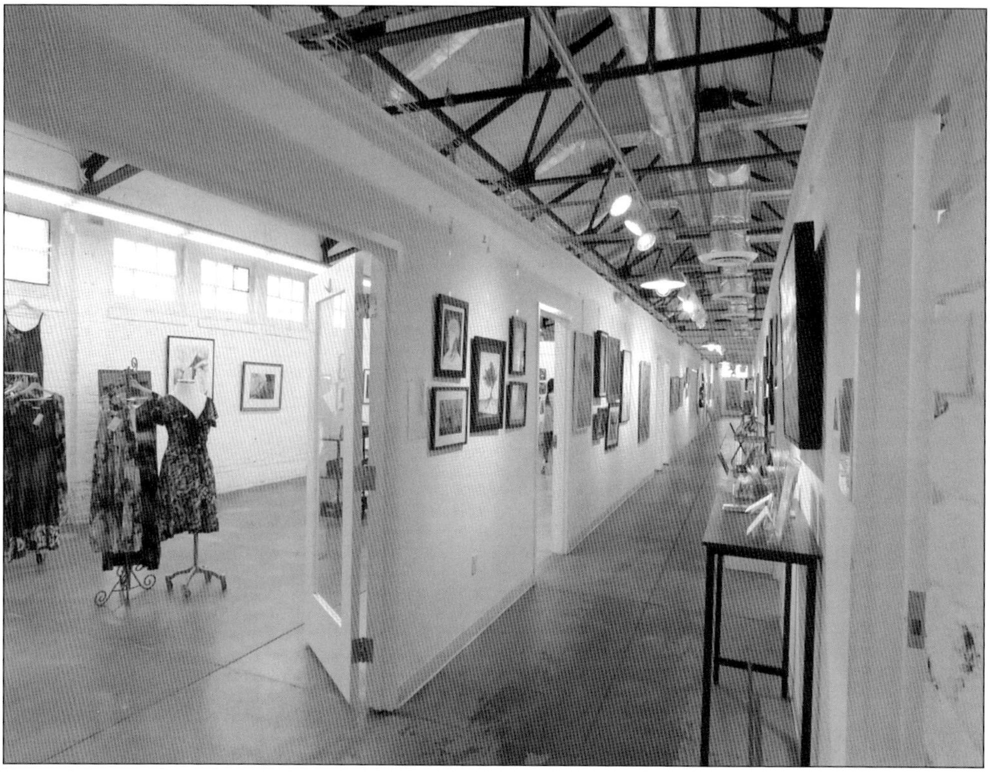

On July 15, 2002, Fairfax County received title to 2,324 acres of the former DC Department of Corrections facility at Lorton for $42 million. In 2006, the Fairfax County Board of Supervisors unanimously approved leasing the Workhouse site to the Lorton Arts Foundation and approved up to $27.5 million in bond funding for renovations to the site. The arts center opened in 2008. It reorganized and became the Workhouse Art Foundation in 2014. (Courtesy of Patrick O'Neill.)

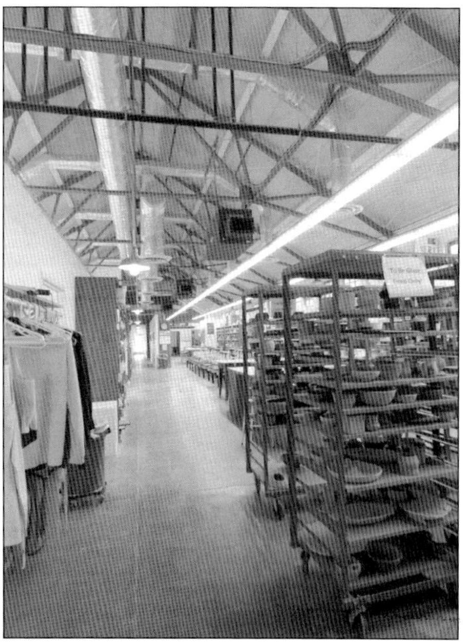

The pottery building at the Workhouse Art Center is one of the busiest. Entering, there is the welcome desk (common to all buildings) and a display of articles for sale. Proceeding, there are the kilns for firing; next is a wide, open area with long work tables for classes at all levels of ability. Shelves for storage and supplies line the sides of the room. The popular ice-cream social is yearly money-making activity each June. (Courtesy of Patrick O'Neill.)

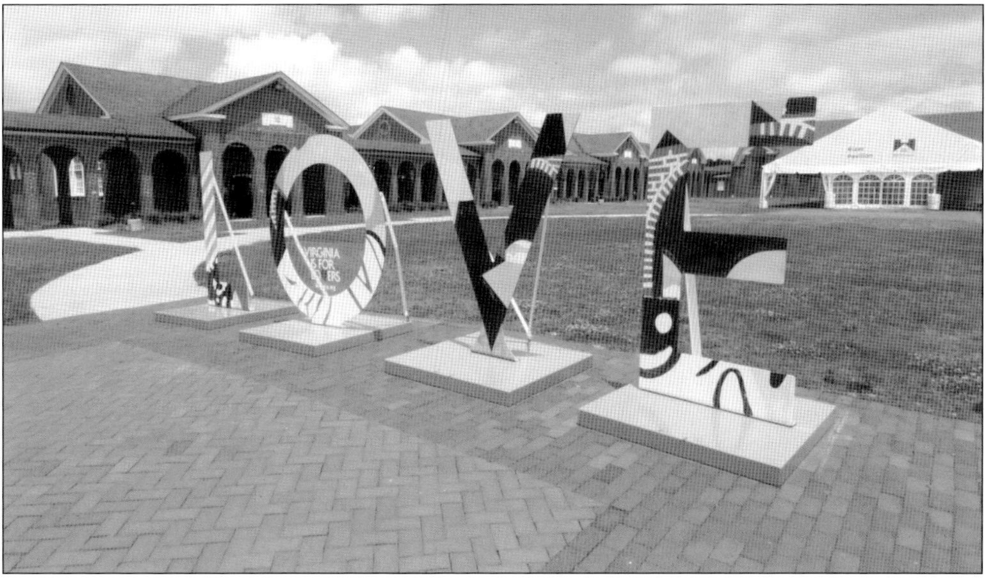

The "Love" sign on the quad at the Workhouse has become a popular picture-taking spot for visitors. In the background is the Rizer Pavilion, which can be set up with a stage for performers and chairs for the audience or with smaller tables and chairs for a picnic A concert series entertains weekly, weather permitting, in the summer. The annual Fourth of July celebration quickly became a tradition. Highway traffic stops once the spectacular fireworks begin. (Courtesy of Patrick O'Neill.)

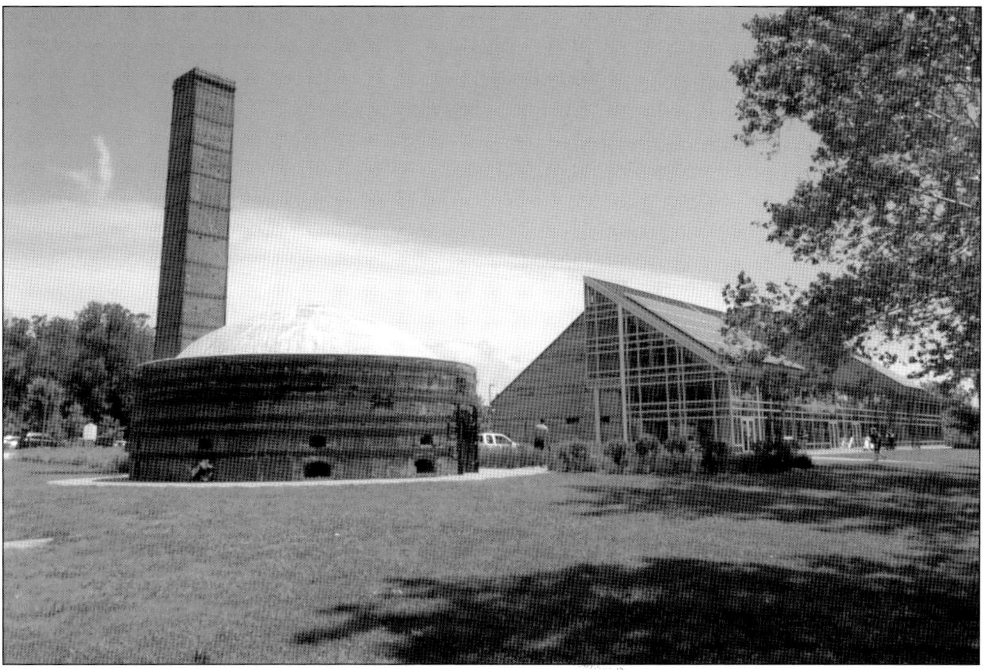

The Fairfax Cross-County Trail (CCT) begins at the wharf on the Occoquan River and ends at Great Falls Park on the Potomac. In its 40-mile journey crossing the entire county, it passes through many tree-shaded stream valleys that support biodiversity in this heavily urbanized area. Along the way, it showcases many of the finest county parks. Side trails add additional miles for hikers, non-motorized bikers, and equestrians. (Courtesy of Patrick O'Neill.)

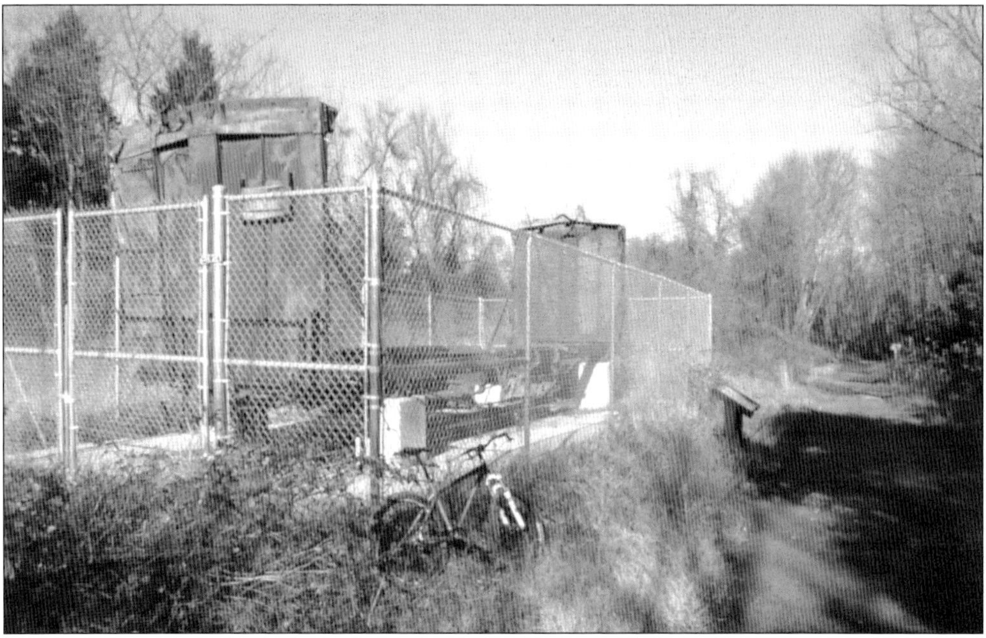

An abandoned railway car was found covered with brush along the track of the old L&O railroad after Fairfax County took possession of the old prison site. It was rescued and restored and now is a favorite stopping place for hikers and bikers along the All-County Trail. (Courtesy of Fairfax County Department of Planning and Development.)

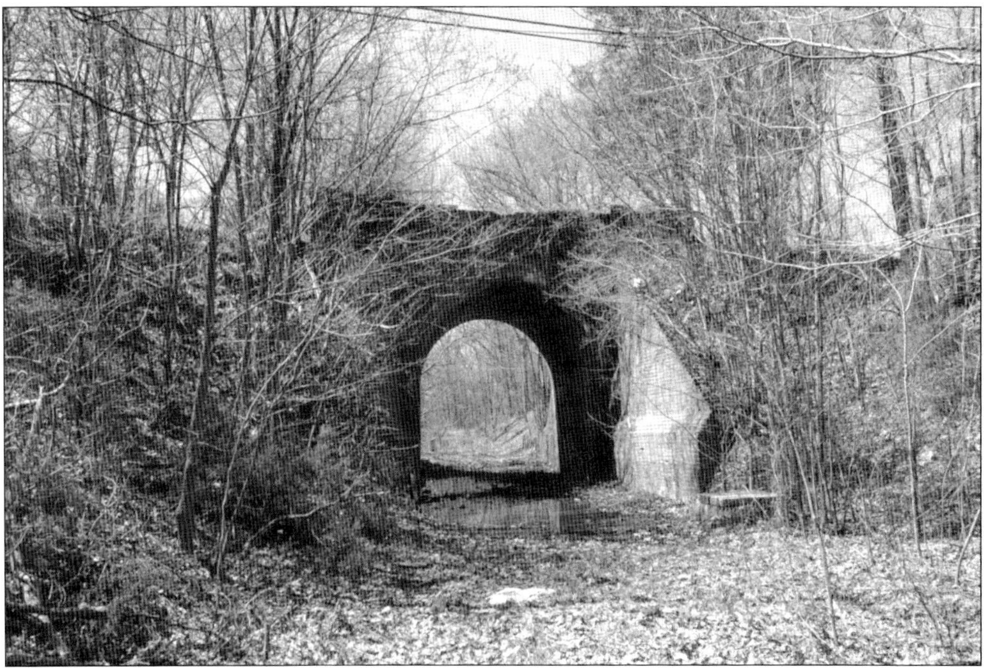

Though one of the most durable construction forms, the barrel arch bridge is no longer used. The one at Lorton was built in 1946 and is the only one remaining in Virginia. When Lorton Road was widened and altered, the bridge was preserved. The railroad bed below it is now part of the Fairfax All County Trail, which begins as the railroad did—at the wharf. (Courtesy of William Koch.)

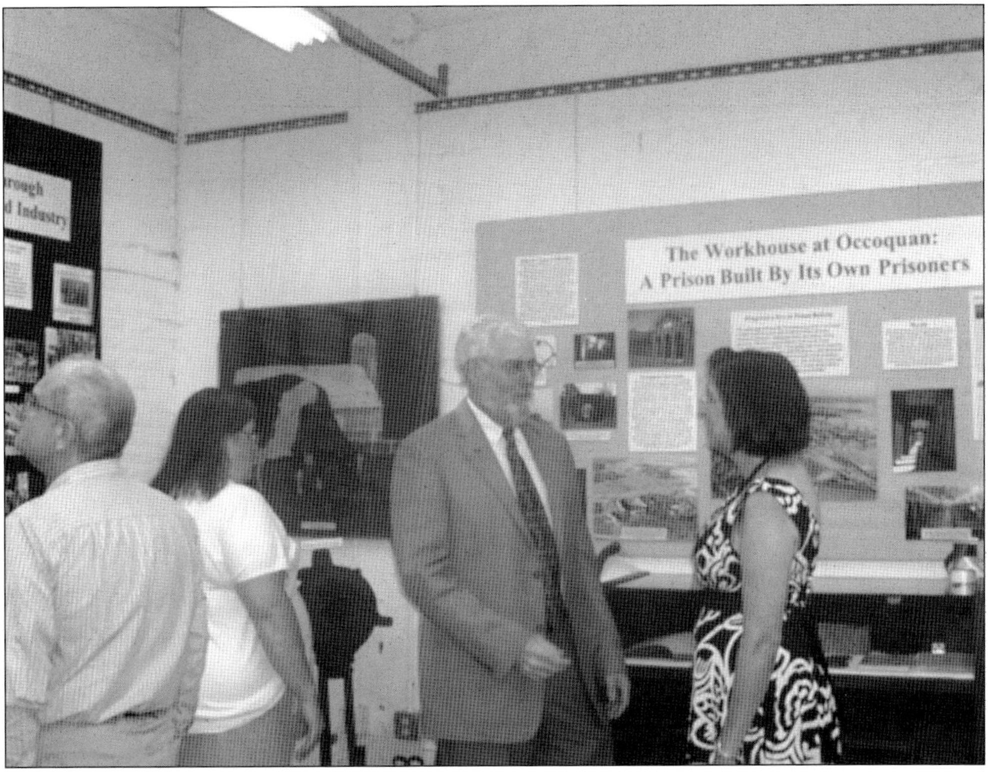

A future museum to preserve the history of the site was always part of the original plans, and a building was set aside for it. As funds were raised for its renovation, Irma Clifton secured one room in Building No. 9 for a docent-designed-and-operated Workhouse Prison Museum. It opened in September 2009; four years later, a second room across the hall was added as its volunteers worked to collect, preserve, and tell the prisons' stories. (Courtesy of Kenena Spalding.)

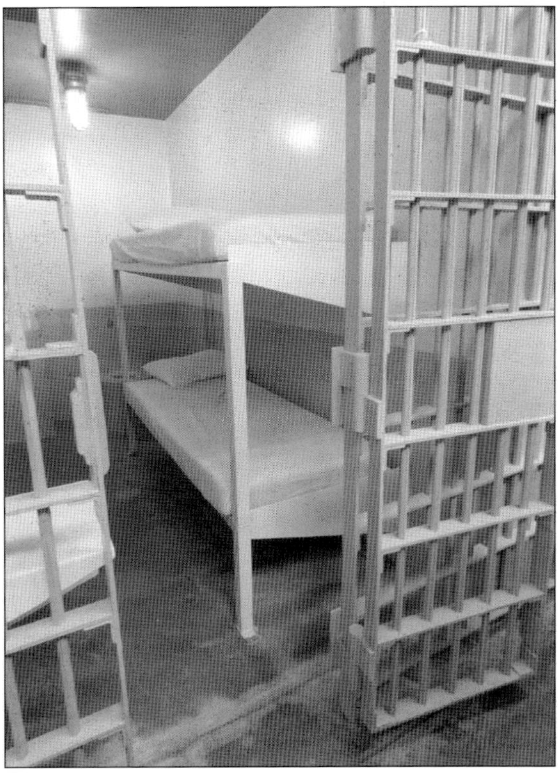

The decision to retain the block of cells was made early in the process of the design for the Lucy Burns Museum. The lead paint was removed from the wall and metal fixtures, and new bedding was purchased. Not originally used at the Workhouse, they were added only to this building during the turbulent, crowded later years. (Courtesy of Patrick O'Neill.)

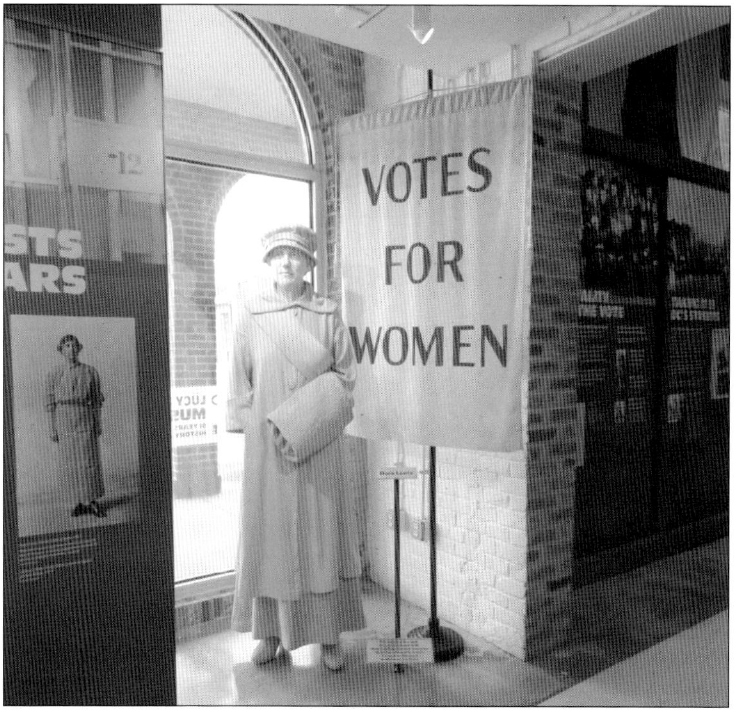

The museum moved to its own building in 2020. It was renamed the Lucy Burns Museum in honor of the cofounder and leader of the National Woman's Party. Professionally designed, installed, and led, it has assumed the charge to research, collect, catalog, teach, and share the history of this place through the stories of the people and events of the century that shaped their lives. (Courtesy of Patrick O'Neill.)

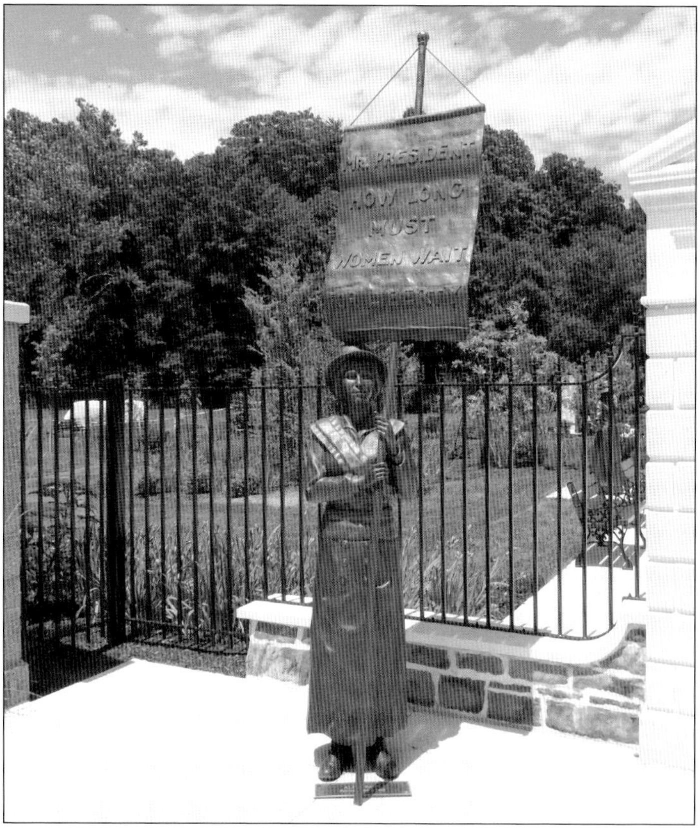

The Turning Point Suffragist Memorial opened in 2021 within the Occoquan Regional Park in Lorton, Virginia. It is across from the lone remaining brick kiln at the wharf. It celebrates all women who participated in the effort to achieve their right to vote in every state. In particular, the memorial honors those who, for the first time, protested at the White House and were jailed or imprisoned at the Workhouse. (Courtesy of Patrick O'Neill.)

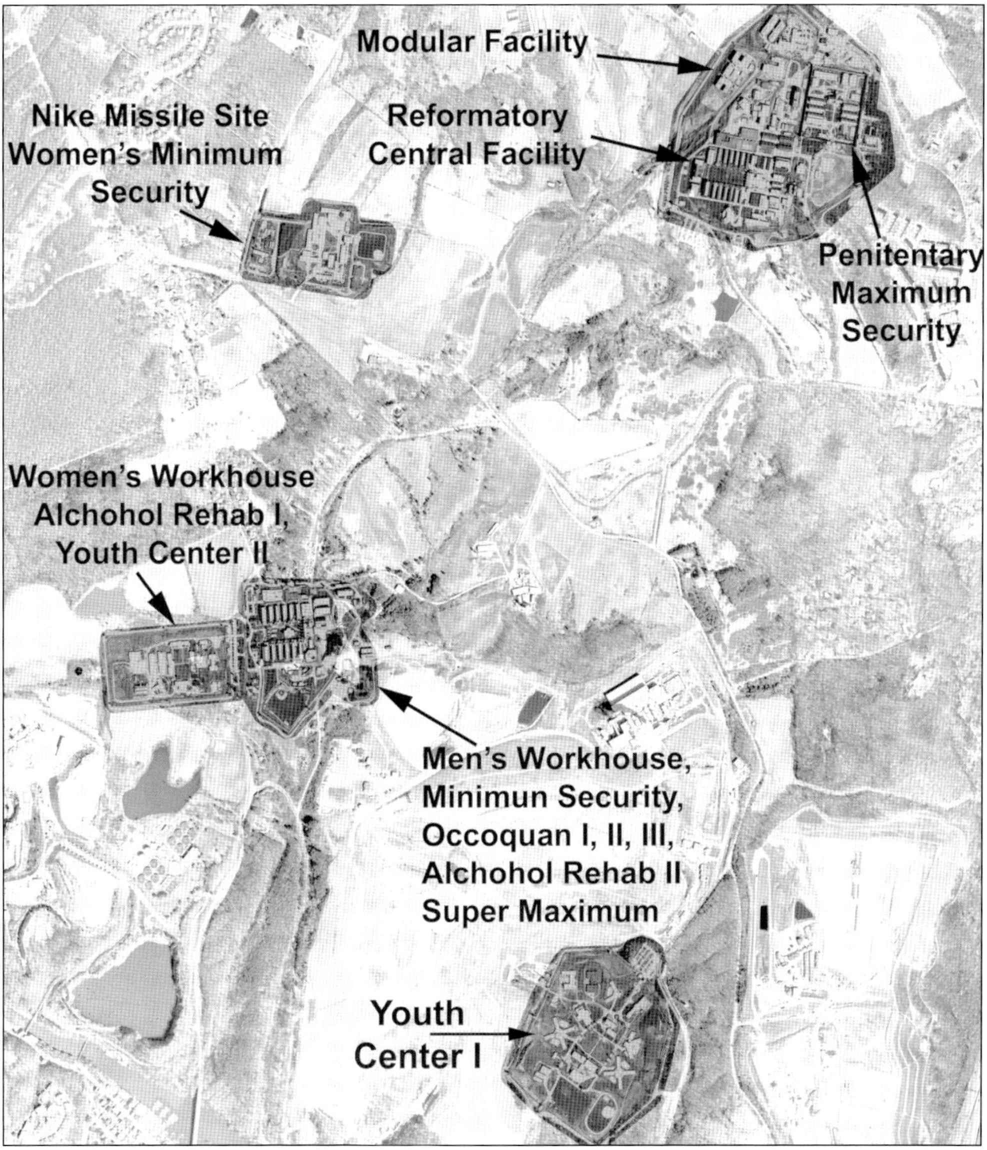

This map shows the location and names of the DC Department of Corrections facilities at Lorton during its near-century of existence. Over time, the names or functions of some of the various facilities changed in response to new ideas, events, challenges, or needs within the system. (Courtesy of Patrick O'Neill.)